Religion, Deviance, and Social Control

Religion, Deviance, and Social Control

Rodney Stark and
William Sims Bainbridge

Routledge
New York & London

Published in 1996 by

Routledge
29 West 35th Street
New York, NY 10001

Copyright © 1996 by Routledge, Inc.

Library of Congress Cataloging-in-Publication Data
Stark, Rodney and Bainbridge, William Sims
   Religion, Deviance, and Social Control / by Rodney Stark and William Sims Bainbridge.
      p.   cm.
   Includes bibliographical references and index.
   ISBN 0-415-91528-7. —ISBN 0-415-91529-5 (pbk.)
   1. Religions—Relations. 2. Religious pluralism. I. Title.
BL410.W54 1996
291.1′72—dc20
                                      95-42245
                                        CIP

Contents

1. Introduction / Religion and the Moral Order   1

Part 1 / **Religion** *and* **Deviance**

2. Religion and Suicide   11
3. Durkheim's *Suicide:* An Inquest   31
4. Rediscovering Moral Communities   53
5. Religion as Context: Saving a "Lost Cause"   67
6. Drugs and Alcohol   81

Part 2 / **Religion** *as* **Deviance**

7. Religious Cults   103
8. Religion and Mental Illness   129
9. Social Control in Utopian Communities   157

10. Conclusion / Brief Reflections on a
    Research Agenda   183

Bibliography   189
Index   207

1

Religion and the Moral Order: An Introduction

As the social sciences emerged from philosophy at the end of the eighteenth century, their founders were unanimous in their assertion that religion reinforced the moral order. Despite this, many of these same founders eagerly awaited the collapse of religion, some because they were equally eager for an end to the prevailing moral order (down with "false consciousness"), and many others because they despised religion, regarding it as a bundle of irrational superstitions incompatible with enlightened thought. Indeed, in his *The Positive Philosophy* (1830-42), Auguste Comte proclaimed that a new science, to be called "sociology," would replace religion as the basis for morality; this science would constitute a sort of ethical calculus.

Of course, nothing of the sort took place, and for most of the twentieth century social scientists have been content to teach that the primary social function of religion is to sustain the moral order. They have therefore assumed that the more religious members of any society will be less apt to violate the moral code (Parsons 1964a; Merton 1968).

Nevertheless, with the exception of studies of the linkage between denomination and suicide (which we will pursue in detail in Chapters 2 and 3), social scientists were mostly content to *assume* that religion was a major factor in social control. Consequently, as research on the

1

correlates of crime and delinquency grew into a major enterprise, little serious attention was paid to religion. For example, a survey of 28 criminology textbooks found that only four included religion in their indexes (Stack and Kanavy 1983). Thus, it was to everyone's amazement when, in 1969, Travis Hirschi and Rodney Stark (reluctantly) struck a blow to social theory as well as to common sense by reporting their inability to find any correlations between measures of religiousness (Sunday school and church attendance as well as belief in Hellfire) and delinquency among high school students in Richmond, California. Soon, this finding was reconfirmed by Burkett and White (1974), who worked with data collected in Oregon.

Social scientists love nothing so much as irony, and Hirschi and Stark's seemed the most ironic finding of them all: that kids were as likely to strip your car on the way home from Sunday school as they were on their way home from the pool hall or the video game arcade. Hence, the lack of a religious "Hellfire effect" on delinquency was enshrined in most introductory sociology textbooks.

Ironically, Hirschi and Stark's finding applies only to the West Coast. As we will see in Chapter 5, studies done elsewhere in the nation unanimously discover strong negative correlations between religiousness and delinquency.

The Social Nature of Religion

Our approach to the topic of religion and the moral order will not pursue a "Hellfire effect." We do not locate religious effects primarily within the individual human psyche, but within the human group. That is, the propositions we will formulate and test stress that the way in which religion sustains the moral order is primarily *social*. Granted that persons having deep religious convictions about sin and divine judgment may strive to lead blameless lives. But, as we shall see, their capacity to do so—indeed, their ability to form and sustain deep religious convictions—will depend greatly on the religiousness (or lack of it) of those around them.

Keep in mind, too, that although religion may generally function to support the moral order, clearly it does not always do so. Often enough, religious organizations and movements challenge the prevailing secular culture, and in so doing can be seen as a source of deviant behavior rather than as a source of social control. The role of churches in resisting and eventually overturning totalitarian regimes in Eastern Europe is a case in point. After the collapse of Soviet-bloc communism, the Roman Catholic Church in Poland or the Orthodox Catholic Church in Russia appear to be bastions of conventional morality. But under the old regimes they were considered sufficiently deviant to prompt serious repression and frequent official condemnation. It also needs to be recognized that many religious movements unsuccessfully challenge secular culture and the state. In doing so they become identified as "cults" and "sects," and mere membership in such groups often qualifies as deviant behavior. We shall have much to say about such groups in the second part of the book.

As these examples illustrate, throughout the book our focus will be on religion as a social rather than as a psychological phenomenon. Thus, for example, we will be far less concerned about whether people holding strong religious beliefs are less apt to commit crimes than we will be to learn whether crime rates vary across communities according to differences in the degree and quality of community religiousness. Indeed, our emphasis will be on the morality of communities, not on individual morality. Consequently, although we will analyze individual-level data, our usual objects of study and comparison will be collective: cities, states, regions, nations, high schools, religious groups, and utopian communes. Such units of analysis are often also referred to as *ecological* units, indicating that they surround individuals.

From time to time we will examine data based on individuals, but even then we will emphasize the effects of denominational membership and church attendance—the social aspects of faith—rather than belief.

There is nothing new about stressing the social role of religion. The earliest social scientists did not limit themselves to the assertion that religion causes people to behave themselves (although they assumed that this was true), but that religion maintains the moral order of society. However, none of the early social theorists claimed that religion was the *only* basis for community morality. As an introduction to the book, it will prove useful to distinguish between *social* and *moral sources* of *social integration*.

Social Integration

The idea of social integration is central to all discussions of social deviance. How do societies hold together? How are people able to pattern their behavior so as to resist temptations and opportunities to harm others to an extent sufficient to permit a relatively orderly social life? In his great work, *Leviathan*, the English social philosopher Thomas Hobbes (1588-1679) postulated an original human situation lacking "society." Had this been the "natural condition of mankind," Hobbes wrote, it would necessarily involve a war of all against all, for no one could trust anyone, and as a result life would be "solitary, poor, nasty, brutish, and short." But, this is not the way things are, Hobbes noted, because people have somewhat subordinated their selfish impulses to society. And the key to this subordination is social integration—*a shared willingness to conform and to cause others to conform to a set of norms or rules defining proper interaction.* To the extent that members of a group can trust one another not to murder them in their beds and/or carry off their possessions, the group is socially integrated. Put another way, the rules governing proper interaction define the moral order of the group, and social integration refers to the extent to which the moral order prevails. It must be noted that rules governing proper interaction are not limited to prohibitions of severe misdeeds against others, but often extend to minor courtesies, such as not belching or picking one's nose in the presence of others.

Social Sources of Integration

It is obvious that the basis of human existence, indeed of being human, lies in relationships with others. Most of what we need and desire we must get from, or in cooperation with, others. Typically, we come to rely on specific others to provide certain rewards—regular trading partnerships arise. Such partnerships often are called *attachments*. We tend to exchange with the same people on a regular basis, and a major part of what is exchanged is emotion. That is, we tend to like and even love those to whom we are attached.

From sociology's earliest days, social scientists have regarded attachments as the fundamental social glue. Thus, when the famous French sociologist Emile Durkheim (1858–1917) argued that humans are moral only to the extent that they are social, he was asserting that people conform to societal norms only to the extent that they are restrained by their attachments. Most of us conform, most of the time, in order to retain the good opinion of those to whom we are attached and to protect these valued relationships. Two propositions follow from this view, the first about individual behavior, and the second about social or collective units.

At the individual level: *Persons will conform to the norms to the extent that they are attached to others who accept the legitimacy of the norms.* Conversely, *people will deviate from the norms to the extent they lack attachments.*

At the group level: *Deviance rates will be higher in groups having a lower mean level of attachments.*

When we are alone, most of us do things we wouldn't do in front of others, especially not in front of others whose opinions of us we value. People deficient in attachments are effectively alone all the time and therefore are free to deviate, since they have no attachments at risk. When there are relatively many such persons in a group, their behavior will generate high rates of deviant behavior.

Many studies have found that the individual level proposition holds. For example, attachments are excellent predictors of crime and delinquency. But, for a long time there was little of value done to test the group level proposition even though it was of substantially greater theoretical interest. In large part this was because it seemed too expensive to assess levels of attachments for a large number of groups having many members—cities, for example. Our efforts to test this proposition in early chapters are based on the recognition that available data—measures of the degree to which a population consists of strangers and newcomers—can serve as an excellent inferential measure of attachments within collective or ecological units of analysis. Nearly all strangers and newcomers necessarily must lack attachments in comparison with people who have resided in the same place for a long period of time.

Moral Sources of Integration

Attachments may give force to the norms, but it is a shared moral conception that *gives the norms coherence and meaning.* It is here that the role of religion always has been stressed. This is because all of the world's great religions not only impose sacred obligations towards the divine, but specify moral demands concerning the behavior of their adherents towards one another. For example, the first four of the Ten Commandments concern duties towards God, but the remaining six are about basic interpersonal morality and specify rules for sustaining social integration.

It has long been recognized that social and moral sources of integration interact. Lack of attachments not only reduces social integration, but weakens religious organizations and thereby the level of moral integration. It is difficult to sustain any form of organized activity, including religious activity, in communities where everyone is coming or going—in communities of strangers (Welch 1983). Indeed, it was the fear that the rapid urbanization that had begun in the nineteenth century would create huge immoral cities of strangers that animated early sociologists. Thus, Durkheim anticipated a society adrift in what he called *anomie*, a condition of normlessness that would arise because societies of the unattached would be unable to adequately teach people what the norms are, let alone induce them to conform. It turned out that these fears about cities were largely groundless—human capacities to create and sustain relationships proved far more durable than Durkheim and his colleagues thought. Nevertheless, the basic claim that attachments are required to sustain organized action is valid—indeed, it is self-evident. In 1891 the pastor of the Collegiate Church in New York City explained his lack of members because of:

> the constant changing of residence by the great mass of the people… Hence a congregation is always changing, and with this its cohesiveness, efficiency and strength are steadily weakening. This uncertainty of residence makes the people reluctant to form any close association with Christian work; and in the majority of cases keeps them from going to church at all. Everybody and everything is strange on both sides, and from day to day there is no firm step taken to establish any church relation. (quoted in Schauffler 1891: 10)

Durkheim went even farther in connecting social and moral sources of integration: he frequently proposed that the latter was only a reflection of the former. As we will see in Chapter 2, Durkheim often argued that religion was but a reflection of underlying social integration, not a contributor to it. Here he echoed Marx, who usually regarded religion as simply a cultural epiphenomenon, a mere reflection of the "real," material bases of society—except when it suited his purposes to argue otherwise, as when he attributed to religion the independent capacity to create false consciousness by serving as an opium of the people. In later chapters we will see whether there are religious effects on moral behavior that are independent of social sources of integration.

We may, therefore, formulate two additional propositions.

At the individual level: *(other things being equal) Religious individuals will be less likely than those who are not religious to commit deviant acts.*

At the group level: *Rates of deviant behavior will vary across ecological or collective units to the degree that they exhibit moral integration.*

The "other things being equal" clause applies to *all* theoretical propositions—although theorists usually treat it as implicit. Here we make it explicit so as to warn readers that, come Chapter 5, we will append a contingent clause to this proposition, indicating special circumstances under which the proposition does *not* hold—circumstances in which other things are not equal.

Part One of the book is devoted to developing and testing these four propositions about religion *and* deviance. Along the way we will explore many other concerns as well, inquiring into Durkheim's "suicide" and examination of the role of religion in the prohibition movement.

In Part Two we will shift our focus from the role of religion in sustaining the moral order to an examination of religion *as* deviance. We will examine the spread and growth of cult movements, claims about religious insanity, and the durability of religious utopian communes.

In the final chapter we will reflect on the neglect of religion by criminologists and sociologists and suggest some potentially fruitful directions for future study.

Finally, we have written this book for the general reader as well as for our social scientific colleagues. Therefore, while most chapters include statistical analysis, and a number of tables have been included to provide other scholars with our precise results, we have written the textual discussions of these results in such a way that one need not examine the actual tables to fully grasp our findings.

Part One

Religion and Deviance

2

Religion and Suicide

Partly by accident, suicide rates played a crucial role in the founding of sociology. At the end of the eighteenth century, several European governments began to collect data to identify and compare various causes of death. When these mortality statistics were assembled it was possible, for the first time, to examine the prevalence of suicide. The data revealed two very shocking patterns.

First, the number of people who took their own lives was extremely *stable* over time: year after year, in a particular place, virtually an identical number of people committed suicide. This stability shocked many early observers because it forced them to recognize that what had up to then seemed the most individual of actions, rooted in each person's psychological makeup and personal circumstances, must in fact be of social origin. Were suicide the sort of idiosyncratic, individual action it had been thought to be, the number of suicides would vary wildly from one time to another. That they did not, but were instead extraordinarily stable, testified to the profoundly social character of human life. The German philosopher Immanuel Kant (1724-1804) was among the first to note the stability of suicide rates, and he immediately recognized that this must mean that society has a certain organic character.

We thank Daniel P. Doyle and Jesse Lynn Rushing who contibuted to an essay on which a portion of this chapter is based.

11

The second shocking revelation about suicide was that the rates *varied greatly* from one place to another. The suicide rate for Paris was more than four times the rate for London, and rates varied from a high of 34.7 per 100,000 population to a low of 0.8 across the 86 departments of France (Guerry 1833). Why? Here too the answer had to be social. Something about life in some places must have been more conducive to suicide than life in other places.

As time passed, a third aspect of suicide rates was noticed: they were *rising*, albeit very slowly. The annual suicide rate for England was 6.3 per 100,000 during the decade of 1830–40, but by 1866–70 it had reached 6.7. During the same period Sweden's rate rose from 6.8 to 8.5 and the rate for Paris rose from 34.7 in 1827–30 to 42.6 in 1872–76. Again the rates demanded an explanation. What was going on?

Not surprisingly, these findings prompted a great deal of theorizing. Perhaps the first serious attempt to account for variations in suicide rates was by André Michel Guerry, possibly the first person to turn the raw numbers of French suicides into rates based on the total populations of various departments and cities. In his pioneering work *Essai sur la statistic moral de la France*, published in 1833 by the French Royal Academy of Science, Guerry stressed the need to "understand to what extent a man who takes his own life may be subject to external influences," and was the first to suggest a systematic analysis of suicide notes. In fact, in his book Guerry included a demonstration analysis of 100 suicide notes obtained from the Parisian police. These revealed a remarkable number of religious concerns, especially about the fact that the Catholic Church condemned suicide as a mortal sin and refused to hold funeral services for people who had committed suicides, or to permit them to be buried in a Catholic cemetery. Here, Guerry's study foreshadowed a major conclusion soon reached by other European studies of suicide: that religion is a potent social factor influencing suicide.

By the latter part of the century, all of the leading students of suicide took it for granted that religion was a powerful deterrent to suicide. Among the more influential of these were Henry Morselli and Thomas Masaryk, whose studies set the stage for the influential work of Emile Durkheim at the very end of the century.

Morselli and Masaryk

In 1879 Henry Morselli published a comprehensive study of European suicide rates, reporting correlations with several factors, both social and geographic. Calling "the influences of religion" among "the strongest motive powers which act on the will of man" (Morselli 1879: 119), he distinguished several ways in which religion might affect suicide. While suspecting that part of "the growth of suicide is to be accounted for by the decrease of religious sentiment," he felt this theory could better be discussed by moral philosophers than in his own empirical work, probably because he lacked data measuring the strength of religious sentiment.

In agreement with earlier researchers, Morselli suggested that members of minority religions showed low rates of suicide because "the spirit of association and the earnestness of religious convictions increase in proportion to the isolation into which any given congregation is cast when in the minority in a country" (1879: 126-127). Aware of the necessity for controlling for other variables, Morselli concluded that Protestantism was associated with high rates of suicide, compared to Catholicism. His explanation was complex, including some common nineteenth-century psychiatric assumptions about culture-induced stress on the nervous system (cf. Jarvis 1850, 1852). But with an oblique reference to the theory of August Comte, it has distinctly sociological qualities:

> The very high average of suicides among Protestants is another fact too general to escape being ascribed to the influence of religion. Protestantism, denying all materialism in external worship and encouraging free enquiry into dogmas and creeds, is an eminently mystic religion, tending to develop the reflective powers of the mind and to exaggerate the inner struggles of conscience. This exercise of the thinking organs which, when they are weak by nature, is always damaging, renders them yet more sensible and susceptible of morbid impressions. Protestantism in the German States further exercises this exciting influence on the cerebral functions in yet another manner; it originated those philosophical systems which are based on the naturalistic conception of human existence, and put forward the view that the life of the individual is but a simple function of a great whole. These philosophical ideas are harmless enough to strong minds and those stored with a fit provision of scientific culture, but in the democratic atmosphere of our times the heart is not educated *pari passu*. The religious apathy with which the present generation is afflicted does not arise from a reasoned enquiry into the laws of nature or a scientific appreciation of its phenomena;

it is not in short a deep conviction of the mind, but springs from a physical inertia and from the little hold obtained by any ideas but such as are directed to material improvement and the gratification of ambition. To our mind therefore the great number of suicides is to be attributed to the state of compromise which the human mind occupies at the present time between the metaphysical and the positivist phase of civilization, and as this transition is more active in countries of marked mystic and metaphysical tendencies, such as is the case with Protestantism, it is natural that in them suicide should have the greatest number of victims. (Morselli 1879: 125–126)

In 1881, Thomas Masaryk published a more theoretical book on suicide and civilization, expressing similar views but placing greater emphasis upon the weakening of religion as the cause of suicide: "Religion… gives man comfort in all situations of life through theism and the belief in immortality, hope in the face of adversity, and the stimulus for the love of mankind. The religious man is therefore joyful in all the circumstances of his life; his faith, his conviction, and his assurance bind him not only to heaven, but also to earth, to life" (Masaryk 1881: 84). For Masaryk, "the modern tendency to suicide has its true cause in the irreligiosity of our time" (1881: 85) and Protestantism was far more accepting of modernism, progress, and secularization than Catholicism. Because of the work of Morselli and Masaryk, when Durkheim came to the topic a decade and a half later, he could not easily cast religion into a subsidiary role.

Durkheim Reconsidered

Despite Durkheim's reputation as a founding father of the sociology of religion, we found his work to display an amazing innocence of elementary facts about religion in Europe at the time that he was writing. Time and again in *Suicide* (1897) his open contempt for and lack of knowledge about religion lead him to frame arguments that are obviously wrong. Nor are these arguments directed towards peripheral concerns. Critical parts of his analysis rest on arguments that never should have passed even moderately informed inspection. That these matters were not recognized long ago probably reflects the persistence among social scientists of the same biases and unfamiliarity that led Durkheim himself into error.

Chapter 3 will examine Durkheim's work in closer detail, but our primary aim here is to engage his key hypotheses with twentieth-century American data. In this chapter we do not exhibit shortcomings in *Suicide* as an exercise in intellectual history, but as a necessary preface to the task of more adequately assessing the relationship between religion and suicide. Having clarified these matters, we attempt more clearly to state the relevant hypotheses and analyze pertinent data.

A lengthy section of *Suicide* is devoted to exploring and explaining the very substantial differences in suicide rates between Catholic areas and most Protestant areas in Europe near the turn of the twentieth century. The discussion is very inconsistent because Durkheim did not regard religion as "real," yet sometimes wanted to attribute to it real effects.

Fundamentally, and in most of his writing, Durkheim preferred to treat religion not as something in itself, but rather as an elaborate reflection of more basic social realities. In *Suicide* he argued that this social reality was integration, that Protestant-Catholic comparisons were but a proxy variable for degree of social integration. In *The Elementary Forms of the Religious Life* (1915) he concluded that religion is actually the symbolization of society itself. Religious rituals are the means by which the group, in effect, worships itself and reaffirms its solidarity. He seems already to have held this view when he wrote *Suicide*, and as we shall see, this made it impossible for him to regard religious pluralism as anything but prima facie evidence of the breakdown of social integration.

In asserting that religion is but the reflection of society, Durkheim was in close accord with Marx, who argued that religion is an illusory epiphenomenon rooted in objective social arrangements. And, like Marx, Durkheim found it impossible to apply this point of view consistently. As Marx grumbled that religion was an opium of the people (thus admitting that an epiphenomenon was potent enough to produce false consciousness), so Durkheim acknowledged that religion has the power to unite its adherents into a "single moral community" (1915: 47). Trying to have it both ways, denying and invoking direct religious effects, is characteristic of *Suicide*.

Durkheim opened his discussion of denominational differences in suicide rates by arguing that theology cannot be the cause of Protestant-Catholic differences because there is no theological variation on this matter:

> ...they both prohibit suicide with equal emphasis; not only do they penalize it morally with great severity, but both teach that

a new life begins beyond the tomb where men are punished for their evil actions, and Protestantism just as well as Catholicism numbers suicide among them. (1915: 157)

This is simply wrong. The fact is that at the time Durkheim wrote, the Roman Catholic Church imposed vastly heavier theological and social sanctions against suicide than did most Protestant groups. For Catholics, suicide was classified as a "mortal sin"—a sin that in and of itself prevented salvation of the soul. To commit suicide a devout Catholic had to decide that life was less bearable than eternal damnation would be. It is true that Protestants also held suicide to be sinful. But they lacked the concept of mortal sin, or indeed the tenet that salvation required absolution—a sacrament that the Roman Catholic Church granted or withheld from the dead and dying. In short, Protestantism lacked the theological means to match Catholicism in prohibiting suicide.

Beyond these marked theological differences were the perhaps even more compelling differences in sacramental practices. For Catholics, suicide brought great stigma and suffering for family and friends. Sacraments such as funeral services and burial in holy ground were withheld from suicides. Since in many Catholic communities there were only Catholic cemeteries, the ban against burial of suicides had a real impact—thus the concern about religious sanctions that Guerry found in the Parisian suicide notes. There were no similar practices among most Protestant groups in the late nineteenth century. Now, it is possible that even these quite dramatic differences in doctrine and practice did not influence suicide behavior. This is a matter that remains to be investigated. The fact that Durkheim ignored these profound differences does not establish their unimportance. We do know that these theological differences seemed to coincide with substantial differences in suicide rates.

In Durkheim's judgment, the "real" causes of Protestant-Catholic differences in suicide were not theological, but social—Catholicism reflects "strongly integrated social groups" (1897: 208-209). Why? Surprisingly, Durkheim attributes this difference to *theology!* Here Durkheim based his argument on crude stereotypes of Catholics and Protestants, and he paradoxically relies upon Morselli's thinking even as he pretends to distance himself from all earlier authors. Hence, "the Catholic accepts his faith ready made, without scrutiny," but the "Protestant is far more the author of his faith." Because Protestants must seek individual salvation without church mediation, there arises among them "a spirit of free inquiry." Indeed, Protestantism and free inquiry are by definition the "overthrow of traditional beliefs" (1897: 158). This line of analysis led Durkheim to his principal conclusion:

> ...the greater concessions a confessional group makes to the individual judgment, the less it dominates lives, the less its cohesion and vitality. We thus reach the conclusion that the superiority of Protestantism with respect to suicide results from its being a less strongly integrated church than the Catholic church. (Durkheim 1897: 159)

Because Durkheim regarded religion as a reflection of society, he was forced to regard religiously pluralistic societies as inherently weakly integrated. It does not seem to have occurred to him (except in the special case of encapsulated Jewish communities) that several faiths could generate independent, co-existing moral communities so that most individuals in a society would experience a high degree of social integration. Nor did he wonder about variations, across nominally Catholic or Protestant nations or regions, in the proportion of the population who actually participated in the religion. Instead, Protestantism per se was regarded as necessarily implying a lower degree of social integration.

Moreover, Durkheim failed to consider seriously the possibility that Protestantism might be only adventitiously associated with secular forces inhospitable to social integration. Thus, when he did note the marked educational differences between Protestant and Catholic nations—knowing that education was positively associated with suicide—he attributed these differences to the impact of the spirit of free inquiry fostered by Protestantism, and did not see them as a possible source of spuriousness.

Indeed, Durkheim's preoccupation with differential Protestant and Catholic suicide rates probably led him away from asking about the impact of religion in general on suicide. As he dismissed the importance of doctrine in inhibiting suicide, so did he ignore the potential of religion to relieve the pressures that, for an irreligious person, might make life not worth living. Indeed, if Marx meant what he said about opium and false consciousness he would likely have agreed with the notion that religion can serve as a potent source of comfort in the face of adversity and suffering. Surely it is plausible that the belief that earthly suffering is but the prelude to immortality has sustained many who might otherwise have lost heart. But of this possibility, Durkheim was relatively silent.

Perhaps the most famous problem in Durkheim's *Suicide* is the confusion between the important concepts of *anomie* and *egoism*. Durkheim explained the apparently greater suicide rate among Protestants in terms of *egoism*—excessive individualism. He also introduced data indicating that stable family relationships and political integration of the community deterred suicide for the same reason: "suicide varies inversely with the degree of integration of the social groups of which the individual forms a part" (Durkheim 1897: 209). We can easily translate this into the terms consistent with the propositions about attachments set forth in Chapter 1: *Egoism is the state in which stable attachments between people are lacking.*

In contrast, *anomic* suicide comes from a disruption of norms or values. The effect of anomie can be discerned in the increase of suicides during abnormal economic times. In especially bad times, and in especially good times, Durkheim said, the suicide rate is higher than in normal times. At both extremes, individuals lose standards by which to judge their own performance. Durkheim believed humans needed the limits imposed by a stable culture, because otherwise they might set impossible goals for themselves. Egoism is the opposite of social integration, while anomie is the opposite of moral integration. Robert Angel has explained that "a high degree of moral integration involves a mutually consistent set of norms derived from common values, norms which members of the group, community, or society have internalized as guides to their behavior" (Angell 1974: 610; cf. Angell 1949: 248).

Today we have good reason to doubt that suicide increases during times of sudden prosperity (Henry and Short 1954). Durkheim's claim that it does is essential to his argument for the existence of anomie. Morselli and Masaryk had already provided the explanation that suicide rates might be low in stable poor societies because they are not undergoing modernization or a decline in the social significance of religion. So, if suicide rates are high only under conditions of sudden economic decline, there is little justification for invoking anomie as the cause. Instead, we might speak simply of despair or introduce a concept Durkheim found so uninteresting that he relegated it to a mere footnote: *fatalism.*

Had Durkheim been committed to a different agenda, he could have argued that higher rates of suicide in Protestant countries were the result of anomie, not of egoism. Religion seems an excellent antidote for both anomie and fatalism. According to Peter Berger, an individual suffering anomie "loses his orientation in experience. In extreme cases, he loses his sense of reality and identity. He becomes anomic in the sense of becoming worldless" (1969: 21). This condition is one of "naked terrors" (Berger 1963: 147) and "nightmare" (Berger and Luckmann 1966: 102). While any of society's institutions might provide a shield against such horrors, religion seems especially designed to make believers feel that existence is orderly, stable, and trustworthy. It sets reliable standards for individual behavior, and it encourages high hopes without stimulating excessive worldly ambition. For those who have been worldless, it transcends the world, and in so doing, restores it.

Unfortunately for clarity of thought, Berger and other writers have seldom distinguished anomie from egoism. We find it convenient to conceptualize anomie as the lack of values and norms, and to define egoism as the lack of social attachments. That is, anomie is a problem of culture, while egoism is a problem of society (Stark and Bainbridge 1987: 61-63). But Durkheim himself often described the two in very similar terms (e.g. Durkheim 1897: 258), and Johnson (1965) has argued that they are indistinguishable concepts in Durkheim's usage (cf. Maris 1969; Pope 1976; Breault 1986).

As noted in the first chapter, we make much of the distinction between moral integration and social integration. Anomie is a lack of moral integration, and we seek data on the power of religion to overcome anomie by creating or sustaining moral integration. Egoism is a lack of social integration, and while religion can provide a measure of social integration through membership in church congregations, other aspects of social life can do the same. Thus, in seeking a distinctive religious influence on suicide, we will often want to control for secular forms of social integration.

In this chapter and the next we empirically examine the possibility that religion as such can have a potent inhibiting influence on suicide. We shall also look to see if, in contemporary American society, there remains any specifically Catholic effect. Moreover, we shall use secular measures of social integration not only to examine their impact on suicide, but to see whether religion is but a proxy variable for this more basic social fact, as Durkheim believed, or whether religion is itself a social fact.

American Data from 1971

In an important but largely ignored paper published back in 1952, Austin Porterfield showed that church membership rates for American states in 1936 showed negative correlations with two sets of suicide rates (r = -0.44 and r = -0.34). What these coefficients indicate is that suicide rates are lower in states where church membership rates are higher. Despite our long professional involvement in the sociology of religion, we were unaware of Porterfield's work until well after we had begun to publish our own, similar studies. We think this reflects the unconscionable failure of sociology generally to subject the works of "the great masters" like Durkheim to serious empirical evaluation. Later we will examine older American data, but our research on suicide began with what was the only recent appropriate data set.

Our research became possible when reliable estimates of church membership for various ecological units of the United States became available (Stark 1980). When the Bureau of the Census was laying plans for the 1970 enumeration, many scholars hoped that a question about religious affiliation would be included. Despite the fact that pilot research indicated that the overwhelming majority of Americans would be happy to answer such a question, protests from a few organizations unleashed a storm of negative publicity around the idea, and this plan was scuttled (Scott 1968: 122). However, in 1971 a privately funded survey assembled membership data for 53 denominations—data adequate for our purposes (Johnson et al. 1974). By adding Jewish synagogue membership and membership in predominantly black denominations, accurate rates for the general population were created. Here we use Standard Metropolitan Statistical Areas (SMSAs) as the units of analysis. Church membership varied greatly across SMSAs in 1971—from 96.6 percent of the population in Provo, Utah, down to 25.0 percent in Eugene, Oregon. The rate for the nation as a whole was 55.7 percent.

Suicide rates for SMSAs are from the Bureau of Vital Statistics report for 1971 and thus are contemporary with the church membership rates. Harsh criticisms have been directed at official data on suicide. Douglas (1967), for example, has argued that all such statistics are but reflections of complex processes of social construction—that whether a given event will be classified officially as suicide depends on many factors that fluctuate by time and place. It would be witless to deny that families, physicians, and coroners sometimes successfully "hush up" a suicide so that it does not turn up in official statistics. But simply to acknowledge some measurement error is not necessarily to conclude that a measure is worthless. The pertinent questions concern the degree of error and systematic bias in the error.

A common concern about bias in suicide rates is that reporting is more accurate for larger cities than for small towns and rural areas. Limiting analysis to SMSAs reduces that problem. A second possible source of systematic bias might be that suicide will be underreported in Catholic communities. But common sense would suggest that if social pressures are strong enough to bias reporting suicides in Catholic communities, such pressures ought also to inhibit suicides. If so, then Protestant-Catholic comparisons might be exaggerated by reporting bias, but it seems unlikely that only reporting differences would be involved. More to the point, as we consider at length below, there seem nevertheless to be good grounds not to expect Catholic-Protestant differences in suicide in the U.S. today.

The nature and operating principles of modern bureaucracies are at considerable variance with notions of covering up suicides for the sake of the family. Bureaucracies operate with an inertia and disregard for individuals that may be highly objectionable, but which ought to produce quite reliable data. We note that crime statistics have also been subjected to harsh charges of bias and inaccuracy, but that the results of massive victimization surveys have made it evident that official crime statistics are in fact quite accurate (Hindelang 1978). Of course, some people commit suicide in ways that evade detection. But there is no reason to suppose that such incidents are a systematic source of error in ecological rates. Admittedly, we cannot demonstrate the absence of systematic bias in suicide statistics. The burden of proof, however, ought to rest with those who postulate systematic bias. And such proof must also be systematic, not anecdotal.

Church Membership and Suicide

Our intention in this chapter is to search for direct religious effects on suicide. Contrary to Durkheim, we think that religious commitment in and of itself ought to prevent a substantial amount of suicide. Elsewhere we present a lengthy deductive theory of religion, why it arises and what it does for people and societies (Stark and Bainbridge 1987). There we offer a detailed argument about the many ways in which religion assuages all manner of human disappointments. Here it is sufficient to but sketch some of the ways in which religion may make life worth living and thus prevent suicide.

First of all, religious organizations are easily accessible to people and are a generous source of affect and self-esteem. Pastors will listen to troubles. Other members rally to the support of those overtaken by misfortune. The lonely find sociability in church. Granted, these are all "this-worldly" aspects of religions and in that sense somewhat akin to Durkheim's reduction of religion to social relations. But it is noteworthy that it is the "other-worldly" concerns and doctrines of religions that make them so much more effective in this respect than other voluntary organizations. Lonely, impoverished widows cannot get the same levels of response from country clubs, welfare offices, or the local Democratic caucus.

But beyond these direct means by which religious organizations can influence people's lives are the truly potent means by which they compensate and comfort people—means that are uniquely religious. Humans are beset with desires and disappointments for which worldly means cannot convincingly compensate. Only by invoking the power of the gods—of the supernatural—can plausible promises of solutions be extended. No one knows how to construct a society in which there is no stratification and hence no relative deprivation. But the gods can offer heavenly glory in return for earthly suffering. No scientific means exist to achieve immortality. But for millennia religions have convincingly promised life beyond death.

The point seems patent. Yet social scientists have ignored religious effects in most areas of research for most of this century. Like Durkheim, most social scientists seem to feel that since they judge religion to be false, it really cannot do anything for people. But one hardly needs to believe in religion to suppose it has effects. W. I. Thomas's admonishment that things people define as real have real consequences might have sufficed to help social scientists to see that for believers faith is real. Put another way, it makes a difference if, on the one hand, one thinks one's problems are overwhelming and cannot be shared or, on the other, if one thinks that Jesus knows and cares.

This is, of course, a wholly testable hypothesis that is not to be taken on faith. If religion does offer real comfort then this surely ought to be reflected in lower suicide rates. Turning to the data, using 214 SMSAs as the units of analysis, we find a very substantial and highly significant negative correlation between church membership and suicide rates ($r = -.36$; significant well beyond the .001 level). If this relationship is not spurious, then religion does have a major deterrent effect on suicide. The church membership and suicide correlation was examined under a series of control variables. None reduced the original correlations. But we must pursue several other variables of interest before we conclude this study.

We have criticized Durkheim for ignoring theological explanations of the differential suicide rates of Protestant and Catholic areas. But theology, in the form of Protestant-Catholic contrasts, may also underlie the relationship we have found between church membership and suicide. There is a modest tendency for church membership rates to be higher in SMSAs with a higher proportion of Catholics.

However, precisely because we suspect that theology can influence behavior, we do not expect to find important Protestant-Catholic differences in suicide today. This is because the Roman Catholic Church no longer stigmatizes suicide as it once did. Catholic doctrine has always held that to sin one must be mentally competent. Thus, for example, the church has held that the mentally retarded are incapable of sin. In modern times psychiatric ideas have had considerable impact on Catholic thought. In consequence, pastors began to take the position that a person who committed suicide while mentally ill did not commit a mortal sin and thus could receive the sacraments of the church. Over the decades it has become increasingly common for Catholic suicides to receive the sacraments. Indeed, pastors now tend to infer an unsound mind from the act of suicide itself. Thus, little remains of the once profound differences, for their theological and social bases have all but disappeared.

The appropriate measure by which to investigate the effects of Catholicism on suicide is the proportion of church members who are Catholic. This is because the proportion of an SMSA's population who are Catholic church members already has entered into the computation of each SMSA's church member rate. Thus the two are confounded. Independence is achieved when we introduce the proportion of church members who are Catholics into the analysis. That is, we are able to hold church membership constant while letting the proportion of Catholic church members vary to see if Catholicism per se has an effect.

When we examined the impact of Catholicism on suicide we found no significant effect. That is, there is a very substantial effect of church membership, but no portion of this is produced by any specific Catholic influence. Religion appears to matter, but it does not seem to matter what kind of religion.

Several interpretations of these findings are possible. First, in Durkheim's time perhaps Catholicism per se did have an independent impact on suicide, as suggested by Durkheim's many comparisons. Since that time the Catholic effect may have vanished because of liberalization of Catholic treatment of suicide. Alternatively, there might never have been a Catholic effect, despite marked differences in doctrine and sacramental practice. Durkheim's Protestant-Catholic comparisons may have reflected mainly differences in church participation rates. That is, Catholic nations and regions in Europe may have had considerably higher church attendance rates than did most Protestant nations and regions—as, in fact, they do today (Iannaccone 1991). A third possibility is that Durkheim may have been right about religion. Thus, it may be that in contemporary America, church membership rates are primarily reflections of more integrated social relations.

Social Integration

For Durkheim, religion reflected no more than social integration. But in order to test his reduction we must resolve ambiguities in his use of that term. Sometimes Durkheim meant social integration to refer to "collective states of mind" (1897: 170). But he also argued that religious beliefs create social integration through their capacity to support an "intense collective life" (170).

Durkheim took it as axiomatic that Catholicism was better able to create collective states of mind and thus to sustain intensive collective life because it did not permit dissent. Catholic communities enjoyed consensus on religion; Protestant communities could not, therefore Protestant communities were less integrated. As noted above, Durkheim fused religion and social integration; yet in order to examine their independent impacts on suicide, we must separate them.

As we developed the concept in Chapter 1, the most conceptually useful way to define social integration is in terms of social networks. The greater the density and intensity of interpersonal attachments among members of a group, the more the group can be said to be socially integrated. Defined in this way, the concept is devoid of cultural content. That is, "intense collective life," as Durkheim put it, is defined as a network of relations without reference to any cultural elements that might support these relations or dominate exchanges among network members. This conceptualization frees us from the grip of tautology. It becomes possible to see if religion, for example, does influence social integration, as Durkheim claimed it did.

Ideally, then, we would want to operationalize social integration in this study in terms of the density and intensity of network ties in these SMSAs. No such data are at hand. But a wholly satisfactory inferential measure is available. Other things being equal, there must be greater social integration, as we have defined it, in communities having primarily a stable membership than in communities made up primarily of newcomers and transients. Hence, a measure of population turnover—the movement of people into, out of, and within metropolitan areas—is a reasonable inferential measure of social integration.

Indeed, this particular measure of social integration is of special relevance in this study because in earlier work we already have found it to be a major factor in variations in church membership rates (Bainbridge 1990). High rates of population turnover erode all kinds of voluntary organizations, including churches. An affiliated person who moves must reaffiliate with a church, a fraternal lodge, a service club, and other such organizations. And a person who moves often must reaffiliate often. At the very least there will be some lag time in reaffiliation, and some people may move again before the normal lag time is up, thus continuing to be unaffiliated. This effect of moving is undoubtedly greatly amplified in communities where large proportions of the population move often. In more stable communities newcomers are more easily reconnected to a church or other organizations by neighbors and fellow workers who are members. To the degree one's neighbors and fellow workers are themselves newcomers and unaffiliated, the reconnecting process is impeded (Bainbridge 1990).

If population turnover has an impact on church membership, it also is easy to see how it would influence suicide. Not only can close attachments to others prevent suicide, but lack of attachments can contribute to the motives for suicide. People with troubles can be helped by others who can share or even solve their problems; lack of close interpersonal ties can be the basis for depression and despair. Indeed, Durkheim's analysis of the effects of marriage and family on suicide is wholly consistent with this line of argument. Control theories of deviance are traced back to Durkheim in part because of the emphasis he placed on the bonds between the individual and the group. As he wrote:

> ...for a group to be said to have less common life than another
> means that it is less powerfully integrated; for the state of inte-
> gration of a social aggregate can only reflect the intensity of the

collective life circulating in it. It is more unified and powerful the more active and constant is the intercourse among its members. (1897: 202)

Clearly, then, we are being fair both to Durkheim's fundamental position and to the needs for a conceptually clean measure of social integration by introducing population turnover into this analysis.

For all SMSAs, only a somewhat crude measure of population turnover was available to us when we began our research: percent change in population size over the past decade. For a more refined measure we were forced to limit the analysis to only the 60 largest SMSAs. Nevertheless, the 214 SMSAs differ greatly in their population change over the decade 1960-70. Undoubtedly, some SMSAs showing little change achieved this without having highly stable populations—they merely had a balance between in-migrations and out-migrations. Still, this group will include those cities with the most stable populations, while the most rapidly growing SMSAs must perforce contain large proportions of newcomers and transients.

Thus it is not surprising to find that this measure of social integration is strongly related to suicide rates (r = 0.32). SMSAs with rapid rates of population growth tend to have the highest suicide rates. Furthermore, rapid population growth is, as expected, very strongly negatively correlated with rates of church membership (r = -0.39).

Is Durkheim correct, then, that religion influences suicide merely as a reflect of underlying variations in social integration? Our first test of his thesis produced a resounding, "No." With population changes held constant, the correlation between church membership and suicide is only modestly reduced (from r = -.36 to r = -.27). Thus, some portion of the original relationship may be spurious. However, the remaining effect is substantial and highly significant.

Rather than reduce the effects of religion to those of social integration, we prefer to see religion as to some extent an intervening variable. That is, one of the ways in which lack of social integration influences suicide is by undercutting religious organizations. This directs our attention to the examination of the correlations between population changes and suicide with church membership rates held constant. This moderately reduces the original correlation (from r = 0.32 to r = 0.21). Thus religion does play a modest role in linking social integration and suicide. Yet here too, the remaining relationship is robust and highly significant. We conclude that both variables play an important and independent role in suicide.

To examine the joint effects of these variables we entered them into a regression equation and produced a multiple r of 0.41. Together, church membership and population change account for 17 percent of the variance in suicide rates.

Population change is, as we have mentioned, a somewhat crude measure of population turnover. For the largest 60 SMSAs a much more sensitive measure could be constructed (Crutchfield et al. 1982). It combines rates of in-migration and out-migration with residential moving within the SMSA to produce the proportion of the population who have been geographically mobile within the past ten years. There was considerable variation among SMSAs in this measure of population turnover. The San Diego SMSA had the highest rate: 55 percent; the Pittsburgh SMSA had the lowest: 30 percent. And the mean was 43 percent.

Since we were now working with only about a third as many SMSAs as in our previous analysis, our first concern was with zero-order relations. Population turnover was found to be very highly correlated with the suicide rate (r = 0.60). The correlation between the church member rate and suicide was much higher in this subset of SMSAs than in the full set (r = -0.61). We were, at first, not entirely sure why these effects were so much stronger in the subset of cases. Since these are the largest SMSAs it is plausible that variations in SMSA size reduced the correlation in the full set. But a control for size did not raise the correlation in the full set. The answer lay in the fact that the rates for the larger SMSAs are based on many more cases, and are thus more reliable. With the measurement error for the less reliable rates for the smaller SMSAs eliminated, the correlations were stronger.

In any event, with two highly significant zero order correlations (beyond the .001 level of significance), the task was to examine the three-variable relationship. With population turnover controlled, the correlation between church membership and suicide was reduced (r =0.37), but remained highly significant. With church membership controlled, the correlation between population turnover and suicide was also reduced (r = 0.33), but likewise remained highly significant. Once again controls for the proportion Catholic among church members had no effect whatsoever on the findings. Using regression to estimate the joint effects of population turnover and religion on suicide produced a multiple r of 0.67 and r-square of 0.44.

A Replication in the
Early Twentieth Century

After completing our analysis of American suicide rates for 1971, we went in search of other data that could extend our research backward in time. We were very conscious of the possibility that differences between Durkheim's findings and our own might be the result of the tremendous social changes that occurred in the intervening century. When Durkheim wrote, the very first automobiles had just begun sputtering along European roads; the data described above were collected after the first human beings had visited the moon. Conceivably, the social influence of religion had changed in like manner. Thus it was with great pleasure that we discovered that good quality American data existed from as early as 1906—just nine years after *Suicide* was published—permitting calculation of reliable rates of church membership.

An extraordinary array of both qualitative and quantitative data on American religion was preserved in a series of enumerations of religious bodies conducted by the United States Bureau of the Census in 1906, 1916, 1926, and 1936. These studies, reported in a number of massive volumes, are notable for scope as well as detail; and yet they languished almost unused by social scientists for many decades. Readers of an authoritative recent history of the census would never guess that they even existed (Anderson 1988). As we have noted, in 1952 Porterfield published an article exploring some connections between suicide rates and the data in these volumes, but the potential of such research never quite sank into the collective mind of sociology, and only in the past twenty years have social scientists begun to take full advantage of these old but excellent data (Azzi and Ehrenberg 1975; Meyer et al. 1979).

The statistical material is of high quality because of the great care and effort that went into the collection process. In the middle of each decade, the Census Bureau contacted every known religious denomination to obtain lists of their individual churches. The bureau used information from ministers, local informants, yearbooks, church publications, and previous censuses to expand the list until they had the names and addresses of almost every religious body in the country. A short questionnaire was then mailed to each local church, accompanied by an aggressive follow-up program to extract data from churches that did not initially respond. In the case of a few denominations, notably the Jews, the census resorted to "special agents" trusted by the denominations to carry out the research. We calculated church member rates for 1906, 1916, and 1926, and comparable suicide rates as well, so we could look back almost to the time when Durkheim wrote.

Table 2.1 reports results of multiple regression analyses for the three years, for cities with over 100,000 population, including the percent of population born in the state as a control for social integration. The zero-order correlation between suicide and church membership is significant for each of the three years, and it strengthens over time: -0.34, -0.36, -0.50. One explanation would be simply that the data collection improved steadily, and religion was more accurately measured in the later censuses. Increasing significance of the correlations is assisted by an increasing number of cases, from 41 large cities in 1906 to 78 in 1926.

In the 1906 data, church membership and born-in-state are equally successful in explaining variations in the suicide rate. The fact that each standardized beta falls short of statistical significance does not compromise the success of the analysis, because together these two variables achieve the 0.02 level. For the other analyses, church membership is always a stronger predictor of suicide than is the percent born in the state, and its beta is always statistically significant. Additional

Table 2.1

Moral and Social Integration and Suicide, 1906–1926 (USA, Cities Over 100,000)

		Correlation (r)	Beta
1906 (n=41)	Church Membership Rate	-0.34*	-0.26
	Born in State	-0.34*	-0.27
	R^2=.18*		
1916 (n=59)	Church Membership Rate	-0.36**	-0.27*
	Born in State	-0.32*	-0.21
	R^2=.16**		
1926 (n=78)	Church Membership Rate	-0.50***	-0.35**
	Born in State	-0.49***	-0.33**
	R^2=.34**		

* Significant beyond .05
** Significant beyond .01
*** Significant beyond .001

analyses, employing different ways of calculating the church-member rate and different control variables, give comparable results (Bainbridge and Stark 1981). Thus, data reaching back to within a decade of when Durkheim wrote his classic demonstrate the importance of religion in understanding suicide rates and refute his claim that it was nothing more than an indicator of community social bonds.

Conclusion

The data suggest that Durkheim was quite right to stress the importance of social integration in explaining suicide. Using population turnover as an inferential measure of the density and intensity of interpersonal relations in metropolitan areas, we found very substantial effects on suicide—effects in accord with the basic arguments developed in *Suicide*.

But Durkheim was quite wrong to claim that religious effects on suicide are no more than a reflection of social integration. We have seen that his arguments against religious effects per se were often dead wrong—our data reveal a strong religious effect on suicide independent of social integration.

In our judgment, these findings provide a striking example of the futility of trying to dismiss religion as an epiphenomenon. Why should it be more "real" to reduce religious effects to those of social integration? When we observe millions of people making considerable sacrifices for their faith, must we maintain that they gain no "real" value from something they appear to value so highly? And, if faith does comfort the faithful, why would it not influence their decision to go on living?

Our failure to find any Catholic effect on suicide raises the possibility either that these differences were spurious when observed by Durkheim, or that changes in Catholic treatment of suicide have led to changes in Catholic suicide rates. In the following chapter we will look for some trace of a Catholic effect in a range of data sets, European as well as American.

Finally, we want to make it clear that our remarks about the reluctance of social scientists to regard religion as a significant social fact do not reflect our private religious concerns. We do not write on behalf of faith, but in pursuit of its social impacts. One need not be faithful to see that faith may have important consequences. Here we have tried to demonstrate that one such consequence is to cushion the despair and desperation that can drive people to take their own lives.

3

Durkheim's Suicide: An Inquest

In 1957 Robert K. Merton credited Emile Durkheim with having discovered sociology's first and thus far its only scientific "Law." This law reads: "everywhere without exception, Protestants show far more suicides than the followers of other confessions" (Durkheim 1897:154), but it is usually cast in terms of a comparison between Protestants and Catholics (Pope and Danigelis 1981). In Chapter 2, we found that American data for 1971 did not support this sweeping claim. Reviewing the literature, we find only one modern study supporting Durkheim (Breault 1986), and this turned out to be in error (Girard 1988). But even as a law about his own time, Durkheim's statement is suspect: Whitney Pope (1976) revealed that Durkheim was, at best, very careless about data.

This chapter is an inquest into Durkheim's *Suicide*. We will first reanalyze some of the same data for European nations that Durkheim used. Next, we will examine data for France and for England that were readily available to Durkheim in sources that he commonly cited. Along the way we will expose the many conscious and flagrant misrepresentations Durkheim wrote about the English in his efforts to explain away a devastating exception to his claims. We will then employ our American data sets, covering much of the twentieth century, to see if Durkheim was a better prophet than he was a sociologist. Finally, we will rescue from obscurity the social scientist really responsible for "Durkheim's Law" and show that it was possible to uphold high standards of methodological rigor even a generation before Durkheim presumed to state the rules of the sociological method.

The Morselli Data

As noted in the previous chapter, many decades before Durkheim, considerable research was conducted on what then were known as moral statistics—so named because they measured actions having clear moral implications. In his pioneering work of moral statistics, discussed in the previous chapter, André Michel Guerry analyzed data on 26 different crimes against persons and on 26 crimes against property, on rates of military desertion, on illegitimacy, and on donations to the poor and to religious establishments, as well as on suicide. Nevertheless, suicide remained the central moral statistic; and some of the best minds of the time devoted substantial effort to understanding its causes.

As we noted in Chapter 2, Henry Morselli published his influential book on the subject in 1879 (with an American edition appearing only three years later). In it, Morselli frankly admits that his work might "resemble too nearly the well-known work of Professor Wagner of Berlin," published in 1864, but justifies his book on the basis of the many new statistics it contains. (We will have much more to say about Wagner, below.) Eighteen years later, Durkheim (1897) felt no need to explain resemblances between his *Suicide* and Morselli's. However, they had far more in common than the same title. As the long passage quoted in Chapter 2 reveals, Morselli argued that Protestants were much more prone to suicide than were Catholics, and, anticipating Durkheim's ruminations on the "spirit of free inquiry," suggested this was because Protestantism tends to develop "the reflective powers of the mind and to exaggerate the inward struggles of the conscience" (1879: 125).

Moreover, Durkheim drew most of his basic statistics on suicide from Morselli, although by judiciously citing Morselli's sources he made his dependence less obvious. Unlike Morselli, however, Durkheim made little effort to use the many newer suicide statistics available to him. Indeed, we shall see that Durkheim seems to have been quite unwilling to make even modest use of primary sources available in every serious library of the time.

In any event, let us look more closely at the Morselli suicide statis-

tics for nations of Europe on which the law of Protestants being sui-
cide-prone was based. Whitney Pope (1976) has noted that there is
some ambiguity about precisely which suicide statistics Durkheim used
from among the alternatives offered in Morselli's volume, which he
refers to as "averages compiled by Morselli." Pope also noted that these
same Protestant and Catholic averages were extremely biased by treat-
ing Germany as a set of independent states in a way that let Saxony's
off-scale rate determine the Protestant group mean.

To reconstruct the appropriate data, we selected the latest figures
Morselli provided for each nation, and merged units to create national
rates as needed. Specifically, we took the rates for seven German states
(Mecklenberg, Saxony, Hanover, Bavaria, Wurtemberg, Nassau, and
Baden), converted them to raw numbers, and then calculated a national rate of 14.8 suicides per 100,000 population for "Germany." We
should note that historically Germany had in fact achieved unification
nearly three decades before Durkheim wrote (Stier et al. 1956: 129).
Table 3.1 shows the Morselli rates for European nations in about 1870.

Before asking what Durkheim should have discovered from these
data, it seems pertinent to ask whether the data are any good. There are
several reasons for an affirmative answer. First of all, record-keeping
and reporting of data like these was remarkably well done in the nineteenth century. In some ways there was even greater emphasis on social
bookkeeping back then. But more compelling evidence can also be seen
in Table 3.1. Parallel to the 1870 data are 1980 data. The correlation
between the two rates is strong (r = 0.62). But two deviant cases can be
seen. Finland had a low rate (2.9 per 100,000) in 1870 but a very high
rate (24.1 per 100,000) in 1980. Since it was geographically peripheral
to Western Europe, Finland underwent relatively greater modernization than any of the other nations on the list during the period, so a
great increase in suicide is to be expected—as Steven Stack (1993) has
demonstrated. But this increase also crushes the correlation. With
Finland removed, the correlation between the 1870 and 1980 suicide
rates rises substantially (r = 0.78).

Over this period, some national boundaries moved. Austria, in particular, declined from a major archaic empire to a modest modern
nation. Take out Austria as well, and the correlation rises toward unity
(r = 0.87). Correlations of this size reflect the well-known stability of
suicide. They also suggest the validity of the 1870 data.

Table 3.1

Suicide and Catholicism in
Western Europe, 1870-1980

	Suicides per 100,000		Percent Roman Catholic	
	About 1870	About 1980	About 1870	1983
Finland	2.9	24.1	0.1	0.1
Norway	8.5	10.8	0.1	0.3
Denmark	25.8	23.9	0.2	0.6
Sweden	8.5	19.4	0.2	1.3
Great Britain	6.6	7.8	9.0	13.0
Netherlands	3.6	9.4	37.0	42.8
Germany	14.8	20.9*	47.5	44.0
Switzerland	19.6	22.0	54.0	51.2
Ireland	1.5	3.8	91.0	90.7
Austria	7.2	22.7	92.0	87.0
Belgium	6.0	16.2	98.0	88.4
France	15.0	15.4	98.0	86.0
Spain	1.7	4.0	99.0	97.3
Italy	4.0	5.8	99.0	86.5

* West Germany only

To establish the religious composition of these nations in 1870, we also consulted Morselli and augmented his statistics from standard sources. The third and fourth columns of Table 3.1 show the percent of each nation's population that was Catholic for about 1870 and for 1983, the latter data coming from the *Catholic Yearbook*. As would be expected, the correlation between the two rates is nearly unity ($r = 0.99$).

Had Durkheim had precisely these data on his desk, he would have proceeded as follows. He would have added up the suicide rates for the eight predominately Protestant nations (Finland through Switzerland) and divided by eight to obtain a Protestant suicide rate of 11.2 (or a rate of 112 per million, following the convention at the time to use a base of one million for figuring such rates). Then he would have summed the rates for the six Catholic countries to obtain a rate of 5.9 (or 59 per million). Then he would have said, "Voila!" People in Protestant nations are twice as likely to commit suicide. However, as Pope (1976) noted, this procedure ignores population size and maximizes the impact of any deviant case. Here, for example, the rate for tiny Denmark is given the same weight as that for large Great Britain. Were Denmark simply removed the Protestant rate would fall to 9.1. Now, shift Switzerland to the Catholic group on grounds that the majority of Swiss were Catholics in 1870, and the Protestant rate falls to 7.3 while the Catholic rate rises to 7.9, and Durkheim's law is repealed by his own data, using his own methods!

But suppose that Durkheim had been able to compute a product-moment correlation on the full set of fourteen nations. He would have found that it was rather weak (r = -0.26) between percent Catholic and the suicide rate, and statistically insignificant. Even so, this is a purely Danish effect. When Denmark is omitted, the correlation crashes to zero (r = -0.05). Clearly, the primary ecological data used by Durkheim (or the closest approximation of them that is possible) offered little real support for his "Law."

Having modern data at hand for comparison purposes, we took the opportunity to assess Durkheim's claim that it is not religion as such that matters, but community solidarity of which religion is but an indicator. In fact, for 1980, suicide is strongly associated with measures of economic development: per capita Gross National Product (r = 0.59) and telephones per 1,000 (r = 0.47). This confirms the belief that modern societies lack social integration. Moreover, there is a huge negative correlation (r = -0.59) between suicide and church attendance. Using regression to control for modernization effects caused only a modest reduction in the impact of church attendance. Thus we see that religion per se, not the particular religious tradition or mere social integration, is what seems to matter.

Although these data contradict Durkheim, in fairness we could not expect him to have used regression, nor, probably, correlations. For one thing, the product moment correlation was an English invention, and antagonism toward English social science was a hallmark of Durkheim and his circle. For another, almost no early sociologists used correlations. But we might have expected a professor at the Sorbonne to know how to read books.

Data for Durkheim's France

Beginning in 1878, the French government began to publish a very lengthy annual volume called *Annuaire Statistique de la France*. These are very like the modern *Statistical Abstract of the United States*, except the French volumes, published up to 1920, are more complete, as they include very detailed criminal justice and educational statistics. Most important for present purposes, each year they offered detailed statistics of suicide for each of the 87 departments of France. These suicide statistics in turn were summarized from a much longer report available annually from the Ministry of Justice. We shall use the suicide rates for all 87 French departments in 1881. Durkheim was aware of these data, because he published a nice map based on them (Durkheim 1897: 394).

The *Annuaire Statistique* did not include data on religious affiliation. It did, however, contain some useful substitutes, which we placed in our data set. Three measures of the relative strength of Catholicism from one department to another are the rate of priests per 10,000 population, the annual number of ordinations per 10,000, and the proportion of primary students enrolled in Catholic rather than secular schools. Interestingly, social scientists long before Durkheim realized that French data on ordinations of priests could be used to examine the effects of religion on suicide (Wagner 1864: 189), although sociologists from Durkheim onward seem to have been oblivious to the fact. Protestantism can be assessed on the basis of the number of Protestant clergy per 100,000 population.

In a footnote added to his famous statement about Protestants and suicide, Durkheim claimed that he lacked "data on confessional influence in France" (1897: 154), but cited a study from one department (Seine-et-Marne) that showed Protestants having twice the rate of Catholics. However, since data on confession are available to us, as they were in fact to him, what do they show?

First of all, they do indicate that where the Catholic Church was stronger, suicide was indeed lower. Table 3.2 shows significant negative correlations between the suicide rate and rates of priests, ordinations, and parochial school enrollment. Secondly, the correlation with the Protestant minister rate is also negative, while Durkheim would have predicted it was positive. The Protestant rate suffers from an excessive number of departments with a rate of zero. Excluding these strengthens the negative correlation (r = -0.24) between Protestantism and suicide. However, when regression is used to control for the priest ordination rate, the relationship between Protestants and suicide crashes to insignificance. In contrast, controls for urbanism did not eliminate the strong effects of the other religious variables.

What implications do these findings have for Durkheim? They fail to support his claims about Protestantism. No positive correlation between suicide and Protestant ministers appears. The strength of the other correlations suggest to us that the operative factor is religious commitment in general, not specifically Catholicism. In any event, Durkheim could easily have used these data. And he could have even more easily used data on suicide in England and Wales.

Durkheim's English Fantasies

The most aggressively misinformed and wrong-headed passages in the whole of *Suicide* concern the English. We suggest that this was not entirely because Durkheim saw it as his primary mission to wrest sociological leadership from the English school headed by Spencer and his anthropologist friends (Pickering 1984). The major reason was, we suggest, that the English presented Durkheim with the most patent evidence that his notions about Protestantism and suicide were simply wrong.

Durkheim was convinced that religious *pluralism* per se was weak integration—that where many faiths competed for the faithful, each was compromised. Since pluralism was a Protestant phenomenon, Durkheim could argue that all Protestant societies lacked moral integration. But England had one of the lowest suicide rates in Europe, a rate less than half that of Catholic France and even lower than that of Italy. How could he explain this? With fantasies.

Table 3.2
Religion and Suicide in the 86 Departments of France, 1881

	Correlation (r) with the Suicide Rate
Priests per 10,000	-0.29**
Catholic Ordinations per 10,000	-0.34**
Percent in Catholic Schools	-0.32**
Protestant Clergy per 100,000	
All Departments	-0.15
Only Departments with 1 or more Protestant Clergy	-0.24*

* Significant beyond .05
** Significant beyond .01

One of Durkheim's fantasies was that the English were a nation of uneducated illiterates:

> England, as we know, is the one Protestant country with the lowest suicides; it also most resembles Catholic countries with respect to education. In 1865 there were still 23 per cent of naval seaman who could not read and 27 per cent unable to write. (Durkheim 1897: 165)

What sailors have to do with it, one doesn't know. What one does know is that Durkheim was well aware that many European nations, including France, kept illiteracy statistics based on couples at the time of their wedding. Indeed, he mentions these data on the same page from which we took the above quotation, and he cites the *Annuaire Statistique* as his source. If we consult this source, we learn that of all French couples who married in 1881, 18.8 percent of the men and 29.8 percent of the women signed the register with an "X." By consulting the English census for 1871 we find that of all English couples who wed in 1870, 19.3 percent of the men and 26.3 percent of the women signed with an "X" too. In each nation literacy correlates positively and strongly with suicide, but since the rates for France and England are virtually identical, this cannot account for England having half the suicide rate of France. Durkheim should have known this, and we think that he did.

His second fantasy is about religion. England is not really a very Protestant nation, Durkheim claimed, for "the Anglican church is far more powerfully integrated than other Protestant churches," despite the fact that "England has been customarily regarded as the classic land of individual freedom" (Durkheim 1897: 160). He then went on to assert that "the Anglican clergy is the only Protestant clergy organized in a hierarchy. This external organization clearly shows an inner unity incompatible with a pronounced religious individualism" (Durkheim 1897: 161). It seems unlikely that Durkheim believed this patent falsehood, and it is hard to understand why his readers would accept such a bizarre statement. Durkheim must have known that all the state Lutheran churches of Scandinavia were hierarchal. Moreover, Scandinavia was much less pluralistic than England and Wales.

Anglicans were not even a majority of English churchgoers, and at the time Durkheim wrote, only 30 percent of British church members were Anglicans (Currie et al. 1977). Surely the presence of a multitude of nonconforming Protestant bodies in Britain and the many conflicts (including civil war) over religious pluralism were not state secrets unknown on the continent. But Durkheim seemed innocent of the rapid and amazing growth of Methodism and of the existence of Scottish Presbyterianism, to say nothing of the many other groups such as Baptists and Quakers. There were even more Mormons in England and Wales in 1851 than there were in the United States. Moreover, Durkheim himself reported that England had the highest rate of clergy per 1,000 population of any Protestant nation, obvious evidence of its immense pluralism.

On all counts, Durkheim's analysis of the relationship between religion and suicide required that England display the highest, not one of the lowest suicide rates in Europe. Yet he could write:

> ...far from weakening our theory, the case of England verifies it. If Protestantism there does not produce the same results as on the continent, it is because religious society there is much more strongly constituted and to this extent resembles the Catholic church. (Durkheim 1897: 161)

In the back of his book, Morselli included several very nice maps of suicide rates. One of these displays the annual suicide rates for each of the 44 counties of England and Wales, based on an average of data for the four years 1872–1876, accompanied by a table of the rates themselves. We can be certain that Durkheim had this map, because he extracted his map of Germany from Morselli (Durkheim 1897: 395). With minor effort Durkheim also could have obtained data on the religious composition of the English and Welsh counties, since a major religious census conducted in 1851 had stirred immense publicity and controversy.

The English Religious Census of 1851

In 1851, Her Majesty's Census Office asked every religious congregation in England and Wales to take a count of attendance at their services on Sunday, March 30. Wherever congregations failed to complete the report form, a local census official did it for them, and more than 30,000 Census Officers took part in gathering up the forms. When the final report appeared in December, 1853, it detailed the numbers of people present for morning, afternoon, and evening services, broken down by denomination, for every county and poor law district. It also provided data on the seating capacity of each religious building.

The report caused a great deal of outrage in the establishment, bringing no end of criticism to its author, Horace Mann. The trouble was that, although the Anglican Church was the subsidized state church, the majority of people at services on March 30 were in nonconforming Protestant "chapels." Some blamed bad weather in the more Anglican counties for this outcome, but records of the weather do not support them. Others said it was due to false counts provided by the nonconformist clergy. Mann refuted this charge on grounds that the ratio of attenders to seats was the same for Anglican and nonconformist reports, indicating no systematic inflation. He also suggested that careful supervision by the Census Officers minimized the opportunity for fraud. Today, scholars accept that the census was quite accurate (Gay 1971). Unfortunately, opposition by Anglican leaders prevented another religious census from ever being conducted.

Although the data are trustworthy, they present problems for generating certain kinds of rates. The trouble arises from the fact that most churches held services three times on Sunday with different levels of attendance at each. Obviously, many of the same people showed up at several services. How do we get a nonredundant total? The answer adopted by Mann, and followed ever since, is to use the total for the service with the most in attendance. Hence, if there were 180 people present during the morning, 128 in the afternoon, and 213 at the evening service, the latter is used to estimate total membership. Anyone who attended one or both of the other services, but not the one with the largest total, is not counted in the membership total. Since we can be sure that people were not counted twice at the same service, this technique gives a solidly conservative estimate; a congregation had at least this many attend on Sunday.

To explore the impact of religion on suicide in England and Wales, we will use denominational statistics from this census. As we saw from data on Europe, religious composition changes very slowly, so there is no reason to suppose that a 20-year gap between the religious and suicide statistics for England and Wales could matter. Other data come from the Census of 1871, making them contemporary with the suicide data.

Table 3.3 offers ironic support for Durkheim's confident claim that Catholicism and Anglicanism were equally proof against suicide: equal and irrelevant. In England and Wales, in the late nineteenth century, there was no correlation between either variable and suicide. But, wherever church attendance was higher, and especially where the proportion of nonconformist members was higher, suicide rates were lower. However, the apparent relationship between nonconformity and suicide is due entirely to the fact that church attendance was higher in nonconformist areas. With attendance controlled in multiple regression, the relationship disappeared. As Durkheim predicted, literacy of people getting married is highly correlated with suicide. But controls for literacy did not wipe out the attendance effect—both remained strong and highly significant. What we find, then, are no denominational effects on suicide in England and Wales. Rather, it is religion per se that matters.

Finally, recall that Durkheim believed that religious pluralism meant a lack of moral integration. This claim too can be tested in the English data. For each county of England and Wales a pluralism rate was calculated using the Herfindahl Index, which is the standard measure of market diversity used by economists (Iannaccone 1991). Notice that pluralism in fact is negatively associated with suicide, entirely contrary to Durkheim's prediction. Moreover, when both church attendance and pluralism are entered into a regression analysis, both retain highly significant, independent effects on suicide and together account for 35 percent of the variance in suicide.

None of these findings supports Durkheim's "Law."

American Suicide in 1926

In Chapter 2, we examined recent American data and failed to find the Protestant–Catholic differences predicted by Durkheim, although we acknowledged that this might merely reflect changes that have occurred over the past century. In the United States particularly, Catholics and Protestants seem to have become quite similar on many counts. However, as we saw, good American data exist from as early as 1906, just nine years after Durkheim wrote. Therefore the next obvious step in evaluating Durkheim's "Law" is to examine these American data.

For 1926, the year with arguably the best data, we can compute the proportion Catholic for 140 American cities that also provide suicide data. The simplest way to do this is to divide the number of Catholic church members by the total number of church members, and multiply the result by 100. This gives us the percent of church members who are Catholics, what we might call the *relative Catholicism* of the city. By this measure, the association between relative Catholicism and the suicide rate is -0.07, completely insignificant. If we restrict ourselves to the 78 cities over 100,000 in population, this coefficient strengthens slightly to -0.14, but this is still insignificant.

Of course, it is possible that some other variable artificially sup-

Table 3.3

Religion and Suicide in the 44 Counties
of England and Wales, 1870s

	Correlation (r) with the Suicide Rate
Percent Anglican	0.06
Percent Roman Catholic	0.08
Percent Non-Conformist	-0.51**
Percent Attended Church	-0.43**
Percent of Couples Literate	0.54**
Pluralism	-0.33*
	Standardized Beta with the Suicide Rate
Pluralism	-0.428**
Percent Attended Church	-0.492**
$R^2 = .35**$	

* Significant beyond .05
** Significant beyond .01

presses a real association between Catholicism and suicide, but we were unable to find one. Perhaps the analysis most worthy of inspection is one that adds the independent variables we found to be potent in the previous chapter: the percent born in the state and the church member rate. We must emphasize that no problem of auto-correlation exists between the church member rate and the proportion of church members who are Catholics. So long as there are some church members in a city, the proportion of these members who are Catholic is free to range from zero to 100 percent.

In Table 3.4 we see that relative Catholicism still explains nothing about suicide, when the two other variables are combined with it in a multiple regression analysis. And the introduction of Catholicism changes nothing significantly about the way that born-in-state and the church member rate combine to explain variations in suicide. The findings were replicated when we used data for cities from 1906 and 1916.

Religion and Attitudes Toward Suicide

In the first chapter we made predictions about the impact of religion at both the individual and the collective levels of analysis. Thus far, how-

Table 3.4

Catholicism, Moral and Social Integration and
Suicide in American Cities, 1926

	Correlation (r)	Standardized Beta
140 Cities		
Percent of Church Members who are Catholics	-0.07	0.02
Church Member Rate	-0.35**	-0.24*
Percent Born in State	-0.43**	-0.34**
R^2 = .23**		
78 Largest Cities		
Percent of Church Members who are Catholics	-0.14	0.07
Church Member Rate	-0.50**	-0.39**
Percent Born in State	-0.50**	-0.32**
R^2 = .34**		

* Significant beyond .05
** Significant beyond .01

ever, our focus has been on collectivities. We have seen that Protestant areas and nations do not adhere to Durkheim's law. However, something called the *ecological fallacy* involves imputing findings based on aggregate (or ecological) units to individual level behavior—in this case assuming that among individuals in the same society Catholics are not less likely than Protestants to commit suicide simply because Catholic and Protestant areas show no consistent differences in their suicide rates. What holds at the collective level may or may not hold true at the level of individual behavior (although usually it will). It is technically possible (if quite implausible) that suicide rates in Catholic areas are generated primarily by Protestants, while in Protestant areas it is primarily Catholics who are killing themselves.

To guard against the ecological fallacy, social scientists like to examine individual level as well as collective data. This is quite difficult in the case of suicide, since it is impossible to interview people who have committed suicide and very difficult to discover much about the biographies of suicide victims. However, it is possible to interview people about their attitudes towards suicide, and a question about suicide has been asked in the General Social Surveys (GSS) for a number of years: "A person has the right to end their own life if this person is tired of living and ready to die?" Respondents can answer "yes" or "no."

We merged three years of the survey (1989, 1990, and 1991) in order to increase the stability of the statistics (n = 2,861). As can be seen in Table 3.5, there is no difference between Catholics and Conservative Protestants in their opposition to suicide—only 8 percent of each group said "yes." Members of Liberal Protestant denominations are less opposed and the difference is significant (p < .0001). However, the really important contrast is between religious people and those with no religious preference, more than a third of whom said "yes." In addition, among both Roman Catholics (gamma = .304) and Conservative Protestants (gamma = .311), opposition to suicide increased with church attendance—the more regular attenders being more opposed. There was no church attendance effect among Liberal Protestants, and virtually no church attendance at all among those giving their religious preferences as "None." Thus, the individual level data give reasonable support to the collective results.

Admittedly this question measures attitudes, not behavior—it is not a measure of actual suicide. But responses to the question are geographically distributed in the same way as the actual suicide rate, which is much higher in the Far West than in the rest of the United States: while 12 percent of persons in the East, Midwest, and Southern regions said "yes," 21 percent of those living in the Far West did so. This sug-

Table 3.5

Attitudes Toward Suicide (General Social Surveys 1989, 1990, 1991)

"A person has the right to end their own life if the person is tired of living and ready to die?"

	Roman Catholic	Conservative Protestant	Liberal Protestant	None
Yes	8%	8%	16%	37%
No	92%	92%	84%	63%
	100%	100%	100%	100%
n=	(719)	(556)	(778)	(219)

gests that the attitude question may tap real differences in social propensities towards suicide. As we will see in Chapter 5, the West also is remarkable for its lack of church-membership.

Plea Bargaining with Durkheim's Attorneys

At this point in our inquest, we can imagine that Durkheim's lawyers have seen the handwriting on the wall, and sense that their client is about to be convicted of willful distortion of the truth and of sociological incompetence. They approach the prosecutor and suggest that they might be willing to plead guilty to a lesser offense: theft. After all, they say, is it not true that "Durkheim's Law" really belongs to somebody else?

Maurice Halbwachs (1930), a disciple of Durkheim, attributed the law not to his master but to Adolf Heinrich Gotthilf Wagner, a German follower of the French moral statistician Adolphe Quetelet. Initial attempts to locate a copy of Wagner's own writings failed until one of us was able to visit the Library of Congress, and we were frankly astonished to discover the high quality of the social data and analysis contained in Wagner's 1864 masterwork, *Die Gesetzmaessigkeit in den Scheinbar Willkuerlichen Menschlichen Handlungen vom Standpunkte der Statistik*. A free translation of the title might be: "The Lawful Regularity of Apparently Voluntary Human Actions Seen from the Standpoint of Statistics." It is a shame that this complex and pioneering work has not been translated into English, and that it appears to have vanished from German scholarly consciousness.

Wagner suggests that regularities can be found in many kinds of data such as, for example, the percentage of letters mailed which carry bad addresses and the results of standardized school examinations. But he particularly emphasizes the regularities in statistics for marriage, suicide, and crime, because abundant data were already available by 1864 and their social significance makes them good for testing theories of human behavior. His book is written in several parts, arranged in progressively deeper layers of analysis covering the same territory. The first section is a public lecture that communicates his findings to a general, educated audience. Twenty-two pages of footnotes to that lecture provide technical support. The next section is a scholarly discourse on the concept of regularity in human behavior. This is followed in turn by a remarkably careful and resourceful analysis of comparative European social statistics, written for Wagner's intellectual peers, who could not have been numerous back in 1864.

While Durkheim is exceedingly vague in citing his sources, Wagner gives precise details about each one of his very many data sources. Where Durkheim sweeps to unsubstantiated conclusions, Wagner carefully weighs alternative explanations. As models for painstaking, rigorous, thorough science, there could hardly be a greater contrast between Wagner and Durkheim, and we fear that the better scientist lost the competition for history's notice.

Wagner himself does not claim to be the discoverer of the Protestant-Catholic difference in suicide rates, noting earlier writers who voiced suspicions that such a difference existed. Rather, he more modestly asserts that his data place this hypothesis on a firm empirical basis for the first time (Wagner 1864: 189).

Based on his wealth of primary sources, Wagner (1864: 125) calculated suicide rates for 128 European states and provinces, 126 of which he was able to characterize in terms of religious confession. If both Protestantism and Catholicism claimed at least a third of the population, he classified the area as mixed. But if fewer than a third were Protestant, he called it a Catholic region. And if fewer than a third were Catholic, he coded it Protestant. Note that Wagner was quite clear about his coding scheme, while a third of a century of supposed progress in social scientific methodology left Durkheim rather vague on how he assigned states to the Protestant or Catholic categories.

None of the 35 Protestant states had suicide rates below 50 per million, in contrast with 32 of the 66 Catholic states. While 19 Protestant states had rates above 150 per million, only 2 Catholic states had such high rates. However, always the judicious analyst, Wagner was not convinced that these data proved that Protestantism, as such, stimulates suicide, compared with Catholicism:

> In order to demonstrate this and to isolate the factor of religion, it is not sufficient to compare purely Protestant and Catholic countries, although here already remarkable phenomena come to light. For the variation in the absolute frequency of suicide of all the countries is without doubt the resultant of all the separate factors which play a part. And while the possibility must be admitted that one factor might exert an entirely overwhelming determining influence, this could not be proven satisfactorily

from comparison of the absolute number of suicides of different countries, because the other contributory factors can also be highly various. More can be gained by so choosing the cases to be compared (countries and peoples) so that the extraneous factors are equally represented as much as possible and therefore can be ignored like continuous entries on both sides of the account, while the chief variation consists of the factor under research. Therefore one should seek comparison countries of equal nationality, as much as possible also tribe, of equal climate, equal culture, education, economy, and conditions of well-being, etc., but populated by humans of different religious confession. More valuable however is determination of suicide frequency among inhabitants of various religions and confessions in the same country, because here presumably all other factors operate with most equal force. (Wagner 1864: 180, our translation)

It seems to us that Wagner was struggling to explain the problem of spuriousness and wishing for multivariate statistical techniques to solve it. Durkheim handled this problem very differently. When the facts refused to fit his argument he either suppressed them or wrapped them in twisted rhetoric. Wagner recognized the problems, worked to the absolute limit of the analytical techniques of his day to find the truth, and expressed honest uncertainty that he had succeeded.

Table 3.6 is copied from Wagner (182), and compares suicides among Protestants and Catholics in particular countries. He also offers more detailed breakdowns for many parts of Germany and Austria, which space does not permit us to duplicate here. In the three German states (Prussia, Bavaria, and Wuertemberg), suicide rates are clearly higher among Protestants than among Catholics. The same is true for the two major portions of the Austro-Hungarian Empire. However in Siebenbuergen, the reverse is true: the rate of suicides is much higher among Catholics than among Protestants.

Siebenbuergen was the remote Eastern end of the Austro-Hungarian Empire, called Transylvania in some later reports (e.g. Morselli 1882: 122). Although a substantial number of German-speakers lived in this Eastern outpost of the empire, it may have been largely outside the culture and society of Germanic Europe (although the same could be said of Hungary). This fact suggests that the familiar Protestant-Catholic suicide differences may have been limited to greater

Table 3.6

Suicide Rates by Denomination in Germany and Austria, Mid-Nineteenth Century

Suicides per Million

State	Years	Catholic	Protestant	Other Christian	Jew	Prot/Cath Ratio
Prussia	1849-55	49.6	159.9	130.8	46.4	322
Bavaria	1844-56	49.1	135.4	-	105.9	276
Wuertemberg	1846-60	77.9	113.5	-	65.6	131*
Austria	1852-59	51.3	79.5	54.0	20.7	155
Hungary	1851-59	32.8	54.4	12.3	17.6	166
Siebenbuergen	1851-59	113.2	73.6	20.5	35.5	65

* There is an error in this row because, if the Protestant and Catholic rates are correct, the ratio should be 146.

Table 3.7

Suicide Rates in Various Countries, According to Durkheim

Suicides per Million

State	Years	Catholic	Protestant	Jew	Source Cited by Durkheim
Austria	1852-59	51.3	79.5	20.7	Wagner
Prussia	1849-55	49.6	159.9	46.4	Wagner
Prussia	1869-72	69	187	96	Morselli
Prussia	1890	100	240	180	Prinzing
Baden	1852-62	117	139	87	Legoyt
Baden	1870-74	136.7	17	124	Morselli
Baden	1878-88	170	242	210	Prinzing
Bavaria	1844-56	49.1	35.4	105.9	Morselli
Bavaria	1884-91	94	224	193	Prinzing
Wuertemberg	1846-60	77.9	113.5	65.6	Wagner
Wuertemberg	1873-76	120	190	60	Durkheim
Wuertemberg	1881-90	119	170	142	Durkheim

Germany. In his more detailed tables, Wagner reported higher Catholic than Protestant rates in the German areas of Merseburg and Frankfort, and in Austrian Galicia and "Grenze" (military frontiers). Of course, as Wagner noted, these deviant cases may merely reflect random variation based on small numbers of suicides in relatively small populations.

Durkheim published data comparable to Table 3.6, given here as Table 3.7, comparing Protestant and Catholic suicide rates for Austria and four German states. He cites five different "observers" as sources, including himself, Morselli and Wagner (cf. Legoyt 1881; Prinzing 1906). But the Wagner data were all copied by Morselli (1879: 122), and thus we cannot be sure Durkheim really read or worked from Wagner's excellent book. Morselli included the three subdivisions of the Austro-Hungarian Empire with higher Catholic rates, however, so when Durkheim chose to quote only "Austria," which had a higher Protestant rate, he was consciously ignoring counter instances without warning his reader that he was doing so (Pope 1976: 71).

Thus, when Durkheim wrote that Protestants have higher rates of suicides than Catholics "everywhere without exception," either he was lying or he assumed that his reader would understand that he was referring only to the geographical units listed in his own table. To be sure, he could easily have attacked the discordant data, saying for example that Transylvania was a remote outpost offering unreliable data (cf. Wagner 1864: 184–185). He could argue that the overwhelming majority of geographic districts in Germany and the Austro-Hungarian Empire proved the superiority of Protestantism with respect to suicide, even if a few cases deviated from this strong pattern. But he did not do this, choosing instead to select only those data that fitted his prediction exactly.

The fact remains that despite his falsely absolutist claim, Durkheim was right that Protestants tended to show higher rates of suicide than did Catholics living in the same district. However, the data were limited to the German cultural region and, as we know, the law did not apply to England or, shortly thereafter, to the United States.

Whitney Pope has expressed the view that these findings might be spurious, perhaps reflecting different levels of modernization of Catholic and Protestant populations even in the same region. He says further that other social differences may have separated members of the two confessions: "To suggest only one possibility, those familiar with Weber…might suspect that Protestants are more involved than Catholics in modern business, particularly at its higher levels; Durkheim…himself suggested, in his well-known analysis of chronic economic anomie, that such involvement leads to higher suicide rates" (Pope 1976: 72).

Interestingly, Wagner (1864: 190-196) immediately follows his discussion of religion with an analysis of education and suicide. His data are entirely from France, so they cannot directly test models of spuriousness in the German and Austrian data, but they show a strong correlation between the suicide rate and high levels of education. Conceivably, in the German cultural area, level of education might correlate with religious confession, which would then show a spurious correlation with suicide.

At this point in our inquest, we face two rather important charges against Durkheim. First, that he stole "sociology's one Law" from Wagner. Second, that the data on which the "Law" was based were far more mixed than Durkheim revealed—the sources from which he took his data do not support his claim that the Protestant suicide rate exceeds that for Catholics *everywhere*.

However, were this an actual inquest, Durkheim's defenders would no doubt bring up the statute of limitations. Whatever Durkheim did, it was done a century ago. Thus, a judge probably would rule: case proven, but dismissed because not prosecuted in a timely fashion.

Conclusion

The failure of Durkheim's "Law" when tested by ecological data is of the utmost importance for sociology, and should be a source of considerable embarrassment for our field. For years, we accepted Durkheim's claims without checking them, even though adequate data have existed all along. For example, one of the best and most widely used textbooks in social statistics presented Durkheim's misuse of data as a prime example of how hypotheses should be tested, illustrating "the proper relationship between theory and data" (Loether and McTavish 1976: 467). At the very least, Durkheim was a poor professor of research methods and a bad role model.

The Law, such as it is, belongs of course to Wagner, not Durkheim. Had Wagner's important work not vanished from scholarly sight before sociology was born, European researchers might have looked further into his tremendously assiduous collection of data, applied multivariate statistical techniques when they became available, and resolved the questions he so carefully raised about the meaning of apparently strong Protestant-Catholic differences in German-speaking nations. Today, we can only hope that quantitatively minded European sociologists with ready access to the original data will be motivated to complete the important work Wagner began a century and a third ago.

Certainly, Durkheim's book harmonized with more recent work that preferred to contrast major denominational groupings, usually simply comparing Protestants with Catholics. Thus, *Suicide* helped retard exploration of other measures of religion, from survey items on belief and practice to ecological data about church membership. Admittedly, the sociology of religion was not at all quantitative when the standard edition of *Suicide* was published in the United States, and Durkheim may have usefully propagandized in favor of numbers. But the largest number employed by many of our colleagues of the previous generation was three, used to count: Protestant, Catholic, Jew.

The public relations success of *Suicide*, both in France soon after it was published and in the United States many years later, boosted the fortunes of a particular conception of sociology. All sociologists agree that *social facts* exist outside the control of the individual, but Durkheim seemed to be saying that it was totally useless to try to analyze these supra-individual factors in terms of social networks, interaction, or any other small-scale phenomena that arise from the actions of individuals (Homans 1967: 60). Put another way: we complain that Durkheim's success discouraged the kinds of sociology that we, ourselves, practice.

A chief purpose of this chapter has been to balance the books on Durkheim as a putative father of quantitative sociology. Let us, then, conclude this inquest by asking (reminiscent of Watergate): what did Durkheim know and when did he know it? The answer is unpleasant. There is ample reason to think he knew way too much about the many exceptions to his theory. But, as was so common among social scientists in his era—Wagner excepted—Durkheim always thought that he knew better. When big ideas are involved, what do some grubby facts collected by little bureaucrats matter, anyway? To insist that this man ought to be celebrated for his role in stimulating quantitative sociology is at best to acknowledge a "latent function." That is, sociology might have gained some benefits from having been mistaken about Durkheim's worth as a scientist. If so, it is not much of a basis for his continuing regard.

Finally, what took us so long? How could generations of sociologists have encountered *Suicide* in college or graduate school and not noticed its many absurdities and slights of hand? Perhaps it was because most sociologists share Durkheim's fundamental beliefs, including his opposition to religion.

4

Rediscovering Moral Communities

If Durkheim's immensely admired study of suicide lacked originality as well as objectivity, the same is true of his equally celebrated *The Elementary Forms of Religious Life* (1915). Durkheim's famous proposition in this book is that the object of religious worship is, in fact, society—that when people perform religious rites they worship, without knowing it, their own reflection. We must admit we have never found any merit in this assertion and have elsewhere dismissed it as an empty metaphor (Stark and Bainbridge 1987). Nevertheless, among our colleagues it has long been one of the most quoted and discussed claims ever made about religion. Despite all this attention, we know of but one mention (Pickering 1984) in social scientific publications of the fact that the *entire argument* was "borrowed" without acknowledgement from Ludwig Feuerbach (1804–1872). Feuerbach was one of the most influential German philosophers of the nineteenth century—a student of Hegel and a teacher of Marx. In his most important work, *Das Wesen des Christentums* (The Essence of Christianity) published in 1841, Feuerbach's primary thesis, argued at great length, was that the object of religious worship is society. This is so well-known among philoso-

Daniel P. Doyle, Lori Kent, Robert Crutchfield, and Roger Finke contributed to essays on which portions of this chapter are based.

phers that it is given careful coverage in the entry on Feuerbach in the *Encyclopaedia Britannica*. But, as noted, Feuerbach's priority is essentially unknown among sociologists.

Methodologically too, *The Elementary Forms* resembles *Suicide*. Durkheim's analysis of anthropological reports about the Australian aboriginals, on which the entire book is based, is marked by the omission of very significant contrary facts, even though some of these had appeared in Durkheim's own, earlier writing on the subject. As the distinguished anthropologist Sir Edward Evans-Pritchard put it: "Durkheim just ignores what does not fit into his picture"(1981: 157). Nor is this a recent discovery. In his review of the book, published in 1915 in the *American Anthropologist*, Alexander Goldenweiser noted that Durkheim's "facts are strangely inaccurate."

Summing up the consensus among anthropologists vis-à-vis Durkheim's work, Evans-Pritchard wrote:

> We have, I fear, come down decisively against Durkheim and to conclude that he may not in any sense be regarded as a scientist—at best a philosopher, or I would rather say, a metaphysician. He broke every cardinal rule of critical scholarship, as well as of logic; in particular in his disregard of evidence, and especially of those evidences which negated his theory. (168)

That being in the record, we now acknowledge that the *definition* of religion proposed by Durkheim (1915: 47) has contributed positively to social scientific studies of the link between religion and conformity: religion is a "unified system of beliefs and practices relative to sacred things" which unites adherents into a "moral community."

Following Durkheim, a number of social scientists attempted to refine the concept of *moral community*. Although Durkheim defined moral communities entirely on religious grounds, it was clear that his additional concerns about secular sources of social integration could usefully be included in the definition. Subsequently, moral communities are identified as those which excel in social integration, having strong social as well as moral sources of integration.

The Metropolis as a Moral Community

During the 1930s and 40s, the study of moral communities was popular among proponents of the University of Chicago version of human ecology (Shaw and McKay 1929, 1931, 1942; Angell 1942, 1947, 1949). Then references to moral communities all but disappeared, with Robert Angell's 1972 attempt to replicate his 1942 research being the only notable publication. A major reason for this was that, because of a perceived lack of adequate data, the studies were virtually tautologies. That is, moral and social integration were not measured directly, but were inferred from their supposed consequences. For example, Angell measured moral integration on the basis of per capita contributions to the United Fund and official crime rates. Even when more suitable measures of integration were used, such as rates of population turnover, the studies suffered from the inclusion of very questionable variables and from the absolute omission of the core of moral integration: religion. Thus, although Angell (1974: 608) defined cities as having greater moral integration the "greater the proportion of native whites to Negroes, Orientals, and Mexicans," as well as "the fewer the mothers who are gainfully employed," he made no use of the easily available census reports on religious membership. In this chapter we attempt to rectify these errors and shortcomings in order to "rediscover" moral communities, an effort we began in 1980. And, not surprisingly, we will give special emphasis to the moral dimension.

As we saw in the chapters on suicide, American SMSAs differ extremely in their proportions of church members. This fact has tended to be obscured by the familiar survey research findings that virtually all Americans will claim affiliation with some religious denomination when they are asked "What is your religious affiliation?" But only about two thirds of Americans are actually carried on the membership rolls of specific churches. That is, while nearly everyone claims a religion, about a third are unchurched. This is not to suggest that unchurched Americans are predominantly irreligious: the majority of them also accept common religious beliefs and engage in private religious practices. For example, three-fourths of the unchurched pray (half of them at least once a day), and about seven out of ten regard the Bible as "inspired" and believe that Jesus rose from the dead (Gallup 1978). But the fact that they are not part of an organized religious body suggests that their religion lacks social reinforcement, just as it lacks social expression. As we have often pointed out, religion gains its power to influence behavior to the extent that it is social. Therefore, we believe that variations in the proportions of church members is an appropriate and direct measure of the religious climate of metropolitan areas.

We readily acknowledge that this measure is not all that we would like. While many unchurched people hold religious beliefs, many churched people are not particularly religious in other ways (Stark and Glock 1968). Hence, it would be especially valuable to have various measures of belief to help portray the religious climate of SMSAs. It would also be desirable to have measures of other aspects of faith: private prayer, scripture reading, and the extent to which religion finds expression in everyday conversations and via the local media. However, since no such data for SMSAs are likely to become available, it is futile to list them. More important, if only one measure of religiousness were available it ought to be one that most clearly reflects social rather than purely individual manifestations of piety. It may well be that a wholly private faith can satisfy the religious needs of many individuals. But such faith may have very slight importance in binding persons to the moral order. For faith to influence behavior it must do so through creating a moral climate, and this requires the social expression of religion. Church membership directly measures the social embodiment of religion.

Crime in 1971

The data on crime rates that we will use are for 1971 and come from the *Uniform Crime Report* for 1972, and thus are contemporary with the data on church membership. Deficiencies in the official data made it necessary to omit 24 SMSAs for which only partial crime data were available. We were also forced to omit 26 SMSAs from the New England region because of well-known problems in how they are constituted. Thus our analysis is based on the remaining 193 SMSAs.

An initial test of our hypothesis produced a highly significant correlation of -0.36 between the church membership rate and the overall crime rate. However, this correlation was somewhat reduced by an uncontrolled suppressor variable. The proportion of the population that is African-American is modestly positively related both to the crime rate and to the church membership rate. With this variable controlled using the partial correlations method, the correlation between church membership and crime strengthens to -0.44, which is significant beyond the .001 level. Moreover, no other variable we examined had such a large effect on the overall crime rate, and we examined all of the standard variables found to be important in other ecological studies of the crime rate.

The overall crime rate included seven fundamental crime categories (plus some additional minor property offenses). However, property crimes constitute so large a proportion of the total of indexed crimes that it is wise to examine each of the constituent crime categories separately. As can be seen in Table 4.1, church membership has considerably more impact on property crimes than on violent crimes (r = -0.45 versus r = -0.20). Moreover, within these categories there is considerable variation in the correlations when more specific offense categories are examined. Thus, among property crimes, high correlations are found for the burglary rate (r = -0.46) and the larceny rate (r = -0.44). But the correlations between church membership and auto theft are much lower (r = -0.18), although still significant above the .05 level.

Among violent crimes, the correlations are significant, but somewhat low, for the homicide rate (r = -0.12), the robbery rate (r = -0.16), and the assault rate (r = -0.14). But the correlation between church membership and the rape rate is quite high (r = -0.41).

It is not novel to discover that variables that influence property crime rates have less effect on violent crimes, and vice versa (Crutchfield et al 1982). Indeed, these rates are not highly intercorrelated (for example, the correlation between the larceny rate and the homicide rate in this data set is only 0.18). This suggests that a major

Table 4.1

Partial Correlations Between Church Membership and Crime Rates in 193 American Metropolitan Areas, 1971

	Partial Correlation with Church Membership Rate (Controlling for % African American)
All Crimes	-0.44**
Property Crimes	-0.45**
Burglary	-0.46**
Larceny	-0.44**
Auto Theft	-0.18*
Violent Crimes	-0.20*
Homicide	-0.12*
Rape	-0.41**
Robbery	-0.16*
Assault	-0.14*

* Significant beyond .05
** Significant beyond .001

conceptual task confronts criminology. While all of these rates measure "crime," the concept of crime may be too inclusive to be of utility for theories of crime causation. Indeed, there is good reason to suppose that these various crimes may have rather different causes. If so, then we will obviously have to construct more narrow and more clearly specified concepts than the legal concept of crime.

In pondering our results, one possible line of interpretation suggests itself. Homicide and assault tend to be crimes of impulse and to occur within family and friendship networks. They typically do not reflect a sustained pattern of deviance (such as a career of burglaries) and thus may be less easily governed by bonds to the moral order. That is, many who commit homicide or assault claim they "lost their heads" in the heat of the dispute, not that they consciously turned their backs on conventional moral codes. Furthermore, acts of violence that tend to occur within social networks (rather than between strangers) will tend to be correlated with community stability—with aspects of communities, such as low rates of geographic mobility, that tend to promote contact with family and friends rather than contact among strangers (Crutchfield et al 1982). However, social forces that sustain community stability also sustain church membership and thus will reduce the impact of religion on these forms of interpersonal violence. We will return to this point.

The impulse versus intentional deviance interpretation is also consistent with the weak correlation between church membership and auto theft—typically juvenile "joy riding" that may not signal chronic patterns of nonconformity. However, there also may be a special problem with ecological analysis of auto theft rates. Professional auto thieves frequently steal a car in one city and drive it a short distance to a different city where it is chopped up for parts or sold intact. The very function of cars is transportation, and thus the rates for nearby cities are likely to be interrelated, often in complex and unpredictable ways. Also, cities presumably differ in the extent to which cars are parked on streets, in locked garages, or in other secure places. Thus the lack of a correlation between church membership and the rate of auto theft may merely represent problems with the auto theft variable itself, although we are also suggesting that much car stealing is impulsive.

Rape, on the other hand, may tend to be a repeated offense and could be more symptomatic of sustained nonconformity than are homicide and assault. Moreover, the kinds of rape most often reported to police are not network offenses, but most typically occur between strangers. These differences may account for the high negative correlation between church membership and the rape rate. Another possibility that we examine below is that religion deters divorce, while a high divorce rate promotes or reflects a breakdown of relations between the sexes, unleashing an increase in rape.

Unfortunately, a reconceptualization of crimes in terms of impulse versus intentional deviance is unable to explain the low correlation between church membership and the robbery rate. Robbery is a career offense and thus indicative of conscious and chronic nonconformity. This would lead us to expect that it would be quite strongly influenced by church membership. Yet it displays the same weak (but significant) level of correlation as do homicide and assault. We are unable to offer an explanation at this point, but will return to the issue when considering 1980 data, below.

To test for possible spuriousness, a number of other variables were controlled both singly and simultaneously. These included population size, age composition, unemployment, poverty, education, and percent Spanish surname. None of these reduced the initial correlations. However, one variable did modestly reduce the correlations: population change 1960-1970. This is a somewhat crude measure of in and out migration and we employ it as a measure of social integration. As such it ought to impact on crime rates, and it does.

Having established a prima facie case for the capacity of religion to deter at least some kinds of crime, we can examine the thesis more closely, providing more details about statistical controls, using data from 1980.

Crime in 1980

The rates of church membership for 1980, provide the basis for an analysis of church membership and crime (Bainbridge 1989, 1990, 1997). Again, the *Uniform Crime Report* gives us information about crimes known to the police. The *UCR* had begun to tabulate arsons, but many jurisdictions had not yet started reporting them, so we could not include this crime in our analysis. We also dropped auto theft from consideration, because of the doubts explained above.

In the following analysis, we focus on the seventy-five large (over 500,000 population) metropolitan areas outside New England. Church membership is measured by our adjusted 1980 rate, but crude rates give very similar results. We will use the most direct control for social integration available in census data, "same house"—the percent of persons over age five who were living in the same house they had lived in five years before the census.

We will also employ controls for family disruption and socioeconomic frustration. We believe it is irresponsible to throw a host of control variables into a multivariate analysis merely because they are available. However, theories of crime stress factors that are probably also related to church membership, and we did not feel we could ignore them. The rates for homicide, assault, and rape undoubtedly include many cases of family violence, and traditionally family disruption has been held responsible for much youth crime. Therefore, we include the percent divorced as a control. Many kinds of crime may be more common where substantial portions of the population experience economic and social frustration. Therefore we also include the percent of families in poverty and the percent African-American.

Table 4.2 shows the correlations linking moral integration (church membership) and social integration (same house) and each of the three control variables with each of six crime rates. There are significant zero-order correlations linking church membership to four of the six crimes: rape, assault, burglary, and larceny. However, essentially zero coefficients reveal no associations with murder and robbery. Social integration is significantly correlated with all of the crimes except robbery. This is not exactly the same pattern we found for the 1971 data, but here we are looking only at very large cities, and below we shall examine how city size affects the results.

The table also reveals that each of the control variables has significant correlations with at least some of the crime rates. We certainly seem to have found many of the factors that would have to be considered in any successful explanation of crime. The next step is to employ them in a multivariate analysis, to see their affect on the apparent influence of church membership. The bottom of Table 4.2 shows the results of multiple regression analysis using all five independent variables. Neither moral nor social integration appear to influence homicide and rape rates, while only moral integration influences assault. Social integration influences burglary, larceny, and robbery. Each equation accounts for a substantial amount of the variation in each crime rate. How, then, are we to make sense of the pattern of associations between church membership and crime, shown in the bottom of Table 4.2? There is good evidence that religion really does deter four of the six crimes: assault, burglary, larceny, and robbery. It appears to have no capacity to deter homicide and rape, unless possibly it deters rape indirectly by reducing divorce.

In the popular mind, murder and rape are crimes of passion. Burglary, larceny, and robbery have in common the fact that all three

Table 4.2

Moral and Social Integration and Crime,
75 U. S. Metropolitan Areas, 1980

	Burglary	Larceny	Robbery	Assault	Rape	Murder
Correlations (r)						
Church Membership	-0.44***	-0.63***	-0.01	-0.23*	-0.38***	0.03
Same House	-0.60***	-0.64***	-0.04	-0.29**	-0.58***	-0.25*
% In Poverty	0.38***	-0.02	0.49***	0.36***	0.37***	0.62***
% African-American	0.12	-0.10	0.44***	0.29**	0.32**	0.55***
% Divorced	0.60***	0.58***	0.21*	0.39***	0.72***	0.38***
Standardized Betas						
Church Membership	-0.22*	-0.39**	-0.23*	-0.26*	-0.11	0.06
Same House	-0.26*	-0.30*	-0.31*	0.08	-0.10	-0.03
% In Poverty	0.40***	0.03	0.37**	0.28*	0.17*	0.39***
% African-American	0.03	0.08	0.29**	0.24*	0.33***	0.34***
% Divorced	0.25*	0.11	0.31**	0.30*	0.59***	0.40***
R^2=	.56	.49	.36	.32	.69	.59

* Significant beyond .05
** Significant beyond .01
*** Significant beyond .001

are forms of stealing, and one might argue that many assaults are committed in the course of robbery. *Exodus* 20:15 says, "Thou shalt not steal," and our data strongly support the proposition that church membership deters stealing. The strongest association is for larceny, the most common crime and probably the one committed by the widest range of people. Burglary and robbery may more often be professional crimes, done by individuals with a generally deviant lifestyle. Thus, acts of larceny may be more readily deterred by religious beliefs. In any case, these crime results give religion an independent power to deter several kinds of deviant behavior in which harm is done to other persons. None of the statistical controls we tried could wipe out the larceny association, and a set of highly reasonable controls left four of the six crimes with the predicted negative associations to church membership.

One limitation of the SMSA data sets is that they exclude New England, where metropolitan areas are not simple assemblies of counties. We were able to assemble a parallel data set of 405 counties, including 27 in New England. The *County and City Data Book* (Bureau of the Census 1983) reports the number of crimes known to police, aggregated into *property* crimes (burglary, larceny theft, and motor vehicle theft) and *violent* crimes (murder and nonnegligent manslaughter, rape, robbery, and aggravated assault). These two gross categories are far from ideal, but they can tell us if the exclusion of New England will greatly affect crime correlations.

For all 405 counties, the correlation between the unadjusted church member rate and the rate of property crime is -0.31, and when the 27 New England counties are removed, this changes only very slightly, to -0.34. The correlation between church membership and violent crime is, predictably, weaker (-0.17), but still statistically significant at the 0.01 level. Removing New England boosts it to -0.21. Certainly, the results are almost identical with New England either included or excluded, and our more detailed results based on metropolitan areas are almost certainly not affected by the fact that we were unable to calculate rates of church membership for New England SMSAs.

Crime in the Roaring Twenties

Like many who do quantitative studies of deviance, we have long bemoaned the lack of older data. The FBI's *Uniform Crime Report* did not come into being until 1930. Worse yet, the *UCR* data for early years are deficient because many jurisdictions simply did not participate. We know of no national data on *reported* offenses from before 1930 that can be made comparable with the UCR statistics, although such data do exist for limited jurisdictions and might be valuable for exploring the rise and fall in crime rates over time. Hence, hopes to extend ecological analysis of crime rates backward in time remain unfulfilled.

However, while searching the census section of our library for other purposes, we discovered an amazing array of data on many forms of crime and delinquency. Taken together, these data sources offer a potentially rich resource long neglected by social scientists. In addition, our historical work using the old manuscript schedules of the United States census revealed that for 1850 and 1860 the census taker was supposed to write down date of conviction and the offense for every prisoner, and while this was not always done, a considerable trove of data about nineteenth-century crime awaits the social scientist who will invest the time and energy needed to extract it. Here we employ crime data from published reports in the Roaring Twenties.

Some of the most useful data on crime early in this century are provided by a series of census studies of individuals held in jails and prisons. Beginning in 1850, the United States census enumerated imprisoned offenders every decade. The census of prisoners conducted in 1923 achieved excellent coverage.[1] Aside from the many obviously attractive aspects of these data, the significant fact is that those who conducted the jail and prison enumerations realized that the most important questions pertained to *offense rates*. Thus the census requested each jail and prison to report on each prisoner *incarcerated* during a given period as well as on all those in the institution on a given date. Thus, if some jurisdictions were giving longer sentences than others for a particular offense, or even across the board, such differences would not inflate the basis for inferring the number of offenses in the enumerations. By limiting reporting to a specific period, any person sentenced, whether to one day or to 100 years, would show up only once in the statistics, as one conviction in the year he or she arrived at the prison door.

Labeling theorists will be quick to suggest that these incarceration rates tell only about differential levels of surveillance and punitiveness

---

1. The Census Bureau continued to provide prison statistics until 1950. After that, the responsibility for prison statistics was transferred to the Federal Bureau of Prisons in the Department of Justice.

across jurisdictions. But if this is so, then one would expect *positive* associations between incarceration rates and ecological measures of social control. That is, incarceration rates ought to be highest in the most stable, integrated, and "tradition-bound" areas, not in the disorganized, "wild," and "wide-open" areas. For example, incarceration rates ought to be high in areas with little population turnover and with high rates of church membership, for it is in such places, according to labeling theory, that even minor infractions of norms ought to be the most certain to provoke sanctions. Thus, labeling theory makes predictions opposite to those of moral community theory, and we shall shortly look at research results that will permit us to decide which theory is better.

The most serious limitation on the prison and jail census data is that they only use states as the units of analysis. The data are not broken down to report which county sent which offenders to the state prison, and jails often served several counties. States are less homogeneous units than cities or counties, and there are fewer of them. This places some limits on the results that can be expected from these data. Nonetheless, to have such good incarceration data from an earlier historical period allows us to test our theories on a data set distinctly different from those we have examined so far.

Table 4.3 shows correlations between the 1926 moral and social integration (population stability) and conviction rate for three specific crimes and the total conviction rate for the 48 states. Both forms of integration are significantly negatively correlated with burglary, larceny, and the total conviction rate (which is dominated by property crimes). And, as we have seen in other data, the correlations with homicide are insignificant.

Individual Level Arrest Data

In Chapter 3 we discussed the so-called "ecological fallacy" and pointed out that although the major thrust of our theoretical interest is directed towards ecological or collective units, when possible it is appropriate to examine individual level data.

The General Social Survey (Davis and Smith 1991) sometimes has included two questions. The first asks: *Have you ever received a ticket, or been charged by the police, for a traffic violation—other than for illegal parking?* Having filtered out traffic stops, the second question asks: *Were you ever picked up, or charged, by the police, for any (other) reason whether or not you were guilty?*

Table 4.3

Moral and Social Integration and Criminal
Convictions for States, 1923

	Burglary	Larceny	Murder	Prisoner Rate
Correlations (r)				
Moral Integration (Church Membership)	-0.441**	-0.430**	-0.157	-0.366**
Social Integration (Population Stability)	-0.334*	-0.429**	-0.190	-0.361**
Standardized Betas				
Moral Integration (Church Membership)	-0.402**	-0.377**	-0.132	-0.321**
Social Integration (Population Stability)	-0.276*	-0.375**	-0.171	-0.315**
$R^2=$	.269*	.323**	0.053	0.231*

* Significant beyond .05
** Significant beyond .01

We combined the data for six years (1973, 1974, 1977, 1980, 1982, and 1984) to get nearly nine thousand cases, and examined the proportion of persons who reported having been "picked up by the police" in each category of church attendance. Table 4.4 shows a rather substantial variation in arrest across the levels of church attendance.

Thus, arrest is four times as common among those who do not attend church as among those who attend every week, and of course with so many respondents there is no question about its statistical significance. This is a very powerful religion effect which confirms on the individual level the strong and robust negative correlations we found on the level of metropolitan area and state. The bulk of the appropriate questionnaire data available concern the criminal behavior of juveniles, and we shall examine that research in the following chapter. Here we have shown that existing survey data on adults fully confirms our findings based on ecological rates. Religion really can deter crime.

T a b l e   4 . 4

Church Attendance and Arrest (USA)

How often do you attend religious services?	Percent Who Have Been Picked up by the Police	n
Never	21%	1147
Less than once a year	18%	658
About once or twice a year	16%	1235
Several times a year	12%	1222
About once a month	11%	622
Two or three times a month	9%	730
Nearly every week	6%	529
Every week	5%	1890
Several times a week	6%	703

C o n c l u s i o n

The data we have examined here suggest that religion plays a central role in sustaining the moral order. Cities with higher proportions of church members have lower rates of crime than do more secular cities. Indeed, low church membership rates help explain a very marked regional difference in crime rates: although the fact has received remarkably little public notice, the Pacific region has a substantially higher total crime rate than do other parts of the nation. And the Pacific region has by far the lowest church membership rates. Those who would celebrate low church membership in California, Oregon, Washington, Alaska, and Hawaii as indicative of enlightenment and as a portent of the future must also recognize the probability that this may be paid for with high crime rates. In subsequent chapters we will examine other "costs" associated with low church membership rates.

5

Religion as Context:
Saving a "Lost Cause"

As quantitative social research on delinquency developed in the first half of the twentieth century, religion was a variable nearly everyone ignored. And, despite the fact that social theorists took it as axiomatic that religion does promote conformity, what little attention was paid to religion often questioned its actual capacity to deter juvenile misbehavior. In 1928, Hugh Hartshorne and Mark May reported no difference in honesty between children who attended Sunday school and those who did not. As late as 1960, one textbook writer relied upon this single study to justify his claim that "there is no automatic transfer for either children or adults from the verbal teaching of moral and religious principles into the desirable overt behavior" (Robison 1960: 164).

Much of the effort that was made to assess the role of religion was wasted comparing levels of delinquency among Protestants, Catholics, and Jews—only gradually did sociologists realize that studies of denominational differences confound religion with ethnicity, neighborhood, social class, and other key variables. Several writers observed that while religion had a powerful potential to shape morality, it might fail to perform that function under the conditions of modern life, and

Lori Kent and Daniel P. Doyle contributed to an essay on which a portion of this chapter is based.

67

noted that conclusions about this issue could not be drawn from the slim and unsatisfactory research literature (Tappan 1949; Neumeyer 1955; Fitzpatrick 1967; Schafer and Knudten 1970).

The problem was exacerbated when competent researchers virtually ignored their own findings about religion. If readers overlooked a particular paragraph in one of the many books Sheldon and Eleanor Glueck (1952: 92) wrote about their famous study comparing a group of delinquents with a matched set of nondelinquents, they would never know that the Gluecks found a substantially higher rate of church attendance among the nondelinquents.

Often too, researchers lacked the methodological tools to analyze their data properly, and filled in the gaps with their own prejudices. Given that social scientists tend to be irreligious and many of them rather militantly antireligious—far more so than natural and physical scientists the majority of whom who tend to be religious (Stark, Iannaccone and Finke, 1996)—these speculations usually disdained religious effects. For example, William Healy and Augusta Bronner concluded:

> church affiliations very frequently were not potent in combating stresses that make for the production of delinquency.... Pastors and Sunday school teachers usually know little of the lives and personal problems of the young people they are endeavoring to influence. The question arises as to whether they are well enough trained in understanding children's problems to be able to aid in solving them. (1936: 70-71)

Yet the data actually collected by Healy and Bronner tell a different story. Their study compared 105 delinquents with an equal number of nondelinquents, and the published results show a higher rate of regular attendance at church or Sunday school on the part of nondelinquents. They applied no analytical techniques beyond comparison of the raw numbers, and we calculate a gamma of -0.33 (significant at the 0.02 level) between delinquency and churchgoing. However, the study is severely marred by the lack of a random sample and by a failure to separate girls from boys, with their different rates of delinquency and involvement in religion. Severely limited in the sophistication of their research techniques, and almost invariably dominated by other research agendas, the studies prior to the late 1960s contributed little to the development of solid knowledge about religion and deliquancy.

William Kvaraceus, surveying the literature in the early 1950s, found substantial methodological problems in the published research and a deep split between sociologists who discounted religion and those who considered it effective in preventing delinquency. Wisely, he commented:

> Someday adequate empirical data on the role of religion in man's behavior may become available. If these data are studied with philosophical insight, ultimate agreement of the opposite parties may be possible. However, most workers in this area will readily concede that the issues related to religion and the church cannot now be resolved on the basis of the available data. (1954: 372)

Given the prevailing biases of the field, it was with considerable satisfaction that social scientists received "Hellfire and Delinquency" (Hirschi and Stark 1969), an apparently conclusive study of religion and delinquency, based on what was probably the best survey data set on delinquency yet collected, and analyzed with then state-of-the-art techniques.

Hellfire and Sociology

Hirschi and Stark reported that religious commitment was not related to delinquent behavior, whether the latter was measured by self-reports or by official records. Young people who believed that hell awaits sinners were no less likely than those lacking such a belief to be delinquent. Young people who attended church and Sunday school regularly were also no less prone to commit offenses than were those without church connections. Nor did the religious behavior of parents have any effect on their children's delinquency.

The Hirschi and Stark paper quickly became the accepted word on the subject, frequently cited and widely reprinted. Although (as Hirschi and Stark acknowledged), several older studies had found some evidence that religion had a slight effect on delinquency, these findings seemed suspect in light of the later study's better sample, better measures of religiousness, and fuller analysis. As a consequence, the belief that religion fails to guide teenagers along the straight and narrow was soon enshrined in undergraduate textbooks.

Yet the findings remained perplexing to those social scientists more concerned with the sociology of religion than with the correlates of delinquency. How is it possible that religion has no effect on behavior that is so intimately associated with fundamental conceptions of sin?

These concerns prompted several replication studies. The first of these led to only a modest amendment of the original Hirschi and Stark findings. In a study of teenagers from several cities of the Pacific Northwest, Steven Burkett and Mervin White (1974) found that religious commitment did reduce the probability that teenagers would use drugs or alcohol, a finding we shall examine further in the following chapter. But the authors found it to have no effect on other kinds of delinquency. And so the mystery of religion's lack of effects persisted.

A few years later, however, two attempted replications (Higgins and Albrecht 1977; Albrecht et al. 1977) yielded very different results. The first of these was based on a sample of teenagers in Atlanta, Georgia. The data revealed strong negative correlations between church attendance and delinquency. The second was based on a sample of Mormon youths living in six wards (congregations) of the Mormon church. Two wards were in rural towns in southern Idaho, where the population is almost wholly Mormon. Two were from a medium-sized community in Utah, again largely Mormon; and two were from suburbs of Los Angeles, both heavily but not as exclusively Mormon. This study also found a substantial negative correlation between religious beliefs and practices and delinquency.

A search of the literature reveals a fifth paper on the topic, published in late 1970 by Albert Rhodes and Albert Reiss. Based on data the authors had collected more than a decade earlier in Nashville, Tennessee, the paper made no mention of the Hirschi and Stark findings; it, in turn, was cited in only one of the three attempts to replicate "Hellfire and Delinquency." Shortcomings in the conceptualization of the "religious factor" used by Rhodes and Reiss seem to have diverted their attention from the data and led them to conclude they had found little of interest.

Rhodes and Reiss were greatly influenced by Lenski's *The Religious Factor* (1961). They followed his lead and gave most of their attention to a search for differences in delinquency rates across major denominational lines (Jews, Catholics, and liberal and conservative Protestant groups). But by the time their article appeared in 1970 most sociologists of religion had recognized that the "religious factor," thus conceived, has little to do with religiousness per se, and is a less than satisfactory measure of ethnicity (Glock and Stark 1965; Stark and Glock 1968; Greeley 1974).

Furthermore, since all these religious bodies foster moral teachings incompatible with delinquent behavior, variations in delinquency by denomination ought not reflect theological differences, but primarily differences in the proportion of highly committed members each group manages to maintain. That is, Episcopalians differ from Baptists not so much in what the respective churches want from their members as in the degree to which they successfully engender high levels of commitment. Which is to say that denomination is also a proxy measure of variations in individual religious commitment (Stark and Glock 1968). There is no point in using proxy variables when direct variables are available.

Distracted by their denominational focus, Rhodes and Reiss ended their paper with this sentence:

> Nonetheless, given problems of measurement where there are low rates of deviance for populations, the crudeness of many sociological measures, and the likely possibility that *religious effects, if there be such, are small*, we would discourage the rather simple analyses that have characterized most of the research on religion and delinquency reported in the literature. (1970: 98; emphasis added)

However, even a cursory examination of their published data reveals a very substantial negative effect of church attendance on delinquency.

As things stood, the empirical findings were contradictory and confusing—two against, three for. Does religion sanction the normative system or does it not? In the conclusion of their paper based on Atlanta, Higgins and Albrecht suggested that a possible reason why their findings differed so from those of Hirschi and Stark might be that "religion is more of a concern in the South than it is in California..."(1977: 957).

In this chapter we argue that this is the key that will unlock the mystery of the contradictory empirical findings. We argue that religious effects on delinquency vary according to an ecological condition—namely, the religious climate of the community studied.

The initial Hirschi and Stark finding, that religion does not constrain delinquent behavior, is puzzling only if we restrict our view to an individualistic, psychological model of how religion influences behavior. So long as we restrict ourselves to thinking that religious beliefs concerning the punishment of sin function exclusively as elements within the individual psychic economy, causing guilt and fear in the face of temptations to deviate from the norms, we may or may not find confirmatory evidence. However, if we take a more social view of human affairs, it becomes plausible to argue that religion serves to bind people to the moral order only if religious influences permeate the culture and the social interactions of the individuals in question.

Religious Contexts and Religious Effects

It appears that an individual's religiousness can limit deviant behavior in some places and not others. How can this be possible? What if we discard the assumption that religiousness is primarily an individual trait, a set of beliefs and practices of individuals, and substitute the assumption that religiousness is, first and foremost, a *group property*—in this instance the *proportion* of persons in a given ecological setting who are actively religious. We suggest that what counts is not only whether a particular person is religious, but whether this religiousness is or is not ratified by the social environment. The idea here is that religion is empowered to produce conformity to the norms only as it is sustained through interaction and accepted by the majority as a valid basis for action. Let us lay this out more fully.

People form and sustain their interpretations of norms in day-to-day interaction with their friends. If most of a person's friends are not actively religious, then religious considerations will rarely enter into the process by which norms are accepted or justified. Even if the religious person does bring up religious considerations, these will not strike a responsive chord in most nonreligious friends. This is not to suggest that nonreligious people don't believe in norms or discuss right and wrong, but they will do so without recourse to religious justifications. In such a situation, the effects of individual religiousness will be smothered by group indifference to religion, and religion will tend to become a very compartmentalized component of the individual's life—something that surfaces only in specific situations, such as Sunday school and church. In contrast, when the majority of a person's friends are religious, then religion enters freely into everyday interactions and becomes a valid part of the normative system.

Let us qualify our position slightly. Even in ecological settings where religious indifference is rife, if religious persons are part of a very isolated and internally integrated subgroup of believers, then religious effects on conformity should appear among them. Urban Mennonites offer an example, and one supposes that individual propensities to "sin" could be predicted from the degree to which individuals conformed to norms of simple dress. Indeed, a strong subculture probably accounts for the fact that Albrecht et al. (1977) found a religious effect on delinquency among Mormon teenagers in Los Angeles suburbs. However, aside from members of self-conscious religious subcultures, people in general do not seem to restrict their close friendships to other believers (Stark and Bainbridge 1985). Consequently, where active religious participation is the exception, the religious person will tend to be encapsulated in secular social relationships.

This view of the way in which religion sanctions the normative system is, in fact, more in keeping with traditional theory than is a purely psychological model. Indeed, in the previous chapters we have not argued that religion makes the individual afraid to sin, but that religion has the potential to bind its adherents into a moral community.

It is, however, important to recognize that this aspect of religion—on which sociological theories rest—is variable. Societies and groups vary in the extent to which they are bound by religion into a moral community. In highly urbanized and geographically mobile contemporary societies, many people may not inhabit a moral community. Indeed, examination of Richmond, California, where the original "Hellfire and Delinquency" data were collected, suggests that it does not much resemble a moral community in which a religious sanctioning system binds residents to the moral order. Burkett and White's (1974) data also came from the West Coast; as we shall demonstrate, they also were drawn from a highly unchurched social climate. On the other hand, Atlanta, Georgia, where the initial findings of a strong negative relationship between religiousness and delinquency were found, would seem more closely to exemplify the moral community as Durkheim conceived of it—a community integrated by shared religious beliefs which sustain conformity. The same can be said of Nashville, Tennessee.

That the five published studies seem to vary not only in their findings but also in the apparent religious climates of the communities studied strongly suggests that ecology influences the effect that religion has on delinquency. In earlier chapters, we have seen that rates of church membership vary substantially across the nation (cf. Stark and Bainbridge 1985). The most prominent feature of American religious geography is the "Unchurched Belt," which stretches up the West Coast from the Mexican border through Alaska.

In most of the nation the majority of the population are official members of a religious congregation. But only about one-third of those living in states along the shores of the Pacific are church members. Indeed, the five states with the lowest church membership rates in 1971 (to select data most contemporary with the research findings reported above) were Washington (33.1 percent), Oregon (33.2 percent), California (36.4 percent), Alaska (37.6 percent), and Hawaii (38.0 percent). Some states in the Mountain region also are quite low in church membership, notably Nevada (39.4 percent) and Colorado (42.4 percent). But Utah, also in this region, has the highest church membership rate in the nation (83.6 percent).

If our ecological interpretation of how religion influences delinquency is correct, then studies conducted on the West Coast will produce negative findings. In contrast, studies done nearly anywhere else will have positive outcomes. Of course, this is precisely the pattern revealed by the published studies.

Our goal in this chapter is to demonstrate how religious ecology affects the correlation, on the individual level, between religiousness and delinquency. To do so we first examine data from two additional communities, selected because they differ greatly in their religious climates, standing first and almost last among American metropolitan areas in terms of church member rates. We then examine data based on a national sample. If we are correct that the effect of an individual's religiousness on delinquency is contingent on the moral climate surrounding that individual, then we ought to be able to make the relationship vary by introducing an ecological measure of religiousness. If this occurs, it would explain the apparent contradiction in the literature, and assign to religion an important role in the prevention of delinquency.

Provo: A Moral Community

We began by searching the archives for data sets on delinquency that contained a measure of religious commitment. We also wanted studies based on communities that represented extremes of religious climate. These conditions were satisfied by the well-known Provo study (Empey and Erickson 1972). The data are based on a sample of boys from Provo, Utah, the home of Brigham Young University. At the time of the study, Provo was a town of about 50,000 people, the overwhelming majority of whom were Mormons. And, while Utah stands first among states in terms of church membership rates, the Provo-Orem metropolitan area stands first among American cities, with a startling rate of 96.6 percent for 1971. This can be compared with the rate of 32.0 percent for the San Francisco-Oakland metropolitan area (in which Richmond, California, is located), where Hirschi and Stark failed to find that religious belief had any effects on delinquency. Indeed, while Hirschi and Stark found that only 37 percent of white boys in Richmond attended church weekly, 55 percent of the boys in Provo attended at least that often and 30 percent of them went to church at least three times a week.

If we are correct that a relationship between religiousness and delinquency is contingent on the moral climate of the community, then such a relationship ought to show up strongly in these data. Table 5.1 confirms our prediction. There is a very strong negative correlation (gamma = -0.46) between church attendance and a measure of official delinquency based on the number of times a boy had been arrested. Similarly, there is a very strong negative correlation (gamma = -0.45) between church attendance and a self-report measure of delinquency.

Seventy-four percent of these boys were Mormons. The others were scattered among many religious groups: Catholics, Jews, and many Protestant denominations. None of these non-Mormon groups contained enough cases for separate analysis. However, there is no reason to suppose that denominational differences are important. When Table 5.1 was recomputed for Mormon boys only, the gammas were unchanged.

As social science research goes, these are very large correlations. Indeed, they are as large as or larger than those typically reported for the variables that are the center of attention in current assessments of delinquency, such as race, sex, IQ, and school performance (cf. Hirschi 1969; Hirschi and Hindelang 1977; Harris 1977). Yet, despite the fact that one might rate Provo as the city the closest to being an ideal moral community of all those studied so far, the correlations in Table 5.1 are not of unusual magnitude. Instead, they are virtually identical to the Atlanta

Table 5.1
Religion and Delinquency in Provo, Utah

	Correlation (gamma) with Church Attendance
Official delinquency	-0.46**
Self-report delinquency	-0.45**

** Significant beyond .01

results: Higgins and Albrecht (1977) reported a gamma of -0.48 between church attendance and an index of self-reported delinquency.

This suggests several things. First of all, the majority of American communities constitute moral communities: it is unusual to find communities so unchurched that an individual's religious commitment has no influence on delinquency. Second, moral climate may well not be a continuous variable. Instead, there may be a threshold effect here. That is, given a sufficient proportion of religious persons in the environment, the potential effect of an individual's religiousness on delinquent behavior may be fully realized. A rise in the proportion professing religious belief and a consequent expansion of the moral community may not increase the effect. We return to these matters later in this chapter.

But before leaving Provo, it is worth pausing to consider what the state of the literature might be today had Hirschi and Stark been employed at Brigham Young rather than at Berkeley, and thus had based their initial paper on data from Provo rather than on data from Richmond. Presumably correlations of this magnitude would have been taken seriously, and religion would not have continued to languish as a "lost cause" in delinquency research.

Finally, anxiety has often been expressed about delinquency research because almost all studies have been based on single communities: would the results generalize to other communities? Similar findings among studies have tended to allay those fears; but here they seem justified. When it comes to the relationship between religion and delinquency, it does appear to matter considerably where the data are collected.

Seattle: A Secular Community

Our next step was to search for a very unchurched community, to see whether we could replicate Hirschi and Stark's nonrelationship. To this end it seemed desirable to have a city from the Pacific "Unchurched Belt." Fortunately, our colleagues Hindelang, Hirschi, and Weis (1981) had just completed a vast experiment to assess the validity of various self-report delinquency measures. In so doing, they administered questionnaires to a sample of teenagers in Seattle, Washington. Of the 216 metropolitan areas for which we had rates, Seattle stood 211th in terms of church membership, with only 28.0 percent of the population belonging to churches in 1971. Thus, it was ideal for our purposes.

In order to make the most precise possible comparison with the original Hirschi and Stark findings, we constructed two measures of delinquency using exactly the same items as used in the original Hirschi and Stark study. And to facilitate comparison with the other studies, we limited the analysis to males.

The results are shown in Table 5.2. Church attendance is only very weakly related to either delinquency measure, the first based on the recency of delinquent acts (gamma = -0.08), the second on the incidence of delinquent acts (gamma = -0.13). When the item "How religious do you consider yourself?" is used to measure religiousness, very small, identical associations result (gamma = -0.14).

We note that these correlations are slightly stronger than those reported for Richmond, California by Hirschi and Stark. Yet they are so weak as to be of neither statistical nor substantive significance.

These findings further confirmed our suspicions that the effects of religion depend upon a community's moral climate. In the "Unchurched Belt" along the West Coast, individuals' religious commitment appears not to sustain conformity to the legal norms. But all the studies we have seen from elsewhere in the nation, where church membership remains the norm, show strong evidence in support of the centrality of religion for conformity. This could explain whay three studies yielded no religious effects, while four did show such effects. All

Table 5.2
Religion and Delinquency in Seattle and Richmond

Seattle	Correlation (gamma) with:	
	Church Attendance	Importance of Religion
Self-report delinquency:		
Recency Index	-0.08	-0.14
Standard Index	-0.13	-0.14

Richmond, California (Hirschi and Stark, 1969)	Correlation (gamma) with:	
	Belief Index	Church Attendance
Self-report delinquency	-0.03	0.02
Official delinquency	0.02	0.06

of the former were conducted in the unchurched Pacific region. These patterns offer very strong support for an ecological interpretation.

It should be pointed out that the West Coast is only unchurched—folks there are not irreligious. Like unchurched Americans in general (see Chapter 4), people on the West Coast are about as likely to believe in God and to pray as are people elsewhere (Stark and Bainbridge 1985). But there is no explicit social basis for their religious beliefs and sentiments, and their religion remains largely unexpressed in public situations.

A Nationwide Sample

To demonstrate that variations in the effect of religiousness on delinquency are ecological in origin, what is needed is a sample that is large enough to permit analysis within regions which differ in their degree of religiousness. Such data exist in the huge surveys that make up what is known as the *Study of High School and Beyond* (our analysis is based on the "essential file" of this study, distributed by MicroCase Corporation). In a national sample including 11,995 seniors studied in 1980 was the item: "I have been in serious trouble with the law." The answer categories were "Yes" and "No." This item has the advantage of offering a highly serious and unambiguous measure of delinquency, unlike most delinquency scales, which are made up of minor offenses (Hindelang et al. 1981). It has the disadvantage of limited variation, as only 3.8 percent of American high school seniors answered yes. However, as we shall see, the immense case base gives great stability to the data and the variation proves to be fully sufficient for analysis. Religious commitment was measured by frequency of church attendance and thus is precisely comparable to the majority of significant prior studies.

The most important aspect of this data set, however, is that it allows us to directly test the proposition that the correlation between religiousness and delinquency holds strongly in all parts of the nation except along the Pacific Coast. This is possible because the sample includes fully 1,566 students from the Pacific region, and thus results should be free of the random bounce that would be found when regional controls are applied to national samples of the usual size.

Table 5.3 shows the religious "climate" of major U.S. regions and the gamma between church attendance and getting into trouble with the law in each region. The results are convincing. In the East, Midwest, and South, church membership rates are around 60 percent. This drops to 48 percent in the Mountain region and to 36 percent in the "unchurched belt" constituting the Pacific region. And as anticipated, the correlations between church attendance and getting in trouble with the law respond to these fluctuations in a very compelling fashion. In the nation as a whole and in the East, Midwest, and South, there are strong negative correlations. The correlation is somewhat attenuated (and falls just below statistical significance) in the less religious Mountain region, and in the Pacific region the correlation vanishes. We think it very important that the gamma does decline in the Mountain region, for it offers evidence that the impact of context may be continuous, at least over a certain range, rather than merely an on-and-off phenomenon.

The large number of cases allowed us to examine the correlations in various subpopulations, hunting for evidence of spuriousness. More males than females in the sample admit to having been in trouble with the law, and we might expect females to be more religious, so it is important to control for sex. Outside the Pacific region, the correlations between church attendance and trouble with the law are almost identical for males (gamma = -0.30) and females (gamma = -0.33), and neither gender shows a significant correlation in the Pacific region (gamma = 0.02, gamma = -0.02).

Another important variable is race, in part because racial composition of the population varies regionally. Because so few of the respondents had been in trouble with the police, reliable results cannot be obtained for racial minorities, but there are sufficient white for separate

Table 5.3
Region, Religion and Delinquency

	East	Midwest	South	Mountain	Pacific
Percent who belong to a church	62%	59%	61%	48%	36%
Correlation (gamma) between church attendance and "I have been in serious trouble with the law."	-0.315**	-0.365**	-0.394**	-0.227	-0.017
n=	(2060)	(2424)	(3871)	(579)	(1566)

* unweighted numbers of cases
■■Significant beyond .01

analysis. Outside the Pacific region, the negative correlation between church attendance and trouble with the law is substantial (gamma = -0.39). And within the Pacific, it is nonexistent (gamma = -0.04)

We regard this as very solid evidence that religion can limit some forms of deviance, but only within a sufficiently religious moral climate. The message for criminologists is clear and comes in two mutually reinforcing parts: you should study the influence of religion, both because it is substantial and very real, and because it operates in some-what complex ways that only a flourishing tradition of social science research can fully explain.

Conclusion

Einstein once remarked that "God does not play dice with the world." By this he meant that we ought not gladly accept random models of phenomena—that we ought instead to search for an underlying logic by which a seeming happenstance becomes explicable and predictable. It would have been all too easy to invoke the dice-rolling assumptions of statistical significance to suggest that contradictory research findings about the relationship between religion and delinquency reflected the luck of random fluctuations in the samples. And it was only the luck of the draw that led Hirschi and Stark (1969) and Burkett and White (1974) to examine data on exceptionally unchurched communities, and thus to argue that the moral sanctions of faith cannot "compete with the pleasures and pains of everyday life" (Hirschi and Stark 1969: 213).

But there seems to be nothing random about variations in the degree to which religion does function to sustain the moral order. An individual's religiousness alone seems unable to constrain delinquent behavior. Only within a significantly religious social climate—a moral community—does the individual's faith generate this power. But the fact remains that the majority of communities in the nation possess such a moral climate, and therefore most studies of delinquency can be expected to find significant religious effects. The cause that was "lost" on the West Coast is alive and thriving east of the Sierra Nevada.

6

Drugs and Alcohol

Sociologists of religion and church members probably agree that religion tends to reduce consumption of alcohol and illegal drugs, thereby reducing the social problems associated with these substances. However, social scientists concerned with deviant behavior have tended to ignore this possibility. In a recent review essay, Peter L. Benson comments:

> Though there is now an impressive body of literature documenting the role of religion in preventing substance use, one would not know it by looking at the mainstream literature on prevention.... As happens too often, the empirical study of religion remains known only to a small circle of scholars, with the consequence that this significant literature is not brought to bear on social policy, community planning, or program development. (1992: 218)

This chapter on alcohol and drugs is included not only to help remedy the situation Benson describes, but also to reveal the interesting and somewhat puzzling contrasts between the impact of religion on alcohol and substance use and the findings of previous chapters. To put it plainly: the effects of religion on alcohol display substantial *denominational variations* at both the aggregate and individual level of analysis, in contrast with religion's general, nondenominational effect on drugs. Moreover, at the individual level these effects exist *regardless of the religious context*. We will begin with historical and contemporary data on moral communities, and then shift to individual level data.

The Road to Prohibition

As we examine historical data on the impact of religion on alcohol abuse, we will also be tracing the rise of the Temperance Movement, culminating in the passage of the Eighteenth Amendment in 1919, which initiated the "Great Experiment" with prohibition. As we shall discuss in detail in the next section, the churches were not of one mind or voice about drinking alcohol, let alone about the virtues of prohibition.

To the best of our knowledge, the first national data on alcohol abuse can be found in the 1860 Census. That year the census enumerators asked at each household whether any member of the household had died during the past year and, if so, the cause of death. The published data detail many causes, among them "delirium tremens" and "intemperance." Louisiana had the highest rate of such deaths—19.9 per 100,000 population. Iowa and Maine were the lowest, tied at 1.3 deaths per 100,000; and for the nation as a whole the rate was 5.6 per 100,000.[1] These rates are probably a bit too low, since the persons most apt to die of alcohol related causes would have been less likely than the average person to leave a surviving household to report their death to the census taker. Nevertheless, the national rate compares reasonably well with the 1992 rate of 9.7 deaths per 100,000 from cirrhosis of the liver.

Table 6.1 shows that church membership had no significant independent effect on alcohol deaths in 1860, but the percent Catholic had a huge effect. That is, alcoholism was not decreased by higher rates of church membership, but it was greatly elevated by the proportion of members who were Roman Catholics.

Table 6.1 also shows data from 1890. Here alcoholism is not measured by deaths (unfortunately, the census no longer asked about deaths), but by arrest rates for drunk and disorderly conduct. Here too we see that church membership as such didn't matter, but that once again Catholicism mattered a great deal. These findings seem entirely reasonable in light of the fact that the Catholic Church has never

1. These figures are based on the white populations since the overwhelming proportion of blacks were slaves in 1860 and had little opportunity for long term alcohol abuse.

Table 6.1

Church Membership, Catholicism and Alcohol
Abuse For States 1860-1890:Regression Results

1860	Death Rate from "Delirium Tremens" and "Intemperance"
	Standardized Betas
Church Membership Rate	0.075
Percent Catholic	0.460**
R^2=.203**	

1890	Persons Charged With Drunk and Disorderly Conduct
	Standardized Betas
Church Membership Rate	0.148
Percent Catholic	0.434**
R^2=.178*	

** Significant beyond .001

Table 6.2

Cirrhosis Deaths, Religion and Social
Integration (119 American Cities, 1916)

	Cirrhosis Death Rate	
	Correlation (r)	Standardized Beta
Church Membership Rate	0.19*	-0.02
Percent Catholic	0.23*	0.27*
Born in State	0.20*	0.24*
R^2=.11*		

* Significant beyond .05

opposed alcohol, while many Protestant groups, particularly in this period, demanded abstinence.

In 1916, only three years before the passage of the Eighteenth Amendment, good data became available on cirrhosis death rates for the major American cities. Table 6.2 shows the familiar finding: percent Catholic obliterates the positive correlation between church membership and cirrhosis deaths. Here too we see that social integration (measured by the percentage of the population born in their state of current residence) has a negative effect on alcohol abuse.

Prohibition and the Temperance Movement

Let us pause here briefly to review the impact of prohibition and the basis of the Temperance Movement. Joseph Gusfield (1963) argued that alcohol policy became the symbol of much larger issues and conflicts throughout a century of American politics. The rural, native Protestants who were politically dominant early in the nineteenth century were people who held strong temperance ideals. Many of the new immigrant groups whose numbers and political strength grew as the years passed had a more favorable attitude toward drinking. The old citizens and new citizens were frequently at odds over economic issues, but because economic conflict takes a muted form in American politics, symbolic issues like alcohol policy came to have an exaggerated importance. According to Gusfield, as they felt their political power slipping, the older ethnic groups tried to assert their superiority over other citizens by promoting their own temperate drinking patterns as the official norm. If their customs became law, their declining social status would be symbolically bolstered. Tensions between ethnic groups and social classes have frequently followed similar patterns (Lipset and Raab 1970).

Gusfield's views have dominated sociological evaluations of prohibition for the past thirty years. They have, however, become increasingly suspect. As we will see, historians have noted that whatever symbolic value prohibition may have had for Protestants, opposition to alcohol had a substantial objective basis. Nor was this opposition limited to a few puritanical activists. Clearly, the Temperance Movement was not merely the expression of the lifestyle and values of one group of citizens. For a time it also represented the views of many reformers and social scientists dedicated to solving serious social problems. At the end of the First World War, George Elliott Howard wrote in the *American Journal of Sociology*:

> At last, after generations of dispute, experiment, and research, clarified public opinion recognizes the liquor traffic as a problem of first-rate national importance whose solution depends upon prevention rather than cure. Alcohol appears as a factor, a chief maker, of the bad social conditions which mar our civilization. It is known to be a direct or contributory cause of degeneracy, pauperism, poverty, disease, and crime. In short, science has cleared the way for an intelligent approach to the drink problem. (Howard 1918: 61)

Howard summarized a great body of evidence that alcohol caused crime, family disruption, illness, and death. With the view that liquor in any quantity was harmful, and with no appreciation for the possible benefits it might have, he was quick to recommend nation-wide prohibition. This sentiment was shared by many progressive Americans who wanted to revitalize democracy and who believed that intoxicating drink debased the virtuous and enslaved the poor (Timberlake 1963). Recently, historians such as James S. Roberts (1984) have begun to argue that the Temperance Movement was a logical response to a marked increase in objective human misery. Distilled spirits became widely available at low cost for the first time during the nineteenth century, so alcoholism and related problems were not common in the poorer social classes until that period. Some kind of social response to these changed objective conditions was warranted, and thus the Temperance Movement was far more than mere status politics.

Christianity did not speak with one voice on the drink question, and the Bible does not offer clear guidance. To be sure, in addition to the famous drunkenness of Noah, the Bible contains many warnings about the evils of heavy drinking: "Wine is a mocker, strong drink is raging: and whosoever is deceived thereby is not wise" (*Proverbs* 20: 1). But other passages cast alcohol in a positive light. Psalm 104 blesses the Lord for his many gifts, including "wine that maketh glad the heart of man" (*Psalms* 104: 15). For the marriage feast at Cana, Jesus transformed water into wine (*John* 2: 8-9).

Thus it is hardly surprising that the churches were sharply divided on the issue. Not only did Catholics disagree with Protestants, and one Protestant denomination with another, but even within the

Temperance Movement there was heated debate over the proper relationship between the churches and the crusade against alcohol. Doubts
of two very different kinds were raised by William Folwell Bainbridge
(1874), a Baptist clergyman and self-described social scientist who
belonged to temperance organizations and whose wife founded one of
the state branches of the Woman's Christian Temperance Union.

First, Bainbridge observed that right-minded people could disagree
about many tactical and procedural issues, even if they agreed that alcohol was a serious social problem. For example, some believed that license
regulations could control alcohol, while others had come to believe in
strict prohibition. Bainbridge feared that debates that divided the temperance forces could spill over into the churches, dividing congregations
and producing un-Christian battles that could harm religion.

Second, the Temperance Movement could divert human and spiritual energies away from work that was more central to the church.
Indeed, Bainbridge believed that the best way to solve social problems
was not to attack their symptoms but their causes, and that the proper
cure for all of them was religion. Thus, he suggested that it would be
more effective to convert drunkards into Christians, which would render them sober and give them many other positive qualities, than to
attempt to cut off their supply of alcohol.

Originally, the Temperance Movement argued only for moderation;
but as the nineteenth century progressed, the goal became the complete
prohibition of alcoholic beverages. As the political winds in the country
blew first one way and then another, alcohol policy shifted several times.
Three separate waves of state prohibition laws were passed and then
repealed—the first in the 1850s, the second in the 1880s, and the third in
the 1910s. The third wave culminated in the ratification of the Eighteenth
Amendment in 1919, and ended when it was repealed in 1933.

Today the common wisdom, enshrined in many undergraduate
textbooks, it that prohibition was an experiment that failed—it was, in
Austin Turk's (1969) words, a "classic fiasco." Moreover, proponents of
the legalization of drugs who argue that this is the only solution to the
problem, constantly cite the failure of prohibition. But, as we shall see,
much of the "failure" of prohibition can be attributed to the fact that it
was never completely tried.

The Eighteenth Amendment and the legislation that accompanied
it never established effective instruments for enforcement. The federal
government felt that the states should foot the bill, while the states

expected federal agents to do so. Two other factors that may not apply with other drugs also contributed to failure: alcohol was a traditionally accepted drug which many Americans wanted, and supplies were very difficult to cut off because alcohol was so easy to manufacture.

Millions of Americans were prepared to defy prohibition. Despite the small number of agents, in the 1920s federal officers seized a total of one hundred and twenty thousand distilleries, over nine million gallons of distilled spirits, fifty-six million gallons of malt liquor, forty-five thousand delivery automobiles, and fourteen hundred rum-runner boats. In accomplishing this, federal agents sustained more than four hundred injuries, and seventy-one of them were killed. A hint of the massive opposition to prohibition is given by the fact that, understaffed as they were, federal agents made a total of more than 550,000 arrests (Merz 1932).

Not only could anyone manufacture their own liquor secretly in the bathtub or basement, but large factories continued to produce legal alcohol for industrial purposes. At the beginning of prohibition, in 1920, 28,000,000 gallons of industrial alcohol were manufactured. By 1925, the annual production had risen to 81,000,000 gallons. The fact is that much of this increase represented alcohol secretly diverted from industry for human consumption.

The federal government devised an imaginative but ethically questionable method of control known as *denaturing*. By law, all industrial grain alcohol had to be mixed with substances that would render it unfit to drink. Some additives were relatively harmless, such as peppermint, menthol, lavender, and soap. But in many cases real poisons were used, including iodine, benzine, sulfuric acid, and wood alcohol. This government tactic became a hot public issue after a large number of people died over the 1926 Christmas holidays, apparently as the result of drinking alcohol poisoned by federal law (Merz 1932).

Among the other unintended costs of prohibition was the stimulus it gave to organized crime. The legendary gang bosses of the 1920s, such as Al Capone, were fundamentally beer barons; they grew immensely powerful through their control of bootleg liquor.

The Success of Prohibition Reconsidered

With the repeal of the Eighteenth Amendment, the prohibition movement practically vanished as a significant political force; and yet there is a sense in which prohibition was a success. Drinking in America did, in fact, decline far below pre-prohibition levels. Indeed, it took many years for per capita alcohol consumption to rise back up to the level of the days before passage of the amendment.

When prohibition went into effect, its advocates were quick to publicize the swift and striking reduction of several social problems that was almost certainly the actual result of reduction in heavy drinking. From 1920 to 1923, the rate of commitments for drunkenness dropped from 185.9 per 100,000 to 83.1, a reduction of 55 percent. Similarly, commitments for disorderly conduct dropped by 51 percent, commitments for vagrancy by 53 percent, and the rate of prisoners in all penal institutions decreased by 18 percent. There were also substantial reductions in the rates of death from auto accidents and pneumonia (Gordon 1943).

The significant medical effect of prohibition can be seen in the rapid decline in deaths from cirrhosis of the liver. We have been able to locate complete data for 194 American cities in 1916, 1926, and 1936. Conveniently, the middle of these three years was right in the middle of prohibition, while the other two were just before and just after it. In 1916, in these cities, the mean annual death rate from cirrhosis of the liver was 15.1 per 100,000, while by 1926 this rate had dropped to 8.8—a very substantial decline. Repeal did not immediately return the rates to their former value, both because cirrhosis of the liver takes some time to develop and because some potential victims may not have begun drinking heavily in the context of reduced consumption of alcohol by the population as a whole. However, by 1936, the rate had risen to 11.2 deaths per 100,000 per year.

These may seem like very low death rates, but upon reflection it is clear that cirrhosis was (and is once again) a substantial social problem. The 1916 death rate from cirrhosis (15.1) was higher than the 1992 death rate from homicide (10.4) and nearly as high as the 1992 death rates from breast cancer (17.3) and auto accidents (16.4). Who would argue that current concerns about *these* death rates are merely masks for status politics, or expressions of "puritanism?"

Looked at another way, 15.1 deaths per 100,000 per year means 150 over a decade, which is one and a half per thousand. Children are unlikely to be affected, so the rate for adults is substantially higher. Assuming that each person knows at least several hundred other adults, there is a strong likelihood that any given person would lose a neighbor, friend, or relative to this disease every few years. At the same time, it is clear that the majority of drinkers do not succumb to cirrhosis, and their pleasure in drinking may have been sufficient to lead most to reject prohibition even in the awareness that the amendment saved lives.

However, despite achieving very significant declines in acute alcoholism and in rates of public drunkenness, prohibition was an experiment that, in many places, was never tried. To examine this aspect of prohibition we can get some estimate of enforcement efforts by examining the 1923 census of jails and prisons. The census reported the number of persons sent to jails and prisons during the first six months of 1923 for violating the Eighteenth Amendment by making, selling, or transporting alcoholic beverages. Such people often were called "bootleggers" from the common practice of selling pints of liquor hidden in the legs of high boots. These totals for each state were divided by the total number of persons sent to jails and prisons during this same six-month period (multiplied by 100). The result is the percent of all prisoners in each state who were doing time for prohibition offenses. This allows for variations across states in their tendency to send people to jails or prisons for any offense.

The result is a measure of local enforcement of the Eighteenth Amendment. Here are the rates for each state (no data were available for Nevada; Alaska and Hawaii were not then states):

Percent of Prisoners Convicted of "Bootlegging"

South Dakota	31	Alabama	19	Connecticut	9
North Dakota	30	Oregon	19	Delaware	9
Idaho	29	Vermont	18	California	9
Indiana	28	New Hampshire	18	Pennsylvania	7
West Virginia	28	Colorado	17	Iowa	7
Kansas	27	Ohio	15	Georgia	7
Oklahoma	27	South Carolina	14	Maryland	6
Wyoming	27	Wisconsin	14	Florida	6
Arizona	26	Nebraska	14	Louisiana	6
Virginia	25	New Mexico	14	Illinois	5
Montana	25	Minnesota	13	Massachusetts	4
Mississippi	24	Utah	12	Rhode Island	4
Arkansas	23	Washington	12	New Jersey	3
Kentucky	22	Missouri	11	New York	1
Maine	21	Texas	11		
North Carolina	21	Michigan	9		

The high rates for the Dakotas and Idaho may partly reflect "rum running" from Canada, and the relatively high rate for West Virginia undoubtedly partly reflects local "moonshining" activities far predating prohibition. The very low rate for Illinois, on the other hand, reflects lack of enforcement and the same is true for Massachusetts, Rhode Island, New Jersey, and New York. Generally speaking, however, this seems an adequate measure of local enforcement efforts.

What accounts for differential levels of enforcement? According to Gusfield, the Eighteenth Amendment was primarily the work of the Protestants in reaction against immigration, industrialization, and urbanization. Presumably, those who pushed it through would have pushed for enforcement. However, as can be seen in Table 6.3, there is no correlation between Protestants per 1,000 population and our measure of enforcement. On the other hand, there is an immense, negative correlation with Catholics per 1,000[2]—which echoes the old anti-

Table 6.3
Enforcement of Prohibition (States, 1923-26)

	Percent of Prisoners Charged With Prohibition Violations
	Correlations (r)
Protestants per 1,000	-0.049
Catholics per 1,000	-0.755**
Population Growth	-.282**
	Standardized Betas
Catholics per 1,000	-0.436**
Population Growth	-0.262*
R^2=.269**	

* Significant beyond .05
** Significant beyond .001

2. It is appropriate here to use the rate of Catholics per 1,000 population rather than relative Catholicism (the percent of church members who are Catholic) since we are not using the total church membership rate in this analysis. Within reasonable limits there is no forced correlation between Catholics and Protestants per 1,000 as the unchurched leave ample room for independent variation between the two.

Catholic slogan about "Rum, Romanism, and Rebellion." Finally, social integration, as measured by population growth (or decline) during the previous decade, also influenced enforcement. States with the most rapidly growing populations were less apt to enforce prohibition. When both Catholicism and population growth are entered into a regression analysis, both have significant net effects and account for a substantial amount of the variation in enforcement.

Having explored enforcement of prohibition, let us now turn to alcohol abuse during prohibition. We have noted that hospital admissions for alcoholism declined following prohibition, but substantial numbers of people still required treatment. Moreover, the rates tended to be highest in states where enforcement efforts were lowest. This can be seen in Table 6.4. There is a very strong, negative correlation (-0.619) between enforcement and alcoholism admissions. There is also a negative correlation between Protestants and alcoholism, while the correlations are positive for Catholicism and population growth. The regression analyses shown in the table reveals that the Protestant effect disappears when Catholicism is controlled. In the second regression shown in the table enforcement is revealed to have a strong negative effect on alcoholism and Catholicism to have a strong positive effect, while the beta for population growth falls just short of significance.

Finally, Table 6.5 generalizes the Catholic effect on cirrhosis deaths to contemporary Europe. Based on the 25 primary nations, the percent Catholic is strongly, positively related to cirrhosis deaths, while church attendance is negatively related to cirrhosis deaths.

To sum up, in many data sets going back to 1860 we have found that in aggregate data, religion in general has no impact on alcohol abuse, but that excessive drinking is strongly related to the proportion of Catholics in the population. However, with aggregate data the possibility always exists that an effect like this does not reflect the behavior of Catholics per se, but perhaps something else—it is statistically possible (if rather improbable) that Protestant liquor consumption is influenced by the presence of Catholics so that in very Catholic communities it is Protestants who supply most of the local alcoholics. In such a case, one commits what is known as the ecological fallacy by imputing an aggregate finding to the behavior of individuals. It may seem extremely likely that our results indicate that Catholics are more apt to drink, but it is not certain. Therefore, we now consider individual level data on alcohol consumption, and broaden the scope of our inquiry to include illegal drugs.

Table 6.4

Alcoholism During Prohibition
(States, 1923-26)

	Hospital Admissions for Alcoholism per 100,000
	Correlations (r)
Percent of Prisoners Charged With Prohibition Violations	0.619**
Protestants per 1,000	0.388**
Catholics per 1,000	0.585**
Population Growth	0.338*
	Standardized Beta
Protestants per 1,000	0.079
Catholics per 1,000	0.540**
R^2 = .347**	
Percent of Prisoners Charged With Prohibition Violations	0.380**
Catholics per 1,000	0.405**
Population Growth	0.205*
R^2 = .553**	

* Significant beyond .05
** Significant beyond .001

Table 6.5

Religion and Cirrhosis Deaths in
25 European Nations (circa 1990)

	Cirrhosis Death Rate
	Standardized Beta
Percent Attend Church Weekly	-0.582*
Percent Catholic	1.035**
R^2 = .480**	

* Significant beyond .05
** Significant beyond .001 (unlike correlations, Betas can exceed 1.0)

Denomination, Religiousness, and Drinking

Is it true that Catholics are more likely than Protestants to drink alcoholic beverages? To some extent, that depends upon what kinds of Protestants are used for comparison. Table 6.6 shows that in the United States Catholics are somewhat (and significantly) more likely to drink than are members of liberal Protestant denominations, but both groups are far more likely to drink than are conservative Protestants. In Canada, however, Catholics and liberal Protestants are equally likely to drink, and conservative Protestants are much less likely to do so. The data for the United States are based on a national sample created by merging the 1989, 1990, and 1991 General Social Survey. The Canadian data are based on the 1988 Canadian General Social Survey.

So, there is no ecological fallacy. The Catholic effect we have observed so often earlier in this chapter is real. Indeed, Table 6.7 reveals just how real. In the United States, church attendance has a relatively robust, negative effect on drinking among both liberal and conservative Protestants, but no effect at all among Catholics. We were able to replicate this lack of a Catholic church attendance effect in other years of the GSS. In Canada, however, church attendance does produce a modest decline in drinking

Table 6.6
Denomination and Drinking (USA and Canada)

	Roman Catholic	Liberal Protestant	Conservative Protestant
United States			
Drinks	82%	72%	53%
Abstains	18%	28%	47%
	100%	100%	100%
n=	(723)	(554)	(838)
Canada			
Drinks Weekly	36%	37%	22%
Sometimes	46%	46%	40%
Never	18%	17%	38%
	100%	100%	100%
n=	(4711)	(3631)	(1267)

Table 6.7

Church Attendance and Drinking Within
Denominational Groups (USA and Canada)

	Correlations Between Drinking and Church Attendance	
	Gamma	**r**
United States		
Catholics	-0.060	-0.018
Liberal Protestants	-0.228**	-0.141**
Conservative Protestants	0.427**	-0.262**
Canada		
Catholics	0.208**	-0.180**
Liberal Protestants	0.213**	-0.198**
Conservative Protestants	0.487**	-0.407**

** Significant beyond 0.001

Table 6.8

Denomination and Drinking Among
U.S. High School Seniors

"On how many occasions (if any) have you had alcohol to drink (beer, wine, liquor) during the past thirty days?"

	Roman Catholic	Liberal Protestant	Conservative Protestant	Total*
None	15%	18%	36%	21%
1 or 2	25%	25%	28%	26%
3 to 5	23%	23%	16%	21%
6 or more	37%	34%	20%	32%
	100%	100%	100%	100%
n=	(3427)	(2397)	(1986)	(550)

* Includes all respondents

Table 6.9

Church Attendance and Drinking
Within Denominational Groups
(U.S. High School Seniors)

	Correlations Between Drinking and Church Attendance	
	Gamma	**r**
Catholics	-0.019	-0.012
Liberal Protestants	-0.130**	-0.111**
Conservative Protestants	-0.209**	-0.163**

** Significant beyond 0.001

among Catholics, as it does among Protestants. But in both nations, the attendance effect is far greater among conservative Protestants than among liberal Protestants or (in Canada) among Catholics.

Returning to the 1980 *Study of High School and Beyond* the national sample of high school seniors analyzed in Chapter 5, we see in Table 6.8 that here too Catholics are the group most likely to drink. Keep in mind that it is illegal for these students to be drinking, but about 8 of 10 had done so in the past 30 days, while a third reported that they drank on at least six occasions or more during the past month. Indeed, although the hypothesized religious effect is evident, even among the conservative Protestants, two-thirds were active drinkers.

However, as Table 6.9 shows, here too there is no church attendance effect on drinking among Catholics, a modest but highly significant effect among liberal Protestants, and a stronger effect among conservative Protestants. Clearly, then denomination matters and, among Protestants, church attendance matters too.

Denomination, Religiousness, and Marijuana

The survey of high school seniors also asked them if they had used marijuana or hash, and how many times they had done so. As Table 6.10 shows, more than half had done so, and 44 percent said they had done so often. There is no significant difference here between Catholics and liberal Protestants, but there is a difference between these two groups and conservative Protestant seniors. Here too one might well have expected large denominational differences.

However, using marijuana is not like drinking for Catholics. While the church has not opposed alcoholic beverages, it has opposed marijuana. And this shows up clearly in table 6.11 where we see that marijuana use is negatively correlated with church attendance in all three denominational groups.

Of perhaps even more compelling interest are the effects of religion on marijuana use generalized to many nations, including non-Christian nations. Table 6.12 is based in the 1990-91 World Values Surveys, in which the same questions were asked of national samples in many nations. One question asked of each respondent was whether he or she regarded herself as a "religious person." Another question asked whether it was ever justified to use "the drug marijuana or hashish." Used as dichotomous variables, gamma is the appropriate measure of association, and Table 6.12 reports the gamma between these two variables for each of 26 nations. In 25 of them there is a strong association between being a religious person and responding that it is "never" justified to use marijuana. In Sweden there is no association, but this is due primarily to a lack of variance—93 percent said it was never justified.

Table 6.13 reveals most perplexing results. Once again using statistics from the 1980 *Study of High School and Beyond* we see that religious effects can be found on alcohol and marijuana use even in the Pacific Coast. That is, while no religious effects on other forms of delinquency turned up within this unchurched context, they did for alcohol and drug use among Protestants and for drug use among Catholics. Nor is this something new. The first replication of the original Hirschi and Stark study was done in Oregon and, while it also failed to find religious effects on other forms of delinquency, it did find that church attendance influenced drinking and drug use (Burkett and White 1974). Since then, these effects have been found many times in other studies done in this region (cf. Cochran et al. 1992).

Why? As to religious effects on drinking, an answer might be found in parental behavior which may, in turn, still be influenced by the historical stand against alcohol associated with Protestantism. We have seen that Protestants are less likely than Catholics to drink, and this is particularly true of members of the more evangelical Protestant bodies. What may be going on here is that even on the West Coast, Protestant teenagers who attend church weekly are disproportionately from non-

Table 6.10

Denomination and Marijuana Use Among
(U.S. High School Seniors)

*"On how many occasions (if any) have you used hashish (hash) or
marijuana (grass, pot, dope)?"*

	Roman Catholic	Liberal Protestant	Conservative Protestant	Total*
Never	42%	45%	50%	45%
Sometimes	30%	29%	31%	11%
Often	28%	26%	19%	44%
	100%	100%	100%	100%

* Includes all respondents

Table 6.11

Church Attendance and Marijuana Use
Within Denominational Groups
(U.S. High School Seniors)

	Correlations Between Drinking and Church Attendance	
	Gamma	**r**
Catholics	0.212**	-0.159**
Liberal Protestants	0.277**	-0.230**
Conservative Protestants	0.201**	-0.160**

** Significant beyond 0.001

Table 6.12

Religiousness and Disapproval of Marijuana
or Hashish in Selected Nations

Correlations between being a "religious
person" and disapproving of the use of
marijuana or hashish

	Gamma
United States	0.505**
Canada	0.439**
Great Britain	0.391**
Ireland	0.485**
France	0.427**
West Germany	0.508**
Netherlands	0.629**
Belgium	0.550**
Spain	0.478**
Portugal	0.536**
Italy	0.657**
Austria	0.407**
Switzerland	0.448**
Mexico	0.362**
Argentina	0.453**
Brazil	0.388**
Chile	0.448**
India	0.618**
Turkey	0.324*
Nigeria	0.550**
South Africa	0.347**
Denmark	0.629**
Norway	0.304*
Iceland	0.485**
Sweden	0.085
Finland	0.232*

* Significant beyond .01
** Significant beyond .001

Table 6.13
Regional Contexts (U.S. High School Seniors)

	Correlations Between Drinking and Church Attendance	
	Gamma	**r**
Non-Pacific Protestants	-0.182**	-0.150**
Pacific Protestants	-0.263**	-0.242**

	Correlations Between Marijuana Use and Church Attendance	
	Gamma	**r**
Non-Pacific Protestants	-0.240**	-0.191**
Pacific Protestants	-0.322**	-0.273**
Non-Pacific Catholics	-0.205**	-0.149**
Pacific Catholics	-0.247**	-0.202**

drinking homes. Hence, what appears to be a direct religious effect is probably, at least in substantial part, indirect, as parents' Protestant backgrounds shape family norms concerning alcohol consumption.

A puzzle remains, however. Church attendance also has a negative impact on marijuana use, and these effects show up in the Pacific region as well as in the rest of the nation. Moreover, the effects apply to Catholics as well as to Protestants, albeit the Catholic effects are a bit weaker. That must mean that this is more than just a generalization of the effects of nondrinking homes to the use of another means for getting high.

We think our ideas about why alcohol use seems immune to contextual effects may have merit, but we simply don't know why drug use is influenced by religion in contexts where other illegal behavior is not. What we do know is that the answer will be found in creative ideas, for data never speak unless spoken to properly. Hopefully, someone else will be able to see what we cannot (cf. Bainbridge 1997: 276–280).

Part Two

Religion as Deviance

7

Religious Cults

Moral communities not only suppress secular forms of social pathology, they also are inhospitable to religious deviance. That is, where moral
integration is strong, it will be very difficult for unconventional religious groups to make headway.

In earlier work on this topic, we proposed that weaknesses in conventional religions were self-limiting in that they generated new, more
vigorous religions to replace them. Subsequent development of a theoretical model of religious economies has produced a more complex view
of interactions among religious groups within societies (Stark 1985a;
1985b; 1996; Stark and Iannaccone 1993, 1994). Briefly, where the religious marketplace is crowded with motivated and efficient "firms," it will
be very difficult for new firms to find a market niche. This will be especially true for small, startup firms offering nonstandard "products." This
leads to the proposition that deviant (nonstandard) religious organizations will not prosper whenever and wherever conventional church
membership and church attendance rates are high, but that such groups
will be common whenever and wherever weaknesses (inefficiencies) in
the conventional churches result in unserved "market segments."

There are two basic forms of deviant religious groups. By far the
most common is the *sect*, which is a religious group within the conven-

tional religious tradition(s) of a society, but one that imposes stricter demands on its adherents than do the mainstream groups. In a sense, sects are regarded as moderately deviant by outside observers on the grounds that they are *too* religious. It must be noted, however, that sects serve to invigorate and periodically revive moral integration as part of a process by which older religious organizations, as they lose their vigor, are replaced by newer, more vigorous bodies. Hence, other things being equal, *sects will prosper in moral communities.*

The second form of deviant religious group is the *cult.* As we define them, cults are religious groups outside the conventional religious tradition(s) of a society. They may or may not impose stricter demands on their adherents, but their primary form of religious deviance does not concern being too strict, but being too different.

Cults can fall outside the conventional religious culture of a society because they reject that culture and seek to replace it with a new religious culture, or because they have added so much to the traditional culture that they are no longer simply another variation on the standard theme. The Neo-Pagans are an example of the first, seeking to replace the conventional Judeo-Christian religious culture of the West with a religious culture claimed to predate Christianity. The Unification Church (often called the Moonies) is an example of the second—they affirm both the *Old* and the *New Testaments,* but add the *Divine Principle* and a series of additional revelations that place the group beyond the Christian boundary (although they dispute this).

Some cults occur through importation—a religion that spreads from one society where it is normal may be deviant in another. For example, various Hindu groups are cults in the United States because they depart markedly from the Judeo-Christian tradition that dominates American culture, but they remain within the dominant and therefore normal religious tradition in India. Similarly, Christianity is a cult in India.

However, many religious groups arise because someone creates or discovers new religious culture and successfully attracts a group of followers. Such groups tend to be cults wherever they occur. But, whether the result of importation or innovation, cults engender far more concern, antagonism, and repressive efforts than do sects—to the extent that even the word cult often is used as an insult or to stir up fear and opposition.

We must stress that we use the word cult in a purely technical way, not as a value judgment. When we identify a group as a cult we do so only on the grounds that its religious culture is quite different from that of the standard denominations in the society in which it is being observed. It is religiously deviant, but it remains to be seen whether it does any harm. Often the form of deviant behavior is quite innocuous. Members of the Transcendental Meditation cult regularly sit quietly for twenty minutes at a time, meditating upon a mantra and feeling that they are in touch with spiritual energies that will restore mental and physical vitality. What could be more harmless? Yet because Western societies do not believe in meditation, the behavior is deviant and may be discouraged by effective social control.

In any event, because cults are the primary form of religious deviance they will be the focus of this chapter. Four propositions inform and guide the analysis.

At the individual level: 1. *Converts to cults will mainly come from the ranks of the religiously inactive.* 2. *People will convert to cults to the extent that their attachments to members outweigh their attachments to outsiders.*

At the collective level: 3. *The success of cults will be inverse to the degree of moral integration.* 4. *The success of cults will be inverse to the degree of social integration.*

The first proposition has been supported frequently—the majority of converts to cult groups report growing up in an irreligious family or at least in an unchurched family (Stark and Bainbridge 1985). The reasons for this are fairly obvious. People who are committed to one faith do not go join another one. It is people lacking such commitments who are free to commit to something new. The second proposition was the first important proposition about conversion to cults to be based on actual field observations (Lofland and Stark 1965) and has been replicated many times (Bainbridge 1978; Kox, Meeus, and Hart 1991).

As to the third proposition, in a number of studies we have previously confirmed the proposition that cults will do best where conventional religious organizations are relatively weak. Using states as the units of analysis we found high negative correlations between church membership rates and various measures of cult activity in the 1920s and again in the late 1970s and early 1980s. We confirmed these findings in Canada, using both provinces and cities as the units of analysis. Finally, we tested the thesis using the nations of Europe as the units of analysis (Stark and Bainbridge 1985). In these earlier studies we did not test the fourth proposition concerning social integration and we failed to convince a number of our colleagues—especially those in Europe—that our European data were adequate. So, in this chapter we do not repeat our earlier analysis, but offer many new tests of the propositions using different data and/or units of analysis.

Christian Science in the 1920s

In *The Future of Religion*, we showed that data on religious cults from the old censuses of religious bodies could profitably be used to test theories about the emergence of deviant organizations. We carefully examined information about the beliefs and practices of various groups included in the censuses to determine which were cults. Then we scrutinized the membership figures the groups reported to make sure the data were reliable and could be used as valid measures of receptivity to deviant religion.

Five groups withstood these tests and were good measures of local receptivity to cults: Christian Science, Baha'i, Divine Science, the Liberal Catholic Church, and Theosophy. Of these, Christian Science provides the best data for testing our propositions. Unlike some of the other cults, it originated in America and is well-suited to this cultural setting. Unlike some other groups, such as the Mormons, it appeared in particular places through local recruitment rather than primarily through migration. Finally, by 1926 the group was large enough and old enough to have smoothed out any idiosyncratic effects, such as the impact of one skilled missionary who went to one particular locale, a problem that does influence rates for small or young groups. Indeed, as early as 1890 Christian Science had overcome all traces of its initial geography. Although the movement was founded in 1879 in Boston by Mary Baker G. Eddy, who continued to focus the group's recruitment efforts in Massachusetts and New York, by the 1890 Census the 10 states with the highest Christian Science membership rates were all in the West. For example, in 1890 California had the highest rate (673 per million population), which was more than three times as high as that of Massachusetts—the latter being 11th highest, while New York came in 13th.

Christian Science is classified as a cult, not a sect, because of the amount of novel culture it added to traditional Christian doctrine. Mrs. Eddy was a student of Phineas Parkhurst Quimby, the founder of New Thought, and she drew on his work to produce Christian Science. Quimby, in turn, had been a student of Mesmerism, the European cult that invented hypnotism and developed a theory of animal magnetism with which to explain it. Mrs. Eddy's sharpest break with traditional Christian teaching was her denial of the reality of matter. Christian

Science maintains that the mind is the only reality. Disease, evil, and sin are the result of erroneous thinking. The mind, misguided by faulty metaphysical ideas, creates a harmful material world. If we can convince ourselves of the truth, the world will be changed in beneficial ways.

Another point in favor of Christian Science membership statistics as particularly good measures of local receptivity to cults is that it was a successful movement in this era (its recent, rather rapid decline did not ensue until the 1950s). Many of the other innovative groups we consider in this book were relative failures that have gone downhill since soon after they were created. Indeed, the vast majority of cults are short-lived; thus, the bulk of the data on cults at any given moment are about groups that have gotten something important wrong, be it doctrine or organizational tactics. Cults that get things right give us the best insights into where cult growth is possible.

The 1926 census located 1,913 Christian Science congregations with 140,081 members, plus another 67,017 members affiliated not with a local group but directly with the Mother Church in Boston. Our analysis is based on members affiliated with a local congregation, for the others cannot be located geographically. The units of analysis are 144 cities having a population of 50,000 or more (mean size was 253,000) and the data come from the 1926 Census of Religious Bodies.

Moral integration is measured as the church membership rate. This is the total number of church members reported by the census divided by the total population (multiplied by 100). Since the cult membership data to be analyzed consist of the number of members of a given cult, divided by the total population, the question of autocorrelation can be raised. That is, each cult membership rate is also a fraction of the total church membership rate and if that fraction were of significant size it could force a positive correlation between the two rates, since a cult rate could, in effect, inflate the total church membership rate.

Two points eliminate this concern. First, since we hypothesize a negative correlation between the two rates, any autocorrelation bias works *against* our hypothesis (as should always be the case in science). Second, even Christian Science comprises such a tiny fragment of the population of any unit as to have no appreciable influence on the overall rate. Overall, Christian Scientists made up less than three-tenths of a percent of the nation's church members in 1926. There were not sufficiently concentrated to have a significant effect on the rate in any unit—removing Christian Scientists would nowhere reduce the church membership rate by more than 0.2 percentage points. As for the small cults to be examined in the next section, altogether they total 14,015 members nationwide and make a statistically undetectable contribution to local rates.

Table 7.1 analyzes variations in the rates of Christian Scientists. The data show that moral integration, as measured by the church membership rate, is very strongly negatively correlated with the rate of Christian Science membership. There also is a strong negative correlation between social integration (measured by the percent of residents who were born in the state in which the city is located) and Christian Science. A third variable, population size, also was included because it has been hypothesized as having an independent impact on the formation of deviant groups (Fischer 1975)—conceivably, potential cultists dwell everywhere, but only in the largest cities are there sufficient absolute numbers to support congregations. However, we see no city size effect on Christian Science.

In addition to correlations, the table shows the results of multiple regression. Both of our collective-level propositions are supported— *both* moral and social integration produce substantial and highly significant betas.

Table 7.1

Integration and Christian Science Membership
in 144 American cities (1926)

	Dependent Variable: Christian Science Membership	
	Correlation (r)	Standardized Beta
Moral Integration Church Membership rate	-0.60**	-0.51**
Social Integration Percent Born in State	-0.45**	-0.28**
Population	-0.03	-0.03
R^2= .52**		

** Significant beyond .01

The Four Smaller Cults

We can now turn to the four smaller cults. Because of their minuscule memberships and diverse histories, each of these groups might have its own peculiarities in geographic distribution. Divine Science is an entirely American creation, with obvious affinities to Christian Science. The other three have some imported elements. Baha'i is an imported cult of Persian Sufi origins that draws upon all the major world faiths and claims to be the universal religion. Theosophy draws upon Hindu traditions but was created by Westerners, while the Liberal Catholic Church is an offshoot of Theosophy with many Christian elements.

The Theosophical Society was tremendously successful in its earliest days, growing rapidly through the 1880s in Europe, India, and America. It quickly stalled, however, suffering innumerable problems of leadership. The founder, Helena Petrovna Blavatsky, engaged in fakery during seances and had many stormy romantic relationship with men, thus inflicting harmful scandals on her movement. In the 1890s, leadership was taken over by Annie Besant, a prominent English radical, and growth resumed. Then schisms arose and dispersed the movement's energies, and Besant withdrew from public activities. In the twentieth century, Theosophy has been unable to grow significantly, although it produced so many schismatic groups that it still casts a long shadow on American and European cultism. The 1926 census of religious bodies counted 223 congregations of the American Theosophical Society, with 6,780 members.

Theosophy is a reasonably good measure of local receptivity to cults, despite its small size and stormy history. First, the group is easily recognized as a cult—it is obviously not a Christian sect. Blavatsky not only claimed to communicate with the spirit world, but she included a great deal of Eastern mysticism in Theosophical doctrines. Therefore, a Theosophist will encounter whatever degree of stigma and sanction is imposed on religious deviants in a given community. Second, like Christian Science, Theosophy recruited its members locally and did not prompt any substantial amount of migration. That is, Theosophical membership rates for a given community reflect local conversion, not in-migration of Theosophists.

Among the offshoots of Theosophy are the Liberal Catholics. By the turn of the century, Theosophy had attracted many English clergymen, especially Anglicans and Old Catholics. The inclusion of Theosophical mysticism in Christian services drew disapproval from Anglican and Old

Catholic bishops. As a result, a number of clergymen formed a new cult movement combining Blavatsky's doctrines with traditional Christian rites, such as High Mass. They took the name Liberal Catholic Church. In 1917, Liberal Catholicism was brought to the United States by Bishop James Wedgwood, who traveled the nation and ordained a number of priests. The Liberal Catholic Church met strong opposition from the Theosophical Society, but in 1926, only nine years after the group began in the United States, the census enumerated 39 Liberal Catholic congregations with 1,799 members. However, these are limited statistics. Many states lack any Liberal Catholics, and no state has a large number.

Divine Science is a New Thought cult that emphasizes healing. It began as two independent movements, one in Denver, the other in San Francisco, in the late 1880s. In 1889, they merged and based their headquarters in Denver. The group has never been very successful. In 1926, it had only 22 congregations and 3,466 members nationwide.

Baha'i is a Persian cult that sprang up among the Sufis in the middle of the 19th century. Its doctrine combines the teachings of all major Eastern faiths and thus claims universality. In 1893, a world parliament of religion held in Chicago drew Baha'i representatives, and this led to the formation of an American branch in that city. The 1926 census located 44 Baha'i congregations in the United States, with a total of 1,247 members.

In 1926, there were on average 233 Christian Scientists per 100,000 population in the 144 largest American cities. But, as Table 7.2 shows, rates for the other cults ranged from a minuscule 1.4 per 100,000 to only 13.7. These small numbers cause problems for analysis. In 1926, 116 of the 144 cities lacked Baha'is, and the fact that zero was the modal rate limits the value of correlational analysis. The same problem affects the four other cults, with 129 cities lacking Divine Scientists, 133 lacking Liberal Catholics, and 55 lacking Theosophists. Indeed, in 1926 fully 52 of these cities lacked all four of these small cults. In contrast, only one of the 144 cities had a zero rate of Christian Scientists.

Nevertheless, Table 7.2 shows that rates of membership in the small cults correlate with Christian Science. This means that the geographic distribution of Christian Science well represented that of cults in general. But this finding also encourages us to analyze data on the small cults further. To maximize the sensitivity of measurement, we combined data on the four small cults in 1926 to make a joint rate.

T a b l e   7 . 2

Christian Science and Small Cults, 1926

	Membership per 100,000 Population	Correlation (r) with Christian Science Rate
Baha'i	1.4	0.29**
Divine Science	5.3	0.23**
Liberal Catholic	2.5	0.38**
Theosophy	13.7	0.54**

** Significant beyond .01

T a b l e   7 . 3

Integration and Small Cult Membership in 144 American cities (1926)

Dependent Variable: Small Cult Membership

	Correlation (r)	Standardized Beta
Moral Integration Church Membership rate	-0.38**	-0.29**
Social Integration Percent Born in State	-0.40**	-0.30**
Population	0.09	0.08
R^2= .34**		

** Significant beyond .01

Table 7.3 shows that the small cults rate can be explained in the same way as the Christian Science rate. Both social and moral integration greatly reduce receptivity to these small cults.

Cults in 1980

When we began our quantitative research on cults over a decade ago, we quickly discovered that it was possible to collect fresh quantitative data on contemporary cults by a variety of means. We shall now analyze a highly varied collection of cult measures: Christian Science healers, writers of letters to an occult magazine, New Age groups and businesses, initiates to Transcendental Meditation, and Scientology "clears." No one of these measures is perfect, but together they allow very powerful tests of our theory of secularization. On balance, do modern cults tend to flourish where the conventional churches are weak?

Above, we saw that Christian Science was a good measure of cultism in the United States of the 1920s and 1930s, and other research has shown the same thing for Canada in 1961 (Stark and Bainbridge 1985: 472). However, Christian Science has been declining rapidly over the past forty years. In 1941 there were 11,200 Christian Science practitioners in the United States, persons trained to provide the church's "medical" therapy. By 1981 that total had shrunk to 3,403, while the population of the nation had increased immensely. Furthermore, the facts that Christian Science has strong roots in the Christian tradition, does not aggressively trumpet its deviance, and has been widely accepted as a variant form of the dominant religious tradition all mean that we cannot presume that it remains a good measure of cultism.

Although recent membership statistics are not available, the monthly *Christian Science Journal* lists the addresses of church-trained Christian Science practitioners (among them Bainbridge's fourth grade teacher) from which we could generate a rate for each metropolitan area, based on a total of 1,653 cases in the largest 75 metropolitan areas outside New England. This magazine also lists churches and nurses, but churches may survive in areas where membership has collapsed, and the nurses appear concentrated around a few special healing institutions. Practitioners are senior members who provide services for other members, and thus they are a good if indirect indicator of membership.

Since its first issue in 1948, the central publication of the American occult has been *Fate* magazine. It carries articles on astrology, ancient mysteries, religious cults, pseudoscience, and many other aspects of the occult milieu. Its plentiful advertisements promote all kinds of cultic businesses and a few religious cults. From the early 1950s, this monthly has carried three letter-to-the-editor columns, with the letter-writer's name and address invariably attached. First, there are the ordinary letters commenting on material published in earlier issues. By their content, the vast majority of these seem to be written by believers in the occult, although on rare occasions an unbeliever writes to complain, including in recent years the anti-occult writers James Randi,

James E. Oberg, Philip Klass, and Paul Kurtz. The two other columns come entirely from believers. "My proof of Survival" reports experiences of apparitions and messages from the beyond. "True Mystic Experiences" covers the whole range of paranormal and occult phenomena. In writing these letters, *Fate* readers are proclaiming their participation in somewhat deviant supernaturally-oriented activities.

In previous research we have calculated *Fate* letter rates and used subscription rates provided by the publisher (Stark and Bainbridge 1985), but the unit of analysis was the state, not the metropolitan area. Furthermore, some letter rates were inflated by multiple missives from the same person. For the present analysis, we have started from scratch, working with all the letters published in the 120 issues from 1975 through 1984, straddling the 1980 census. Each letter-writer's name was written on a card, and then these were sorted by author, so that we could count letter-writers rather than letters, finding a total of 1,182 in the 75 SMSAs. In the event that a letter-writer used two or more addresses, we coded him or her as residing at the address given in the majority of the letters, and ties were decided randomly.

For years, a cult group in San Rafael, California, has published traveler's guides to New Age and occult groups and businesses. Their best coverage of the United States was achieved in the 1974 *Spiritual Community Guide* (Singh 1974). A well developed, extensive communications network and efficient, computerized data management produced a high quality listing. Earlier editions had achieved wide distribution, being sold by many occult bookstores and carried by many cultic pilgrims, so groups that could have been included had the opportunity to make themselves known to the editor. Later editions charged for each listing, and coverage was substantially poorer.

This guide emphasizes the "natural" and "oriental" aspects of the New Age Movement, a subculture that overlaps with the traditional occult but is somewhat distinct from it. Not simply a duplication of the *Fate* data, the *Guide* listings are a sizable data set of their own. While several oriental religious cults are listed, many American cults are not—for example, Christian Science and Scientology. Over half of the *Guide* listings are what the editor calls "centers" and "communities"—organizations often indistinguishable from full-blown religious cults providing meditation and various other practices designed to raise spiritual consciousness. The rest of the listings are bookstores, foodstores, and restaurants—businesses of a more limited scope, but still dedicated to the New Age and occult subcultures.

Again, earlier research had examined rates for American states (Wuthnow 1978: 10; Stark and Bainbridge 1985), but we did a fresh tabulation by metropolitan area. Because the *Guide* organizations rely on clienteles to keep them in business, they tend to concentrate in larger cities, and thus fully 1,471 could be placed in our 75 major metropolitan areas.

The religious cult in which the largest number of Americans participated in the 1970s was probably Transcendental Meditation, although the TM organization struggled (unsuccessfully) in the courts to avoid being labled as a religion, and many participants may not have seen it as such (LaMore 1975). Founded by Indian guru Maharishi Mahesh Yogi, this group achieved wide publicity, partly because the Beatles participated in it, and offered a simple brand of meditation said to improve mental, emotional, and physical health (Wallace 1970; cf. Pagano, Rose, Stivers, and Warrenburg 1976; White 1976a, 1976b).

By the end of the 1970s, about one million Americans had been "initiated" into Transcendental Meditation, although only a few thousand became full-time, dedicated members of the cult. From near the very beginning, this group kept excellent, computerized records of all persons trained in TM, mainly to make sure local offices sent the proper fees to the central organization.

With the help of Daniel H. Jackson, we were able to obtain a printout of some of these data from the central organization, including a vast table of the number of people initiated into TM for each of about 3,200 urban areas for each of eight years, 1970–1977. For the present study, we scoured maps of the nation to locate these urban areas and combine their statistics into the right SMSAs. Altogether, 454,328 Americans were initiated into TM in the 75 large metropolitan areas during this time period.

Finally, our data set includes information on Scientology, the famous new religious movement founded by science fiction writer L. Ron Hubbard (Wallis 1976; Stark and Bainbridge 1985; Bainbridge 1987). First presented to the world as Dianetics in the May 1950 issue of *Astounding Science Fiction*, Scientology has become a constant source of amazement to journalists, frequently becoming the center of furious public controversy (Hubbard 1950a, 1950b; Gardner 1957; Malko 1970; Cooper 1971; Miller 1987). Years ago, Bainbridge carried out six months of observational research on Scientology that convinced him that it functioned as a religion for most members, and Scientologists have called upon him to testify to this fact in court proceedings.

Scientology suggests that each person has hidden godlike powers that can be unlocked by its extensive training and therapy techniques. Scientologists aspire to a status known as *clear*, where they not only gain honor and influence in the organization but believe themselves to gain high levels of health, intelligence, and creativity. The public relations officer for Scientology of Boston obtained for us a computer printout from the Los Angeles headquarters listing the number of clears in each three-digit postal zip code area as of November, 1985. While zipcode areas and metropolitan areas have different boundaries, working with detailed maps we were able to place 7,888 clears in the correct SMSAs and obtain reasonably accurate rates.

The rates for these five cults are entirely independent of each other. Only one, the TM rate, is based on the total number of participants in a group. The Christian Science and Scientology rates are based on leaders in these organizations. *Fate* letter writers represent the readership of the magazine, which generally sold in the vicinity of 100,000 copies of each issue. And the Guide data reflect the density of cults and cultic business- es of the New Age Movement. Because they are so different, we may wonder if these five rates really reflect a single phenomenon: the recep- tivity to cults in each metropolitan area. But the rates correlate highly.

The strongest correlation (r = 0.75) is between the *Spiritual Community Guide* rate and the TM rate; this is not surprising because these two share a similar cultural heritage, being based substantially on Asian religion. The lowest correlation (r = 0.47) is between the *Guide* rate and the *Fate* rate. We suspect that this merely reflects the fact that the *Guide* businesses are concentrated in the biggest cities with the largest markets for their offerings, while the *Fate* rate is the most inde- pendent of the size of the urban area, being substantial even in some rural states, because subscriptions can be mailed to any address. The mean correlation linking pairs of cult rates is 0.58, and all correlations between cult rates are highly significant, far beyond the 0.001 level.

Table 7.4 shows that all five cult rates have substantial negative cor- relations with *moral integration* (the rate of church membership) rang- ing from -0.49 to -0.62. The impact of *social integration* also is quite pronounced (measured by the proportion who do not live in the same house as they did 5 years before), ranging from 0.46 to 0.60. The lower section of Table 7.4 shows a multiple regression analysis examining the effects of moral and social integration on each cult rate. In all five regressions, moral integration has a significant and substantial effect, but in three of them the social integration effect is insignificant.

Table 7.4
Integration and Cult Rates in 75 Standard Metropolitan Statistical Areas (1980)

	Christian Science	Fate Writers	Guide Listings	TM Members	Scientology Clears
Correlations:					
Moral Integration Church Membership	-0.58**	-0.62**	-0.49**	-0.59**	-0.55**
Social Integration % Different House	0.60**	0.47**	0.53**	0.46**	0.48**
Standardized betas:					
Moral Integration	-0.32**	-0.56**	-0.24*	-0.52**	-0.41**
Social Integration	0.38**	0.09	0.37**	0.10	0.20
R^2 =	0.41**	0.38**	0.32**	0.35**	0.33**

* Significant beyond .05
** Significant beyond .01

Table 7.5
Integration and Christian Science Practitioners, States, 1995

Correlations	Christian Science Practitioners Rate
Church Membership	-.575**
Population Change	.391**
Standardized betas	
Church Membership	-.503**
Population Change	.153
R^2= .350**	

** Significant beyond .01

In 1995 there were 1,820 Christian Science practitioners listed for the United States. These were sufficient to create rates for each state. Table 7.5 shows that here too the expected correlations between moral and social integration appear. And, here too, regression results fail to sustain effects of social integration, while moral integration is strongly related to Christian Science. Together, these variables account for 35 percent of the variance in the Christian Science rate.

A Canadian Replication

Canadian data are of exceptional value for social scientific studies of religion because the nation-wide census conducted every 5 years (during the second and sixth year of each decade) always asks each person's religious affiliation. The statistics are reported in exquisite detail for the nation overall and for each of the 10 provinces—335 Canadians gave Satanism as their affiliation in the 1991 census, 95 of them residing in British Columbia. For smaller units, the data are less detailed, but they still permit examination of cult movements in each of the 25 Census Metropolitan Areas.

In an earlier study we found strong support for our proposition that moral integration suppresses cult activity in Canada (Bainbridge and Stark 1982), and our findings subsequently were replicated by David Nock (1987). The 1991 census allows additional analysis.

We will measure moral integration as the proportion of the population who claim a religious affiliation—hence, the larger the percentage of the population who reported their religion as "None," the lower the level of moral integration. Even though the data are based on only 10 cases—the provinces—in Table 7.6 we see incredibly large correlations between the percent "None" and membership in 7 cults.

Here again the possibility of autocorrelation does not arise because the contribution of these cults, even added together, to the overall proportion claiming a religious affiliation is insignificant. In all of Canada, 23,607,680 people claimed a religious affiliation in 1991. Of these, 17,390 belonged to one of the groups shown in Table 7.6, or about 0.07 percent. Were every single one of these cultists to move to Ontario, they would increase that province's level of religious affiliation by less than two-tenths of one percent.

The last three measures of cult strength are based on data prepared for our initial study. Although they are from a decade earlier than the other measures, each exhibits a huge, positive correlation with the percent

Table 7.6

Irreligion and Cult Membership in Canada's
10 Provinces (1991)

Correlation With % Giving "None" As Their Religious Preference

Membership Rates For:		
	New Thought	.97**
	Satanism	.95**
	New Age	.93**
	Paganism	.93**
	Spiritualism	.89**
	Scientology	.85**
	Theosophy	.79**
	Fate rate (1979)	.88**
	Fate letter writers (1951-1980)	.88**
	Cult Centers (1980)	.83**

** Significant beyond .001

Table 7.7

Moral Versus Social Integration in Canada's 25
Metropolitan Areas (1991)

Dependent Variable: Para-Religious Group Membership

	Correlation (r)	Standardized Beta
Moral Integration		
% None	.82**	0.89**
Social Integration		
% Not Moved	-.52**	0.11
R^2= .66**		

** Significant beyond .001

"none." Overall, it would be very difficult to obtain more potent empirical support for the proposition that moral communities are inhospitable to cults.

The data published for the 25 metropolitan areas do not detail the individual groups reported in Table 7.6. Instead, statistics for these groups are collapsed to form a category designated as "para-religious groups." Table 7.7 shows that both moral (.82) and social (-.52) integration are correlated with membership in these cults. But the results of regression analysis show that, in these Canadian cities, moral integration is the source of both correlations since the standardized beta for social integration is tiny and insignificant.

Once again we find strong support for the proposition that moral communities are inhospitable to religious deviance. However, we have found inconsistent evidence that social integration has an independent effect on cults. Sometimes an independent effect appears, sometimes it does not. This may be a misinterpretation of the findings, however. We may be confronting a more complex causal chain here. That is, the impact of social integration on cult activity may be restricted to an indirect effect wherein weak social integration results in weak moral integration and this, in turn, leads to cult activity. In more technical terms, moral integration may be the crucial *intervening* variable linking social integration to religious deviance. If this is the case, then the correlation between social integration and religious deviance ought to disappear when moral integration is controlled. And that is what we have found for some cult rates for American cities in the 1980s and in recent data for Canadian cities and for the 50 states. Admittedly, the findings are mixed, but we think them generally supportive.

What About Europe?

In our first article on the ecology of cult movements (1980), we acknowledged that many would cite Europe as a contrary case. Given that many nations of Europe exhibit very low levels of church attendance, then these same nations ought to abound in new religious movements. Indeed, other things being equal, such movements ought to be more prevalent in most of Europe and Great Britain than they are in the United States or Canada. To meet this potential challenge, we noted that

> a closer look at Europe supports rather than weakens our
> analysis. Although it receives little attention from intellectuals

and less coverage in the press, cult activity seems to be *quite widespread in Europe.* (Stark and Bainbridge 1980c: 114)

To justify this claim, we presented fragmentary data to show that England probably had a substantially higher rate of new religious movements per million population than did the U.S., and that involvement in astrology was higher in France than in America.

Needless to say, such data failed to satisfy many social scientists—indeed, we were not satisfied with them either. And they certainly could not have been expected to give pause to European social scientists, most of whom were certain that new religious movements, which are so abundant in the United States and Canada, fail to find fertile ground on the other side of the Atlantic. Describing the European literature on new religious movements, Thomas Robbins and James Beckford (1988: 19) noted "a widespread but questionable assumption that NRMs [cults] are relatively rare and unusual phenomena."

In response, we searched for means to offer a more adequate picture of the real situation in Europe. Using data from a great variety of sources, on many different groups, we demonstrated that many parts of Europe abounded in new religious movements, often having rates far above those found in the United States and Canada (Stark and Bainbridge 1985). For example, the rate of Indian and Eastern cult centers was higher for Europe (1.8 per million population) than the United States (1.3 per million). Moreover, many European nations, especially those where church attendance rates are lowest, had rates far higher than America's. Switzerland's rate was 3.8, Scotland's 3.2, Denmark's 3.1 and England and Wales' 3.0. Indeed, only Belgium (1.0), Italy (0.7) and Spain (0.6) had rates lower than that for the United States.

Unfortunately, the responses of our European colleagues to these findings were primarily methodological rather than substantive. Thus, the late Roy Wallis repeatedly noted that many of the rates were based on very small numbers of cases (Wallis and Bruce 1984; Wallis 1986a; 1986b) and suffered from other grave defects. This prompted Karel Dobbelaere (1987: 120), one of the continent's finest sociologists of religion, to use the occasion of the Paul Hanly Furfey Lecture to dismiss our claims as "empirically refuted."

We were not unsympathetic to these objections because we knew, as a result of our own searching, how woefully crude and incomplete were the available data on religious groups in Europe, and especially on unusual groups. In fact, we had been forced to patch together data from such diverse sources as the back cover of an ISKCON magazine, a New Age travel guide, a Mormon almanac, a book published by Scientology, and from yearbooks published by the Jehovah's Witnesses and the Seventh Day Adventists. Whatever one believes about the prevalence of religious movements in Europe, it is certain that such groups have received scant scholarly attention compared with their American counterparts. As we noted:

> We could not simply go to the library and find material on cults and sects in Europe even slightly comparable with such works as J. Gordon Melton's *Encyclopedia of American Religions*, with its more than 1,200 entries. (Stark and Bainbridge, 1985: 477)

This is no longer true. A three-volume *Religions Directory International* is nearing publication (as our book went to press it was not clear when this valuable work would be published, or by whom). Assembled by J. Gordon Melton and his associates at the Institute for the Study of American Religion, these directories attempt to list all religious groups currently active in each European nation—adding up to thousands of groups. In addition, for each nation, religious groups are sorted out by "families" following the same scheme that Melton developed for his American listings. Thus, it soon will be possible to consult a standard source to count various kinds of religious groups active in European nations—just as we made our earlier computations for American religious groups. We have been privileged to have access to a nearly final draft of each directory.

These new data offer an opportunity to better resolve the dispute about the prevalence of new religious movements in Europe. Before taking up these matters, however, it seems prudent here to offer a brief account of how these international data were gathered.

Hunting for Religious Organizations in Europe

Melton has gone about getting information on European religious groups in much the same manner as he has done for more than 30 years in America—by cultivating local informants and by ransacking bookstores (especially religious, occult and New Age bookstores) for directories, magazines, tracts, and newsletters. In some places he was given very effective assistance, as in the United Kingdom where he had access

to the excellent files created by Eileen Barker and her INFORM colleagues. In other places he was on his own. After several years and a
number of trips to Europe, Melton was joined by Gary L. Ward and
Isotta Poggi. More trips to Europe followed, and each visit expanded
the number of religious groups found in any given nation.

On Undercounting

It must be abundantly clear from the above that the time and effort
invested in locating European religious movements still has been minor
compared with that devoted to American religion. Not only has Melton
been actively engaged in gathering American data far longer, but he had
the benefit of a very solid and voluminous literature from which to begin.
Moreover, Melton has had time to gain the trust of many smaller, more
obscure American religious groups, which accounts for the increase of
nearly 400 additional groups between the first edition of his American
encyclopedia, published in 1979, and the third, published in 1989.

The above discussion leads to several very important caveats. First,
European religious groups will have been significantly *undercounted* thus
far. Second, the undercounting will primarily apply to the kinds of religious
movements of greatest interest vis-à-vis the current debate about new religious movements, for these groups are often secretive and usually obscure.
Finally, undercounting will be greater in some nations than in others, thus
producing a significant but unknown degree of *spurious variation in rates*.

Defining Europe

The directories include the nations of Eastern Europe. However, aside
from Poland, the data from the Eastern bloc include only conventional
religious bodies. Indeed, until very recently, anyone searching for
unusual religious groups in most of Eastern Europe was attempting to
outdo the secret police. For this reason we eliminated all of Eastern
Europe (including East Germany), except for Poland. We also decided
to exclude the tiny nations such as Liechtenstein, Andorra, and
Monaco. In the end we settled on 18 nations—15 on the continent plus
the United Kingdom, Ireland, and Iceland.

Europe's New Religious Movements

We excluded from our counting procedures all Christian and Jewish
groups, but we did count Christian Scientists and the Mormons. We

also eliminated a number of Islamic groups composed of Moslem immigrants or guest workers. We counted all other groups active within each of the 18 nations, but *only if* the directory contained their current address. Those lacking a current address might no longer exist, so we excluded them all.

We then turned to the third edition of *The Encyclopedia of American Religions* (Melton 1989) and applied the same criteria. For the United States it was necessary to exclude some Buddhist and Hindu as well as Moslem groups because they were composed mostly of immigrants. That is, we counted Zen Buddhist groups based on congregations primarily of non-Asian backgrounds, but did not count those based on Asians. In counting American groups we also eliminated all that were listed as defunct and those for whom a current address could no longer be found.

The results are shown in Table 7.8. Overall, these European nations have *twice* as high a rate of cult movements as does the United States. Moreover, many European nations have rates many times that of the United States—in fact Switzerland has a rate about ten times that of the United States. Keep in mind too that, not only are European cult movements undercounted, but the nations with the lowest rates are mainly those where Melton believes the undercounting to have been the greatest. As an example of the magnitudes that might be involved in some of these undercounts, consider that in the draft initially available to us, Melton and his associates reported 32 cult movements in Italy, for a rate of 0.6. Subsequently it became possible to dispatch an Italian-speaking researcher to look again. She found an additional 34 groups during a four-week stay, thus doubling Italy's rate.

So much, then, for data that are "empirically refuted." Compared with the United States, Europe is awash in nonstandard religious movements.

As it turns out, however, these rates are not adequate for statistical analysis, probably because of the extent to which variation is caused by undercounting. In contrast, the European rates we assembled previously may have been based on crude sources, but they displayed high and appropriate correlations. That is, the rate of Eastern and Indian cults correlated 0.77 with the rate of Mormon membership and these, in turn, correlated highly with rates of Scientology staff members. Moreover, all three of these rates correlated very negatively with church attendance rates. In contrast, the rates shown here do not correlate with current European Mormon membership rates or with any of our earlier rates.

Table 7.8

Cult Movements in Europe and America

	Cult Movements Per Million	Number of Cult Movements
Switzerland	16.7	108
Iceland	12.0	3
United Kingdom	10.7	604
Austria	7.9	60
Sweden	6.8	57
Denmark	4.5	23
Netherlands	4.4	64
Ireland	3.9	14
West Germany	2.5	155
Belgium	2.4	24
Norway	1.9	8
Greece	1.5	15
Italy	1.2	66
Portugal	1.0	10
France	0.9	52
Finland	0.8	4
Spain	0.7	29
Poland	0.5	17
Europe*	3.4	1,317
United States	1.7	425

*Total based only on the nations listed in the table.

This suggests that, while the new data are far less limited in scope than were the earlier data, they are not as well-counted. That is, the data on Mormon membership, on Scientology staff members, and on the location of Indian and Asian cult centers seem far more reliable as a basis for *ranking* European nations. But because of their limited scope they are far less valuable for addressing the question of whether European nations tend to have more new religious movements than does the United States.

In any event, the spurious variations caused by undercounting mean that we cannot replicate the analysis presented in our earlier work. But the results more fully justify the proposition that Europe's *true rate* of cult movements is far higher than that of the United States.

Groups or Members?

Roy Wallis (1986a) as well as Robbins and Beckford (1988) have objected to our use of data on the number of cult *movements* as a basis for comparison. Robbins and Beckford argued that statistical evidence concerning the number of new religious movements in Europe and America

> ...totally begs the question of the relative *strength* of the movements in terms of their resources, property, standing and power in the two places. It seems perverse to make assessments of Europe's receptivity to NRMs [cults] without taking these things into account. (1988: 220)

Wallis also made much of our admission that of course "a count of cult movements is not a count of cult members." First, he perceptively noted that the numbers would reflect "a variety of different groups and movements which are quite likely to wish to be represented in every major nation. This would automatically produce higher rates per million for small population countries" (497). His second objection was that just because someone opens "an office does not mean that he has any customers," a view shared by Robbins and Beckford who suggested that temples and staff members may only represent "missionary activity," not results (22).

The point that movements may lack customers has merit, but surely it applies as fully on either side of the Atlantic. As for the claim that groups will seek a presence in European nations even without local supporters, it *could* apply *if* the groups at issue were primarily larger movements with an international base, such as Scientology and ISKCON. But the vast majority of groups involved in these national rates are tiny, with only a single location. Indeed, this militates against the more general criticism that we have counted groups such as Scientology with a single location in France, for example, and 23 centers in the United States, as but a single cult in each nation. For every larger group in America, such as Scientology, there are scores that consist of only 100 or fewer people.

Moreover, our original data for Europe showed that Scientology had multiple centers in many European nations—5 in Great Britain. Wallis regarded this as proof that Scientology was anemic in Britain compared with the United States, choosing to dismiss the fact that, in terms of Scientology staff members, the comparison was far closer— Britain had 10.5 per million population in contrast with America's 17.9

(circa 1975). He also thought it unfair of us to suggest that, as an American-born movement, Scientology should be larger here, since it had been recruiting far longer on this side of the Atlantic.

In any event, Wallis (1986a) successfully prevailed upon the Church of Scientology for current membership statistics (circa 1985), and reported that there were 4 million members in the United States. If so, that would have made Scientology the fifth largest religious body in the nation at that time—the Lutheran merger was not yet complete. That is, Wallis accepted that there were more American Scientologists than Mormons, more Scientologists than the combined totals for the Episcopalians and the United Church of Christ. As for Britain, Wallis reported 336,000 Scientologists, and he placed another 624,000 of them in the rest of Europe. Turned into rates, America was far ahead with 16,427 per million, compared with 6,011 for Great Britain and 3,684 per million in the rest of Europe. Thus, Wallis found our statistics about Europe's receptivity to nonstandard religious movements to be "entirely wanting."

At the time we judged it unnecessary to respond, since these data were so obviously fantastic. They are reminiscent of the claim by a Toronto magazine in the early 1980s that there were 10,000 members of Hare Krishna in that city. When Irving Hexham, Raymond Currie, and Joan Townsend (1985) investigated, the actual number turned out to be about 80. Fantastic or not, we should have responded, for we have since learned that many of our colleagues took (and still take) these data at face value.

Recently, more realistic data on Scientology membership have become available. Barry Kosmin (1991) and his colleagues conducted the largest survey ever devoted to American religious affiliation. Based on responses from 113,000 randomly selected Americans, Kosmin calculated that there were approximately 45,000 American Scientologists, or slightly more than 1 percent of the total reported to Wallis. In contrast, the 1989-1990 edition of the *United Kingdom Christian Handbook* (which is much like the *Yearbook of American and Canadian Churches*, except that it recently began to collect and print data from non-Christian groups) reported that there were 48,000 Scientologists in Great Britain. While this too is but a fraction of the number proposed by Wallis, it is sufficiently large to completely reverse the comparative rates, there now being far more Scientologists per million in Britain

(845) than in the United States (182). Based on the 1991 census, there are 45 Scientologists per million in Canada.

In addition to these survey data, Peter Brierley (1993) has reported that approximately 40,000 persons in France gave their occupations as professional astrologers on their income tax returns. In contrast, examination of the 1994 Yellow Pages (in electronic form, from American Business Information, Inc.) for the entire United States revealed 220 astrologers, 43 Tarot Readers, 20 Fortune Tellers, and 441 Psychics for a total of 724 or 2.8 per million population. The French rate based on tax returns is a staggering 706.7 per million. Brierley also reported that there are 90,000 fortune tellers and witches registered in Germany—consistent with the fact that a third of Germans believe in their abilities (Stark 1993).

Perhaps, even added together, these data are not definitive. Data seldom are. But they are the best data available and they all suggest that Europe is fertile ground for deviant religious movements. Indeed, we suggest that the burden of proof now rests on those who wish to believe otherwise.

Conclusion

For decades, despite the ready availability of excellent data, the sociology of religion ignored cults. To be sure, few people belonged to them, but then very few people in any time or society are engaged in radically creative activities of any kind. And the many sociologists of religion with ties to bland, conventional denominations were uncomfortable with the thought that radical cults might contain within them the seeds of the future of religion. Most new religious movements fail quickly, but a very few of them throughout history have become the great religions of the world. It is unlikely that in the aftermath of the Crucifixion there were more than 1,000 members of the obscure cult group who came to be known as Christians. Three centuries later there were probably more than 30 million, and Christianity dominated the Roman Empire (Stark, 1996). And in 1830 there were only six Mormons—members of an obscure cult in rural New York State. At the end of 1994 the Mormons numbered nearly 9 million. If we want to understand how religions begin and what determines whether they survive, we must study contemporary cults.

This field of scholarship has also been limited by a tendency on the part of researchers to avoid statistical analysis of quantitative data. To be sure, sociology can accomplish much with both historical and ethnographic qualitative data. Indeed, both of us have done extensive qualitative field observations of cults, and each of us has invested a great deal of time working with qualitative historical materials about religious movements as well. But, the fact is that much statistical information has been lying around, some of it for many decades, waiting for sociologists to make use of it. On top of that, nothing prevents industrious sociologists from quantifying other kinds of data, or from bringing more rigor to qualitative analyses.

8

Religion and Mental Illness

From the start, social scientists have interpreted religion as essentially irrational, rooted in "hallucinations" (Comte 1896: vol II: 554) and "neurosis" (Freud 1927: 88). Not surprisingly this has inspired an immense amount of effort to link religion and mental illness. Two basic themes have dominated. First, the claim that religion *causes* mental illness—a view that flourished in the nineteenth century. Second, the view that religion *is* mental illness—a view that remains common, especially among orthodox Freudians.

Should either claim have substance, religious mental illness would be an excellent example of religion as deviance. In this chapter we will assess both claims. We begin with the earlier of the two theses, that religion can drive humans insane.

Religion as a Cause of Mental Illness

In the nineteenth and twentieth centuries, as psychiatry has undergone various fads and revolutions, it has frequently blamed religion for causing substantial amounts of mental illness. In Chapter 2 and Chapter 3, we examined Durkheim's thesis that Protestantism stimulates suicide, and it is not uncommon for particular brands of religion to be accused of mental and emotional harm.

129

The accusation that religion can corrode mental health has appeared in so many guises, from so many quarters, that it is impossible to cover all of them in one chapter. Here we shall look at the historical roots of the antagonism between psychiatry and religion through the theory of religious insanity held by American *alienists* (psychiatrists) of the nineteenth century. One reason for this choice is to show once again what marvelous historical data exist, ready for sociological analysis, and we have discovered treasuries of quantitative data from as long as a century and a half ago. The data derive from a most significant period in the history of psychiatry, when psychiatrists were first emerging as trained professionals and the first substantial number of insane asylums (as mental hospitals then were called) were being built. In many respects, subsequent dramas between psychiatry and religion have been merely replays of the events of this period.

Another reason to pursue these particular issues is to show that students of religion and deviance need not always concern themselves primarily with causes of deviant behavior. A substantial task undertaken by many sociologists is to document the ways that social groups define deviance, and this chapter proves that we are in sympathy with this approach. Only when societal reaction becomes the sole topic of study, to the exclusion of the causes of the behavior itself, do we take issue with our colleagues.

Religious Insanity in Nineteenth-Century America

On July 16, 1860, William S. Allen languished in the Tennessee state asylum at Nashville, a victim of religious excitement. A forty-five year old tailor from Virginia, Allen had been committed the year before and was but one of the 212 inmates and 30 staff who lived at the hospital. Rebecca Hester, fifty-two, was also a Virginia native driven mad by religion, while Ann J. Pickett, the wife of a physician, had lost her sanity to the Spiritualism craze of the 1850s. Methodist-Episcopal preacher Thomas B. Craighead was not among the 11 inmates crazed by religion, because his affliction was diagnosed as hereditary. We know these intimate facts because Dr. William A. Cheatham, director of the institution, told them to Davidson County assistant marshal J. B. Corley when he came to count the residents for the 1860 census.

When we first discovered such records, quite by accident, we assumed that either Cheatham or Corley had taken it upon himself to add these tidbits of information to an otherwise dull enumeration of the population. But then we found similarly rich reports from other institutions revealing, for example, that a victim of religious excitement known only as Moses wandered the halls of the asylum at Stockton, California. Further research revealed that it was the official policy of the federal government to tabulate causes of insanity at the 1860 census and that the official psychiatric theory of the time considered religious excitement to be an important source of psychopathology.

Microfilm copies of the original census enumeration schedules are now available at a dozen federal archives around the country, and a growing body of social-scientific research has exploited this unexpectedly rich trove of data (Laslett 1977; Johnson 1978; Perlmann 1979; Hirata 1979; Bainbridge 1982, 1992b). A guide book published by the Bureau of the Census (1979) purports to give the full instructions to enumerators in 1860, but in fact this is an eviscerated abridgement. The extensive original instructions state, in part:

> In all cases of insane persons, you will write in the space where you enter the word "Insane," the cause of such insanity; and you will in every case inquire into the cause or origin thereof, and write the word—as intemperance, spiritualism, grief, affliction, hereditary, misfortune, etc. As nearly every case of insanity may be traced to some known cause, it is earnestly desired that you will not fail to make your return in this respect as perfect as possible. (Department of the Interior 1860: 16–17)

The instruction does not suggest religion per se as cause of insanity, but does name spiritualism, the prominent religious deviance of the 1850s. The published volume of summary statistics for the 1860 census (Kennedy 1864) contains a long essay on insanity, written under the direction of the distinguished alienist and social scientist, Pliny Earle. Here, in the widely read official report of the best social statistics of the time, the theory that religious excitement often caused insanity was stated at length and presented as fact.

However, only a single table of data from the 1860 enumeration of the insane was published, and it gave merely their numbers by state, "slave" and "free." A table reporting the supposed causes of insanity in a large number of cases came not from the census but from hospital reports previously summarized in a popular almanac (Earle 1863).

Apparently, the rich information about supposed cause recorded by the enumerators was never tabulated, and one purpose of this chapter is to bring these interesting data to scientific attention.

Of course, we need not accept the theory of mental illness reflected in the nineteenth century etiological judgements. Indeed, the chief modern use of these data is ethnographic: to help us understand the theory of insanity which prevailed over a century ago and learn the role which religion played in it. While no society achieves full consensus in its views of madness (Edgerton 1966; Finkel 1976), the theory of religious insanity had the status of official truth for more than fifty years, promulgated by the leading psychiatrists and social scientists, accepted by popular media like the almanacs from which opinion leaders took their information, and enshrined by the census as the official position of the United States government.

Psychiatric theories may serve four functions, quite apart from their capacity to explain the cold facts about insanity known at the time of their popularity. First, they may assist professionals in asserting special claims to power and status (Hollingshead and Redlich 1958: 163; Strauss et al. 1964). Second, they may be used as rhetorical tools to discredit political opponents and members of devalued classes or subcultures (Gursslin et al. 1959; Goode 1969; Medvedev and Medvedev 1971). Third, they may be used as media through which the culture consensually expresses and modifies its basic conceptions of human nature and social values (Benedict 1934; Ackerknecht 1943; Opler 1959; Edgerton 1966; Bastide 1972; Kiev 1972). And fourth, they may provide legitimation for humane treatment and hope for patients and their families (Szasz 1961; Parsons 1964b; cf. Haley 1963). It may be that the theory of religious insanity served each of these functions.

Sociologists have long argued that science itself may have cultural roots in the very religious tradition to which the nineteenth-century alienists belonged (Westfall 1958; Merton 1970), and until the end of the period under consideration here, religion worked through science as much as against it (Gillispie 1959; Toulmin 1982). Religion provided Americans with an interpretive framework for understanding humans and society, yet it was slowly giving way to secular perspectives. The alienists mixed piety and science in a way which aided this transition while condemning religious deviance, raising the alienists in status, and giving comfort to many sufferers.

This chapter will examine the 1860 data on supposed cause of insanity, together with comparable statistics found in official reports and scientific publications of the time, in the light of these hypotheses. We will learn the psychological theory that encouraged alienists to believe that religion can cause nervous breakdowns, and we will consider a number of social functions this conclusion may have served. While fascinating from a purely antiquarian standpoint, this topic has relevance for understanding the contemporary psychiatric antipathy toward religion. In the middle of the nineteenth century, when psychiatry was emerging as a profession supposedly based on scientific principles, the enduring psychiatric suspicion of religion took root.

Statistics on Religious Insanity

Persons labeled insane can be found throughout the 1860 census manuscripts, and cases attributed to religion appear in many different residential contexts. For example, Moses Smith, a thirty-five year old shoemaker driven mad by religious excitement, lived at the town poorhouse of Monson, Massachusetts. Galen Weston, a farmer who lived at home with his wife Judith in Duxbury, Massachusetts, lost his wits to Spiritualism. While such cases are numerous nationwide, they are rare in any given town, and a search for a large sample of uninstitutionalized insane would be prohibitively expensive. But in 1860 there were forty-two major insane asylums in the United States, and we were able to locate census records for every single one of them.

Despite the care with which the assistant marshals generally did their work, supposed cause is not given for twenty-four asylums. We think the cumbersomeness of the hospital records often made it very difficult to extract special information except in a concerted study such as the occasional statistical reports prepared by asylum directors or treasurers. Such reports typically described the patients who had been admitted during a given year, or all those admitted since the founding of the institution, while the census wanted data on the inmates present on the day of enumeration. Several of the asylums which do not give cause in the 1860 census did so in their own publications, and they may have found it far too inconvenient to redo the work on short notice for the census taker.

In one case, the Auburn Asylum for Insane Convicts in New York, the criminal offense of each inmate is named instead of cause of insanity, the enumerator having followed the instruction to report offense and date of conviction for all prisoners. The federal microfilms were not completely legible for the asylum at Taunton, Massachusetts, but a duplicate handwritten copy preserved in the Boston State House provided these data. For seventeen major asylums, we know what was believed to have caused insanity in 2,258 cases.

The summary volume of the 1860 census gave the supposed cause for fully 9,473 admissions to four hospitals in Massachusetts, New York, Pennsylvania, and Connecticut. Of these 740, or 7.8 percent, were attributed to "religious excitement" (Kennedy 1864: lxxxix). These data span three decades or more, and some individual patients were counted more than once because of readmissions to the hospital. Data from the seventeen asylums in 1860 represent a wider range of asylums, including recently built institutions in southern and western areas of the country, and they count actual persons, without duplication, at a single point in time. However, hospital reports are valuable both because they reach back further in time and because they were public expressions of a professional psychiatric ideology aimed both at political leaders and at the general public.

Table 8.1 gives the percent of insanity cases attributed to religion in approximately fifteen thousand cases, data taken from two of the most comprehensive hospital reports, three almanacs contemporary with the 1860 census, and the census itself.

The first four annual reports of the State Lunatic Hospital at Worcester, Massachusetts, offered lists of all patients admitted, their identities hidden by code numbers, with a variety of information about each, including individual ascriptions of cause (Calhoun 1837). Reaching back to 1833 when the hospital was opened, they offer an obvious comparison with our census reports.

A retrospective report of very high scientific quality concerning the Bloomingdale asylum of new York City was issued in 1848 by Pliny Earle, aggregating the supposed causes of patients' insanity into 85 categories. The Bloomingdale report clearly counts separate persons, rather than tabulating the same patient repeatedly upon readmission to the hospital, and we can use Earle's data with great confidence because his many social-scientific publications reveal him to be an accomplished statistician and a researcher of high professional standards.

Since colonial days, almanacs had been among the most important sources not only of statistical and scientific information but also of

Table 8.1

Persons Hospitalized for Insanity Attributed
to Religious Causes

Source of Data	Asylum	Dates	Percent Attributed to Religion
Calhoun (ed.), 1837	Worcester, MA	1833-36	3.7%
Earle, 1848	Bloomingdale, NY	1821-44	7.8%
American Almanac, 1860	Augusta, ME	1858	14.6%
American Almanac, 1861	Augusta, ME	1859	6.0%
National Almanac, 1864	Augusta, ME	1862	4.8%
	Concord, NH	1862-63	5.1%
	Taunton, MA	1854-62	5.4%
	Hartford, CT	1824-63	6.3%
	Philadelphia, PA	1841-62	6.1%
	Harrisburg, PA	1851-62	1.3%
	Indianapolis, IN	1848-61	14.4%
	Jacksonville, IL	1860-62	5.2%
Census Manuscripts	17 Asylums*	1860	6.1%

* Somerville, MA, Staunton, VA, Worcester, MA, Blackwell's Island, NY, Nashville, TN, Concord, NH, Baltimore, MD, Fulton, MO, Stockton, CA, Mill Creek, OH, Taunton, MA, Jackson, MS, Newburg, OH, Dayton, OH, Raleigh, NC, Northampton, MA, Kalamazoo, MI.

ideas and values from which Americans created a national culture. Thus it is very interesting that they confidently promulgated the theory of religious insanity, supporting it with statistics sufficiently official to be appropriated by the authors of the census volumes. In *American Almanac* and *National Almanac*, these data are included in reports on the operations of the various state governments, in amongst lists of state officials and tables of budget expenditures.

Often, we find fragmentary comments which indict religion as a cause of insanity without giving us quite enough information to compute rates. Two examples from the 1860 *American Almanac* are the Indiana Hospital for the Insane and the Worcester Asylum, each of which appears in our table with data from another source. For the former we are told, "The alleged probable cause of insanity in 86 cases were religious excitement and anxieties; in 35, spiritual rappings; in 31, intemperance; in 23, tobacco," but we are told nothing about other causes, nor given the total number of cases assigned a cause. Worcester reported twelve common supposed causes, with 289 cases attributed to religious excitement, 25 to Spiritualism and 10 to Millerism (a religious movement which expected the world to end at any moment).

For the Maine Insane Asylum at Augusta the 1860 almanac says that 126 admissions occurred in the year following November 30, 1857, with no attribution of cause for 30 of these admissions religious excitement accounted for 11 cases and Spiritualism for 3, meaning that a total of 14, or about 15 percent of the 96 assigned cases, were blamed on one or another manifestation of religion.

As Table 8.1 shows, the percent of cases attributed to religion among those which were assigned some sort of cause ranges from a low of near one percent to a high of nearly fifteen. To be sure, doctors may have differed in their readiness to blame religion, so the rates could vary greatly across institutions. But most of the reports range narrowly around 6 percent, and the rate for the seventeen asylums is 6.1 percent.

The census records actually present approximately 300 different etiological comments. Indeed, an exact count is impossible because differences in spelling and grammar shade imperceptibly over into real differences in meaning. To get the total of 138 cases attributed to religion, we added together 57 cases of religious excitement, 53 of religion, 2 of religious perplexity, 1 of religious, 6 of Millerism, 17 of Spiritualism, and 2 of spirit rappings. Only two of the seventeen asylums, those in Baltimore and Kalamazoo, contained no patients whose illnesses were attributed to religion in some terms or other.

Nervous Breakdown from Overpowering Religion

To understand the hypothesis that religion could cause madness, we must discover the general etiological theory of which it was a part. Pliny Earle's essay in the 1863 *National Almanac* provides a succinct statement of the standard theory of insanity of his day:

> Inasmuch as insanity is almost uniformly a disorder connected with bodily debility, a fact apparently never learned until within the last half-century, it necessarily follows that all customs, habits, occupations, or other agencies whatsoever which exhaust the power of the brain and nerves, bringing the body to

a weakened condition, may thus become the origin of mental disorder. Such influences are, indeed the ramified root from which insanity springs. (Earle 1863: 56)

In the summary volume of the 1860 census (Kennedy 1864), Earle detailed the "principal methods by which the religious sentiment is aroused to that point at which it can produce mental disorders," citing first the "extraordinary and spasmodic" religious revivals in which "the excitement, both mental and corporal, is long–continued, and necessarily produces nervous exhaustion—the condition most favorable for an attack of insanity." Here Earle echoed charges often directed towards revivals and "religious enthusiasm" by liberal Protestant clergy. According to Sydney Ahlstrom, "a firm opposition to revivalism and the whole pietistic emphasis on a religion of the heart was a settled conviction with liberals" (1975: I: 474). Thus, in 1778, having newly been appointed president of Yale University, the Reverend Ezra Stiles offered his opinion that revivals such as those conducted by George Whitefield (one of history's greatest revival preachers and a close friend of Benjamin Franklin's) were accomplished by driving people "seriously, soberly, and solemnly out of their wits" (in Ahlstrom 1975: I: 490).

Earle also condemned the intensity of meetings of small church groups and especially warned against "solitary reading and meditation upon religious subjects, until personal demerit and its consequent punishment become the sole occupants of the thoughts, to the exclusion of those consolations which the spirit of Christianity guarantees" (xc-xci). Earle's admonition to ministers in the census volume cited the healing as well as the pathogenic powers of religion:

By that denunciatory and, as appears to us, intemperate style of preaching, wherein the terrors and consequences of Divine wrath are portrayed with all the vigor and the force of a vivid imagination, giving over the minds of the young, the sensitive, the susceptible, and the strongly-conscientious, to the dominion of despondency and fear, the action of which is powerfully depressive to the vital energy, and, consequently, strongly promotive of an invasion of mental disorder; while the solemn and awe-inspiring rites of some services are sore trials to the minds of the sensitive and superstitious, contribute their influence to the subversion of reason, and would be even more frequently fatal but for their rapidly and strongly contrasting variations, so illustrative of the

remedial power attributed to the administrators of these imposing ceremonies, which modifies their effect. (Kennedy 1864: xci)

In 1841, after a visit to thirteen European asylums, Earle contend-
ed that religious excitement was a distinctively American cause of
insanity, noting that none of 1,557 cases admitted to the Asylum at
Charenton near Paris were attributed to religious excitement, compared
with 53 of the 678 cases treated at the Massachusetts state hospital
(Earle 1841: 119). He suggested that the more lively and widespread
religious debates in the United States promoted insanity here, while a
differentiation of the French into obediently superstitious "lower
orders" and confidently unfaithful "higher orders" left no one prey to
private indulgence in religious obsessions. However, American psychiatric thought was an extension of British and French doctrines, and the
theory of religious insanity took firm root in all three nations.

A Manual of Psychological Medicine by British doctors John Bucknill
and Daniel Tuke was "by far the best general treatise upon insanity in
the English language" (Earle 1886: 60). It "quickly became the standard
work in the field" of American psychiatry (Dain 1964: 150), cited extensively even by the 1860 U.S. census publication (Kennedy 1864: lxxix).
The fourth edition of this text holds religious excitement responsible
for about 425 of 14,152 English asylum admissions and 20 of 2,068
French admissions (Bucknill and Tuke 1879: 91–93). The authors commented, "Doubtless, in many instances it was in reality the initial symp-
tom of the disorder. Still we cannot for a moment doubt that the form
in which religion is but too frequently presented is a serious cause of
Insanity" (Bucknill and Tuke, 1879: 99).

Supposed Causes of Insanity

The standard nineteenth-century theory of insanity had the marvelous
capacity to connect under a few general principles the most diverse set
of specific ideas. To see how it did so and to discover the conceptual
context in which the idea of religious insanity flourished, we shall survey the main etiological categories revealed in the 1860 census data and
in Earle's report of the Bloomingdale asylum covering 1821 to 1844.
Table 8.2 gives supposed cause for the seventeen asylums and for
Bloomingdale, collapsed under large conceptual headings of the type
used by Earle and his colleagues.

Religious excitement and Spiritualism are treated as one category;

however, there were no cases attributed to Spiritualism at Bloomingdale, since this religious movement did not begin until after the period covered by the Bloomindale data. Males and females seem about equally prone to religious insanity.

If excessive intensity of religious emotions can cause madness, then overpowering feelings and experiences generated by family problems, occupational difficulties, and other disasters of social life should also be pathogenic. The next section of Table 8.2 lists several categories of such social-psychological problems. In the technical language of the day, these were known as *moral* causes.

Each of these categories includes many particular etiological comments. For example, pecuniary trouble includes pecuniary embarrassment, loss of property, money matters, and failure in business. Domestic trouble includes such family problems as abuse by husband, adultery, infidelity of wife, and recent marriage. Loss and grief includes death of children, death of husband, death of wife, loss of parents, and, in one case, witnessing brothers drown. The most common of the "other" intense emotions was jealousy. Traditional gender roles are reflected in the fact that men were more apt to suffer from pecuniary or business trouble, while women more often suffered domestic problems plus loss and grief.

The gender differences in the next four categories—of hedonistic self-indulgence—also may reflect traditional sex roles, although the greater propensity of males to be accused of onanism may have physiological causes. Throughout the nineteenth and early twentieth centuries, medical science and religious moralism conspired to prohibit this autoerotic behavior. The first superintendent of the Worcester Asylum, Dr. Samuel B. Woodward, fulminated against masturbation both in the *Boston Medical and Surgical Journal* and in a book titled *Hints for the Young in Relation to the Health of Body and Mind*. There he said, "From the hand of God himself we receive the noble attributes which distinguish us from the animals around us. This vice reduces us below their level" (Woodward 1840: 7). In *Genesis* we read that the sin of Onan was so wicked in the sight of the Lord that it was punished with death. But religion, like medicine, may merely have been the vehicle for a more broadly-based Puritanical culture.

Woodward's theory of how masturbation produced insanity provides an interesting contrast with Earle's analysis of religious insanity, because Woodward expressed an allegedly scientific discovery in the rhetoric of a thundering sermon:

Table 8.2

Diagnosed Causes of Insanity

	Seventeen Asylums (1860)		Bloomingdale Asylum (1821-1844)	
	Males	Females	Males	Females
Religious excitement or Spiritualism	6.6%	5.6%	7.4%	8.5%
Pecuniary trouble	5.4%	2.3%	18.7%	3.0%
Disappointment	3.3%	4.9%	2.3%	5.8%
Domestic trouble	3.7%	10.7%	3.2%	8.7%
Loss and grief	1.6%	4.7%	2.3%	5.4%
Love	1.2%	0.7%	0.1%	0.6%
Fear	1.3%	1.5%	2.3%	5.0%
Other intense emotions	2.2%	2.1%	3.6%	3.4%
Intemperance	15.0%	4.4%	14.1%	4.0%
Drugs	1.1%	0.9%	0.7%	1.6%
Masturbation	17.7%	2.1%	5.4%	0.0%
Sin and bad habits	2.0%	0.6%	1.3%	1.4%
Overexertion	3.8%	2.2%	4.9%	0.0%
Hardship	1.0%	1.4%	0.0%	0.0%
Ill health	11.8%	21.9%	21.6%	15.7%
Childbirth	0.0%	8.2%	0.0%	18.9%
Feminine problems	0.0%	7.7%	0.0%	13.7%
Epilepsy	9.5%	5.1%	2.8%	0.8%
Paralysis	0.4%	0.1%	0.0%	0.0%
Injury	4.1%	1.1%	5.8%	0.8%
Exposure	1.3%	0.5%	1.3%	0.0%
Hereditary	5.7%	7.1%	1.3%	0.0%
All other causes	1.3%	4.5%	2.0%	2.6%
	100%	100%	100%	100%
n =	(1,230)	(1,028)	(689)	(497)

It is a vice which excites, to the greatest activity, the strongest and most uncontrollable propensities of animal nature; and these are rendered more active by indulgence, while the power of resistance and restraint is lessened by it in a tenfold degree. The moral sensibility becomes so blunted as to retain no ascendancy in the character, to control and regulate the conduct. Under such circumstances, the best resolutions to reform, and the firmest determination to abandon the habit, fail of accomplishment. In spite of himself, the victim sinks deeper and deeper in pollution, till he is overwhelmed at last in irretrievable ruin and disgrace. (Woodward 1840: 7)

In Table 8.2, overexertion and hardship are mixed categories describing patients who had succumbed to nervous exhaustion brought on by too much labor, whether mental or physical, or by terrible circumstances which are not readily assigned to one of the other categories in the table. From ill health to exposure we tabulate a large number of cases attributed to purely physiological causes. Official psychiatric nosology of the nineteenth century attempted to make a strict distinction between *moral* (or social-psychological) causes and *physical* causes. If moral causes exhausted or overtaxed the nervous system, physical causes attacked it directly or undermined it by debilitating vital organs of the body.

Many doctors considered the vices, as well as many forms of hardship and exertion, to be physical causes of insanity because the immediate effect is on the body, even if conscious human behavior is a more ultimate cause. When Edward Jarvis, one of the best social scientists of his century, placed Mesmerism among physical causes he was guided by the view current at the time that Mesmerism actually dealt in animal magnetism rather than social suggestion (Jarvis 1852: 23; cf. Darnton 1970).

Another distinction, maintained by some alienists and ignored by others, described certain causes as *predisposing* and others as *exciting* (Earle 1848: 76; cf. Durkheim 1897). In compiling his Bloomingdale data, Earle considered heredity to be the ultimate predisposing cause in many if not all cases, and the causes listed in Table 8.2 were all considered to be proximate exciting causes—final straws, as it were, breaking a naturally weak nervous system. In particular, Dr. Isaac Ray, director of several major asylums during his illustrious career, felt that persons who had inherited weakness of the nervous system should be especially careful to avoid the emotional dangers of religious revivals (Ray 1863: 191).

Etiology and Patient Characteristics

Data from the old records are quite adequate for many kinds of statistical analysis, and Table 8.3 reveals an interesting pattern in the cure rates for the Worcester and Columbus mental hospitals, reported in 1850 by Edward Jarvis. While "cure" here meant merely that the patient seemed improved and was discharged from the institution, and did not necessarily mark a complete end to the illness, inspections of cure rates for cases with different supposed causes should reflect real differences in the nature of the afflictions.

The very high cure rate for religion suggests that interpersonal theories of mental illness might well apply to many of these cases. In contrast, the very low cure rate for epilepsy undoubtedly indicates serious neurological impairment. The low cure rate for masturbation suggests that these cases were schizophrenics placed on the back wards, unrestrained by social control—people apt to masturbate in full view of the hospital staff, their behavior being a sign rather than a cause of serious pathology. The other etiological categories included a wide range of problems, some of a temporary nature, whether episodic and leading to false announcements of cure or really ending in a restoration of health. For example, many cases of intemperance were delirium tremens brought to an end by the enforced sobriety of the asylum (Earle 1848).

Table 8.3
"Cure Rates" for Mental Illnesses by Cause (Jarvis 1850)

Percent "Cured"

Religion	72.2%
Pecuniary	58.2%
Intemperance	57.7%
Masturbation	29.7%
Epilepsy	11.1%
All Cases	57.6%

Religious Aspects of the Theory

The most comprehensive dissertation on religious excitement was *Observations on the Influence of Religion upon the Health and Physical Welfare of Mankind*, published in 1835 by Amariah Brigham, one of the most learned and progressive physicians of his day and founding editor of the first psychiatric journal in the United States. Brigham urged a mixture of good physical hygiene and religious moderation, believing "that whatever was established and enjoined by our Savior, is beneficial to mankind, and not injurious to health" (Brigham 1835: 104).

However, he surveyed the history of religious fanaticism and found it thoroughly antagonistic to Christ's teachings. In his view, protracted revival camp meetings were unhealthy and unscriptural, resulting "in the multiplication of diseases of the nervous system, in the increase of epilepsy, convulsions, hydrocephalus and insanity, and in a generation of men and women, weak and enfeebled in body and mind" (1835: 178).

Brigham explained the psychological power of revivals and camp meetings in terms of the then-current theory of social imitation or sympathy (1835: 256) that could produce mass hysteria (cf. Mackay 1852; Le Bon 1895). Thus, the spiritual manifestations allegedly experienced by participants in revivals were illusions, the consequences of overtaxed nervous systems. In a numbered, italicized, formal proposition he expressed the root concept of the theory of religious insanity: *"I. All long continued or violent excitement of the mind is dangerous, because it is likely to injure the brain and nervous system"* (1835: 284).

Brigham connected this proposition to religion in a classic theological-medical argument, stated in six further propositions (1835: 330–331). First, he said, religious sentiments are innate in humans, but they may act blindly unless guided by reason and knowledge. Secondly, Christ established no rites or ceremonies but instead laid down principles of virtuous conduct; unfortunately, to Brigham's mind, religious denominations grafted rituals onto Christianity, which became sources of discord. Third, revivalists misled ordinary people by suggesting that the supernatural currently intervened in worldly affairs, and thus created fanaticism. Fourth, religious revival meetings were both unscriptural and unhealthy and ought to be abolished; the excitement they produced could create madness. Thus, the doctrines of revivalists and sects promoted unreasonable expectation of miracles, which could unbalance judgement, and the nervous system could be broken by the emotional intensity of camp meetings and similar unregulated excitements.

While the first four statements in his argument castigated sectarian religion, the final two emphasized the healthful qualities of orthodox Christianity. His fifth point was that the Sabbath should be a day of rest, thus restoring frayed nerves. And sixth, he asserted, "religious worship and the cultivation of devotional feelings, are beneficial to man, when not carried to an unreasonable extent" (Brigham 1835: 331).

When Brigham first made these views public, "he brought upon himself a charge of skepticism and infidelity" (Hurd 1917: 361). Despite the piety in which they were couched, his psychological theories challenged popular religious notions, as did the entire enterprise of scientific study of the mind. In a popular book on mental hygiene, Dr. Isaac Ray was forced right at the beginning to consider the challenge psychiatry gave to the Christian theory of the soul, commenting that the idea that the mind

> could be affected by any merely physical conditions seemed to be degrading to its dignity, and indicative of the coarsest material-ism. If the mind may be diseased, then it may perish, and so our hopes of immortality be utterly destroyed. This startling conclu-sion has been sufficient to deter the mass of mankind from admit-ting very heartedly the facts which physiological and pathological inquiries have contributed to this subject. (Ray 1863: 1–2)

Those who held both religious and scientific views had long resorted to the hypothesis that the nervous system was the means by which the immortal soul expressed itself in the material world, that the brain was the instrument through which the soul plays its tune. Like Brigham, Ray says that madness may be produced by overexcited religious senti-ments but not by the more sober and dignified variants of religion. Often he defends psychiatry against potential charges of infidelity, in an essay that is both scientific and theological. Despite these pious dis-claimers, psychiatry and the social sciences have from the beginning played roles in eroding religious faith, and their theories do often chal-lenge the doctrine of the soul.

Psychiatry as a Tool of Social Control and Status Assertion

In the days of Brigham and Ray, psychiatrists opposed not religion in general but only its sectarian, high-tension varieties. Although

Brigham criticized Catholic practice, the only denominations mentioned by name as causes of insanity in any of the reports examined by us are Spiritualism, Millerism, and Mormonism, three deviant religious movements. The camp meetings, revivals and winter baptisms by total immersion attacked as unhealthy by Brigham and his colleagues were all practices emphasized by high-tension sects, in those days primarily the Baptists and Methodists.

The theory of religious insanity flourished in a period when medicine was largely unregulated, often pseudoscientific, and of dubious social status in the community (Kett 1968). The alienists named here were highly educated men who had been given high public trusts as directors of asylums and chairmen of governmental commissions. While medicine groped toward respectable status, the alienists wished to be seen as scientists, scholars, humanitarians, and community leaders. Yet they were doubly marginal. First, they were doctors when doctors were justly suspected of quackery. Second, they were alienists when their specialty was seldom included in medical educations.

In 1867, Pliny Earle told the Berkshire Medical Institution that a course in psychiatry was essential for the general practitioner, both to guide him in diagnosis and treatment and to give him information on mental hygiene with which to indoctrinate his community. In support, Earle conjured up vivid images of the danger to social status when unprepared doctors were called upon to testify in court upon the issue of mental competency:

> Some, with sufficient sagacity to perceive, after they went into court, the meshes of the net, and the cat beneath the meal, were wise enough to be very suddenly and unexpectedly called home before the court was ready for their testimony; while but too many others, supplying their deficiency of knowledge by a complement of confidence, have tied themselves to the Promethean rock with a cord of blunders, and the lawyers have torn from them, strip by strip, their bleeding flesh, until nothing was left but dry and disjointed bones, dangling and rattling in the wind. Were psychological medicine properly taught in the schools, such mistakes, which bring odium upon the profession, would not be likely to occur. (Earle 1867: 19)

But for the period under consideration here, medicine was generally taught in proprietary medical schools which set their own standards and seldom cooperated to provide organizational or conceptual coherence to their profession. As Joseph Kett commented, "Operating without outside restraint, their activities quickly took on molecular characteristics, bouncing about at random, smacking into each other, forming chance alliances, and breaking into still smaller particles" (1968: 65). One sign of the widespread desire among physicians to appear scientific and to assume a respected role in their communities was the almost perfect rate of participation (99.7 percent) of 1,319 Massachusetts doctors asked to carry out a state census of the insane and mentally retarded (Jarvis 1855: 15).

In his massive, influential *Treatise on the Medical Jurisprudence of Insanity* (1871), Isaac Ray argued that only experienced alienists could diagnose insanity and be proper experts to testify in legal proceedings. Thus, the psychiatrists struggled to attain honor and status from elite and respectable sectors of American society. In terms of religion theory, they sought to reduce their tension with the sociocultural environment. The scorn for high-tension religion expressed through their theory of religious insanity served perfectly this attempt by the alienists to achieve low tension, and may in part have been a rhetoric designed with just this purpose in mind.

But there is more to it than that. However comfortable the alienists may have been with diagnoses of religious insanity, the published cases suggest that these judgments were usually made first by family and friends of the afflicted, with the doctors often merely accepting these lay diagnoses. Indeed, the enumeration instructions for the 1860 census assumed that most causes of insanity would be readily apparent to household members. Thus, the ideology of religious insanity was part of national culture, accepted by ordinary members of the community, as well as by national opinion leaders.

Some theorists in the labeling theory or antipsychiatry traditions would suggest that psychiatry was merely used by families to punish deviant members and was an instrument of the community to suppress religious deviance (Goffman 1961; Scheff 1966; Laing 1967; Szasz 1970). The high reported cure rate for religious insanity is consistent with this interpretation. But only a deep study of hospital records or autobiographical accounts could tell us for sure if some of those labeled insane merely held unpopular views.

The possibility remains that sometimes the alienists were right and religion was in some way the proximate cause of psychiatric disorder. So-called "hysterical states" in preliterate societies often involve delusions of spirit possession or other apparently religious experiences. I. M. Lewis (1971) interprets these phenomena as oblique redressive strategies, instrumental roles adopted by oppressed persons as means for forcing their families and neighbors to treat them better.

While hysterical use of supernatural symbolism is not an effective strategy in modern society, it probably still had its place in nineteenth-century America. Some hospitalized mental patients may have been hysterics dramatizing their struggle with social conditions through religion. Since hysteria is impossible without a suitably scripted role to play, religion would be properly implicated as an enabling cause.

Furthermore, it is clear that many particular symptoms are really attempts by the patient to cope with a deep-seated problem. People beset with mental illness often fall back upon basic coping strategies rooted deep in their culture (Opler and Singer 1956; Breen 1968). Religion provides plans and interpretations for dealing with the greatest and most terrifying challenges of life (Stark and Bainbridge 1985, 1987). Thus, some patients respond to their illnesses as religious problems, thereby manifesting symptoms of religious insanity, even though religion was a response rather than the cause of the problem.

The idea that physical or emotional shocks could drive susceptible persons into madness was well adapted to an age that held high hopes for the cure of insanity (cf. Langfeld 1939). The asylums proliferated in this period, nurtured by propaganda that speedy removal of the afflicted to a place of care and rehabilitation could restore most to sanity (Rothman 1971). An optimistic "cult of curability" dominated psychiatry, not incidentally helping the psychiatrists sell their services to the public (Earle 1886).

If excessive religious excitement had caused a nervous breakdown, the calm environment of the idealized asylum, augmented by sober religious services, could heal nerves and restore sanity. The suspicions "respectable" people held of revivalism rendered the concept of religious insanity plausible and, in turn, facilitated their acceptance of psychiatry.

Dominance and Decline of the Theory

The official nineteenth-century theory of insanity was a marvel of eclecticism. The root concept was the idea that stress could exhaust a constitutionally weak nervous system. Were the stress great enough, even the strongest mind would succumb. The sources of stress and exhaustion were many but could be grouped under the headings *physi-*

cal and *moral.* Under the gross categories were finer ones, like *religion*, and within these were even finer divisions, like the three hundred different etiological comments we found in the census records. Thus the system possessed great flexibility, because one could focus either on general categories and over-arching concepts or on specific causes in particular cases.

The great flexibility of the system in turn permitted the high degree of consensus it achieved for the better part of the nineteenth century. A doctor who believed mental illness was primarily an inherited trait could happily agree with one who held that religious revivals and other social-psychological shocks were responsible, because the official theory fit both ideas together in a way which minimized debate.

Everything was a matter of degree, because all popular ideas on madness were incorporated in a single ideological structure. The ordinary citizen and the trained psychiatrist could share the same perspective, because the most specific concepts in the system referred to everyday ideas like grief over the loss of a loved one, while the general structure of the theory gave it the appearance of a science fully comprehensible only to highly trained specialists.

The official theory of which the concept of religious insanity was a part may have had especially benevolent consequences for patients, not only because of its basic optimism, but also because it saw patients as *individuals* driven mad by very particular circumstances rather than as faceless multitudes swarming in vast herds named by a few diagnostic terms. The three hundred etiological terms used in the 1860 census records describe 2,258 human beings. Thus, on average, there are only eight people per diagnostic category, and in fact there were many instances of individuals possessing unique etiological comments. But by 1880, when we find 629 inmates in the census records for the Cleveland asylum, only six diagnostic terms are found, one for every hundred. This reflects a total revolution in the medical conception of insanity.

Throughout the nineteenth century, alienists worked to construct a system to categorize the *forms* of insanity, quite separate from the theory of causes—a typology based on symptoms (Bucknill and Tuke 1879: 142–305). The 1860 census report was able to assert: "The five great generic terms, Mania, Monomania, Melancholia, Moral (or Emotional) Insanity, and Dementia, constitute a grouping, which, for general purposes, is as good as any which has been devised" (Kennedy 1864: lxxx).

The enumerator who visited the Mississippi asylum in 1860 wrote such terms down for all the inmates, as well as the supposed causes. But by 1880, alienists were no longer expected to distinguish patients through a long list of distinct causes, so at the Cleveland asylum we find 3 inmates suffering from imbecility, 5 from dipsomania, 6 from paresis, 210 from melancholia, and 369 from mania. These technical terms gave added scientific lustre to the psychiatric profession (although we can doubt they promoted deeper real understanding of insanity) and they were superseded by a different set of terms a few years later.

The system of supposed causes, including religious excitement, was not completely abandoned until well into the twentieth century. For example, patients sent from Alaska to the Oregon asylum, and others in Washington state, were still described in this way as late as the 1930s. But as an official national ideology, this theory lost its dominance in the two decades after 1860, being replaced by pessimistic agnosticism and hereditary explanations, as the asylums developed into custodial institutions with far lower expectations of cure.

With the decline of the theory, American culture lost a doctrine of mental hygiene that mixed scientific and religious concepts with traditional moralism and humane optimism. The theory of religious insanity was a tool of "mainline" religion against sects and revivals, and a means by which psychiatry promoted itself toward respectable scientific status. But for many Americans it was also a system which rendered madness comprehensible in familiar terms and offered considerable hope that the great suffering of insanity could be overcome.

Religion as Mental Illness

As the theory that religion causes religion faded, social scientists outside the psychiatric tradition promulgated the view that religion *is* mental illness—or is caused by mental illness.

From the beginning, social scientific studies of religion have been shaped by a single question: *What makes them do it?* How *could* any rational person make sacrifices on behalf of unseen supernatural entities? Or as Henri Bergson (1932: 103) put it, how can it be that "beliefs and practices which are anything but reasonable could have been, and still are, accepted by reasonable beings?" The answer: because, when it comes to religion, apparently reasonable beings are unreasonable—religion is rooted in the *irrational*. Keep in mind that claims about the irrationality of religious sacrifices have not been limited to great sacrifices such as asceticism or martyrdom. At issue are such ordinary activities as prayer, observance of moral codes, and contributions of time and wealth.

Whether it be the imputation of outright psychopathology, of groundless fears, or merely of faulty reasoning and misperceptions, the irrational assumption has dominated the field. The notion that normal, sophisticated people could be religious has been limited to a few social scientists willing to allow their own brand of very mild, "intrinsic," religiousness to pass the test of rationality.

The irrationalist premise has taken many forms. The most influential of these equates religion with psychopathology and is notable for the open contempt and antagonism expressed towards its subject. Consider Freud, who managed to characterize religion as a "neurosis," an "illusion," a "poison," an "intoxicant," and "childishness to be overcome" all on *one page* of his famous book on the subject (1927: 88). Not to be outdone, Michael P. Carroll (1987: 491) recently filled many pages in the *Journal for the Scientific Study of Religion* with claims that praying the Rosary is "a disguised gratification of repressed anal-erotic desires"—a substitute for playing "with one's feces."

Another convinced Freudian, Mortimer Ostow (1990), asserts that Evangelical Protestants are unable to accommodate "the realities of modern life" (100) and remarks on "the vacuous smiles seen on the faces of cultic converts that so exasperate their parents and that betray their fear of dealing with the real world" (102). Returning to his "analysis" of Evangelical Protestants, Ostow blames it all on regression to infant mentalities:

> the fundamentalist is also regressing to the state of mind of the child who resists differentiation from its mother. The messiah and the group itself represent the returning mother. (113)

Moreover, the diagnosis of religion as psychopathology has not been limited to Freudians; clinicians of many persuasions have expressed this view. Consider A. Ellis:

> Religiosity is in many respects equivalent to irrational thinking and emotional disturbance....The elegant therapeutic solution to emotional problems is to be quite unreligious...the less religious they are, the more emotionally healthy they will be. (1980: 637)

Or Wendell Watters, who traces all manner of incapacities to Christian belief:

Christian doctrine and teachings are incompatible with many components of sound mental health, notably self-esteem, self-actualization, and mastery, good communication skills, related individuation and the establishment of supportive human networks, and the development of healthy sexuality and reproductive responsibility. (1993:140)

Because of Freud's immense influence on anthropologists, purely psychopathological explanations of religion have been popular among them too. Thus, Weston La Barre (1972: 19) confidently explains that "A god is only a shaman's dream about his father." And, whether influenced by Freud or not, from the start anthropology has been and remains a bastion of antireligious commitment. No one has put this better than E. E. Evans-Pritchard, writing about the famous founders of the field, including Spencer, Tylor, Frazier, Levy-Bruhl and Durkheim:

The persons whose writing have been most influential [on the subject of religion] have been at the time they wrote agnostics or atheists....They sought, and found, in primitive religions a weapon which could, they thought, be used with deadly effect against Christianity. If primitive religion could be explained away as an intellectual aberration, as a mirage induced by emotional stress, or by its social function, it was implied that the higher religions could be discredited and disposed of in the same way....Religious belief was to these anthropologists absurd. (1965: 15)

That this continues today can be seen in data showing that anthropologists as well as psychologists differ greatly from other social scientists in terms of personal religiousness, and that social scientists as a group are far less apt to be religious than are natural and physical scientists, the substantial majority of whom are actively religious. For example, in a huge national sample of American college and university faculty, only 27 percent of those in mathematics, statistics and in physical sciences claimed to have "no religion," as did 29 percent of those in life sciences, and 30 percent of economists and political scientists. In contrast, 48 percent of psychologists and 57 percent of anthropologists reported having no religion. In addition, substantial majorities in all fields said they considered themselves "a religious person," but only 33 percent of psychologists and 29 percent of anthropologists did so (Stark, Iannaccone, and Finke 1996). These differences are of such magnitude that one can scarcely imagine their not influencing the tone of conversation, instruction, and research involving religion in these two fields. Indeed, having served on the faculties of several of the most distinguished universities in the nation, each of us has encountered social scientists who openly expressed their opinions that religious people shouldn't be awarded advanced degrees because they clearly were incapable of logical or independent thought.

It will be evident that the various mind control and brainwashing theories of conversion are only unusually vulgar versions of the same basic psychopathology premise—since it is "self-evident" that no one would *choose* to join an unusual religious group, converts must have been "hypnotized" or otherwise have taken leave of their senses.

An additional version of the irrationalist approach is focused on the "religious mentality." Proponents of this view don't claim that religious people are mentally ill, exactly. Instead, they are content to claim that sincerely religious people just don't think very well, having very rigid intellectual processes. Thus, Johnson and Tamney (1988) discovered that large numbers of Americans could both oppose abortion (on some grounds) and approve of capital punishment. They tried to discover "how some antiabortion people can hold inconsistent life views by advocating preservation for one form of life (an embryo or fetus) but not another (a human being convicted of a capital crime)" (44). The bias of these authors becomes obvious when they find nothing inconsistent in the life views of those in their sample who oppose capital punishment, while favoring abortion. Either both views are inconsistent, or neither. Given their prejudgments, it is not surprising that Johnson and Tamney concluded that those opposed to abortion and in favor of capital punishment "tend to be authoritarians and dogmatic authoritarians tend to ignore or compartmentalize inconsistent beliefs." They offered no data in support of this claim and, as we shall see, there are none to be found.

The invocation of authoritarianism to explain "fundamentalism" has been common since World War II. It began when T. W. Adorno (1950) and his colleagues wrote about an "Authoritarian Personality" for whom religious belief relieves pressures stemming from their inability to tolerate any intellectual contradictions or ambiguities. Indeed, it was claimed that authoritarianism not only made people religious, but that the two factors combined to make them bigots as well. Gordon W. Allport (1963) made similar claims about what he called *extrinsic* religion. As James Dittes (1971) made abundantly clear, Allport's motives were polemical, not scientific. Allport's writing on the subject amounts to little more than claims that his own brand of liberal social values tinged with vague notions of the sacred is *good* religion, while anything involving serious belief in the supernatural is *bad* religion. Slowly, other psychologists have begun to recognize the fundamental biases in Allport's work, most recently Kirkpatrick and Hood (1990).

A variant of the "religious mind" theory is the ignorance and poor reasoning theory of religious belief. This view has been especially popular among social scientists holding liberal religious views. Thus, in book after book, H. Paul Douglass (cf. Douglass and Brunner, 1935) identified the "emotional sects" as "a backwash of sectarianism" found only "in certain quarters," especially "the more backward sections of the nation." His colleague at the Institute of Social and Religious Research, Edmund Brunner (1927: 75–76), described one evangelical congregation as "a poor class of mixed blood and of moronic intelligence." And Warren Wilson, another member of the Institute, blamed the growth of evangelical Protestant groups in rural America on the fact that "among country people there are many inferior minds" (1925: 58). He further explained that revivalism was bound to persist in these regions "until we can lift the administration of popular institutions that are governed by public opinion out of the hand of the weak brother and the silly sister."

But what do the data really show?

The Research Literature

Despite the confident claims that religiousness is rooted in psychopathology, the data have been uncooperative. In a study based on a sample of persons diagnosed as being in need of immediate psychotherapy and a matched sample of the population, Stark (1971) found that those diagnosed as ill were far less likely to attend church or to score high on an index of religious orthodoxy. He also reported that the published empirical research offered no support for the claim that more religious people are prone to authoritarianism.

Subsequently, in a survey of all published, empirical studies, Bergin (1983) found that most reported a positive, rather than a negative, relationship between religiosity and mental health, and that the studies that did report a negative association between religion and mental health were tautological, having included religious items in their psychological measures. For example, Barron (1953) included five pro-religious items in his Ego Strength Scale, each of which counted against a person's ego strength and thus "discovered" that religious people had weak ego strength. Thus, only in worthless studies and in nonempirical speculation is the link between mental malfunction and religion sustained.

Finally, Christopher G. Ellison (1993) has assembled an imposing empirical literature that strongly supports the conclusion that religious belief and practice greatly *improve* self-esteem, life satisfaction, the ability to withstand major social stressors, and even improve physical health.

A moment's reflection should reveals why religion ought to be neither a form of mental illness nor a source of such illness. Religiousness is statistically normal—most people are religious. It is utterly illogical to attribute abnormal behavior to normal sources—by definition abnormalities cannot be sufficiently common to be caused by normalities. In similar fashion, that religious imagery and preoccupations are common among persons in mental hospitals is without significance since this would be equally true of persons hospitalized for purely physical problems such as broken legs or cancer. That is, "if religiousness is normal in a given culture, one would also expect to find it common in the insane asylums of that culture. Indeed, [large numbers] of mental patients in American are probably Democrats, but that has led very few to consider party choice as a source or consequence of insanity" (Stark 1971: 166).

Conclusion

For the decades straddling the year 1900, psychiatry was a strictly biological discipline that had little use for psychological, social, or religious concepts. The fact that it lacked effective treatments and could promise practically nothing to the mentally ill and their families left a market open for penetration by alternative ideologies. By the middle of the twentieth century, a variety of psychotherapies had come to dominate public consciousness, despite the fact that they were designed for mild emotional problems and had relatively little to contribute to the cure of institutionalized populations.

The rise of psychoanalysis was in many respects a re-enchantment of psychiatry that rendered madness again a moral issue that might have religious implications. Throughout their history, schools of psychiatry have been marked by many of the features of sectarian religion, including not only strange beliefs and practices but also a marked tendency toward dogmatism and organizational schism. From this perspective, hostility of some psychiatrists toward religion is nothing more than the tension that always exists between competitors for a limited clientele, augmented by the strains that often exist between high-tension religions of different traditions. Biologically oriented psychiatry is not in the same business as religion, while psychoanalytically oriented therapies probably are.

It is stretching the concept of religion beyond its useful boundaries to conclude that psychotherapy is a religion (cf. Frank 1961; Tennov 1975). The term religion ought to be reserved for systems of thought that postulate that there are supernatural beings or forces (Stark 1981). But in many ways psychotherapy directly competes with religion. This is most obvious for psychoanalysis and related treatments. Psychotherapists often function as evangelists who must first convert their congregation before ministering to its spiritual needs. In one of his many tirades against religion as a "shared delusion," Freud (1927) admitted that his own system might be an illusion of the same order, and the evolution of psychotherapies into religious or quasi-religious cults is today a well known phenomenon (Rieff 1966; Fodor 1971; Wallis 1976; Bainbridge 1978).

Millions of people successfully integrate direct contact with the supernatural into lives filled with worldly success. Most of the time they work, play, raise their children, and deservedly enjoy the respect of their neighbors, but on occasion, especially when encouraged by their church, they hear the voice of the Lord. There is something profoundly perverse about diagnosing insanity in such patently healthy lives.

Of course, if religion has power, then it has the power to harm. But there is no evidence at all that religion produces madness, and the diagnosis of religious insanity seems more an expression of the prejudices of psychiatric infidels than it is a scientific judgment. Ironically, the sociology of religion can go a long way toward explaining why psychiatrists might do this: leaders of cults often disparage the traditional churches.

9

Social Control in Utopian Communities

In its most perfect form, a moral community is a completely cohesive group sharing a single, comprehensive system of beliefs and norms. To achieve absolute social integration, it will need to be rather thoroughly encapsulated, having few social relations with outsiders and thus needing to be a nearly self sufficient economic unit. To achieve absolute moral integration, it must be dominated by an intense form of religion that reaches into all aspects of people's lives. In previous chapters, we have seen that far more diverse and open societies can function to a great extent as moral communities, but in this chapter we shall consider the extreme form of moral community, in order to know what limits may exist to its power over individual behavior.

If religion has some power to suppress deviant behavior in loosely-structured secular societies, that power should be all the greater in tightly organized sacred communities from which all traces of secularism have been banished (Fitzpatrick 1967). Throughout American history, significant numbers of religious intentional communities have sought to overcome selfishness, thus serving as natural experiments evaluating religion's capacity to control individual desires and enforce behavioral uniformity.

Western religions generally teach that perfection cannot be gained in this world, and the only real utopia is Heaven. However, participants

157

in religious communes believe that God has made them an exception to this rule. About their own group, the Shakers commented, "It is certain that nothing short of Divine Wisdom could ever have devised a system of equalization, so just and equitable, and yet so contrary to the partial, aspiring and selfish nature of man" (Green and Wells 1823: 62).

John Humphrey Noyes, the founder of the Oneida commune, offered a more scientific argument: "Judging from all our experience and observation, we should say that the two most essential requisites for the formation of successful Communities, are *religious principle* and *previous acquaintance* of the members" (Noyes 1870: 57). Note that he attributes a power to religion, as a human institution, quite apart from the divine power of God. Previous acquaintance means strong, existing social bonds. This analysis anticipated Durkheim's distinction between anomie and egoism by nearly three decades. Noyes was writing about the American communes of his century, but by extension his theory applies to all forms of moral community.

Given the immense amount of recent work on utopian communities, it seems remarkable that the finest research study was published more than a century ago: *The Communistic Societies of the United States: From Personal Observation*, written by Charles Nordhoff (1875). Both as ethnography and as a foray into social theory, Nordhoff's work far surpasses more recent monographs. He noted that the well established communes he visited in the 1870s "have as their bond of union some form of religious belief" (387) while almost all American secular utopias had evaporated before he could visit them. He also took sharp issue with the popular belief that religious utopias were peopled with "fanatics," and that only fanatics can sustain utopian ventures. Instead, the utopians he had seen were people whose faith seldom gave rise to "outward religious observances," but was tacit and taken for granted. He wrote that "none of them can properly be called fanatics, except by a person who holds every body to be a fanatic who believes differently from himself" (388). Moreover, there was no need for the religious utopians he observed to be fanatics. For what he discovered were the immense benefits these communities were able to provide—material and social as well as spiritual benefits.

Religion transcends the mundane concerns of ordinary life and therefore promotes the transcendent goals of utopianism—a promise of a sublime future. It can thus support self sacrifice and altruism essential to communal society. The hope it offers can preserve members' commitment during rough times that might bring a secular experimental community to ruin. Furthermore, religion may regulate community leadership, placing a higher power over the potential tyranny of the founder or governing board. Parsons (1964a: 342) called religion one of the *evolutionary universals* required by every successful society to embody regulatory cultural traditions, and utopias by definition seek to be autonomous societies. Of course, one may impose communism by force with a police state, but religion may achieve as much by encouraging voluntary submission to a higher ideal.

Given the tremendous amount that has been written about historical utopian experiments, and the substantial number that can be readily located in the contemporary world, it should be possible to test the hypothesis that religion strengthens such communities. Most studies that have attempted to do this have contrasted the longevities of religious and secular communes, following the logic that whatever other measures of success there might be, living is more successful than dying.

Quantitative Studies of Utopian Longevity

By far the most influential sociological study of commune longevity was Rosabeth Kanter's book applying theoretical ideas about "commitment mechanisms" to a list of 30 American communes of the nineteenth century. Nine of the thirty lasted twenty-five years or longer, and Kanter called these groups "successful" in comparison with the twenty-one groups that died more quickly. Partly because she wanted to test a number of hypotheses unrelated to religion, and we think also because she was looking for lessons to guide modern secular communes, she downplayed the importance of religion. She noted that "all of the nine successful communities that I studied began with some kind of religious base," but she dismissed this with the comment, "this was also true of a large number of the unsuccessful communities" (Kanter 1972: 136).

However, it is hard to find a variable in the long list Kanter examined that can equal religion in its power to explain success among the communes. Even among her twenty-one unsuccessful cases, religious communities lasted on average 7.3 years, compared with just 4.7 years for the secular ones, and the mean lifespan for the nine successful religious communes was fully 74.3 years (Bainbridge 1985b).

To put this important point another way: being religious was a necessary condition for success among Kanter's communes, although it was not sufficient to ensure longevity. There is some doubt that Brook Farm, which lasted 7 years, should be placed on the ledger, because it went through a religious phase. Remove it from consideration and there are 29 cases, 16 religious and 13 secular. Expressed in terms of gamma, the correlation between being religious and being successful is perfect (gamma = 1.00). If one prefers a restrictive definition of causation (Bainbridge. 1992b: 195–196), there is still a huge correlation between the two variables (phi = 0.60). By chi-square, the association would be significant at the 0.01 level, were it not for the conventional restriction that this test of significance does not work when the number of cases expected in a cell of the table is fewer than five. But this is true for all of Kanter's tables, and may be one reason that she did not report tests of statistical significance anywhere in her book.

To be sure, these are only 29 cases from a single era in American history. Does this finding generalize? More compelling results can be found in a massive coding of American utopian ventures by Karen and Edward Stephan (1973) that, curiously, resulted in only a brief research note. The data overlap those of Kanter, and tabulate survival rates of 143 cases that occurred in the United States between 1776 and 1900. Of these, 71 were religious, and 72 were secular.

After ten years, 63 percent of these religious communes were still in existence, compared with just 17 percent of secular ones. Thus there is a powerful correlation between religiousness and survival (gamma = 0.79, phi = 0.48) which solidly achieves the 0.001 level of statistical significance. After forty years, all the secular communes were defunct while 35 percent of the religious communities were still thriving (gamma = 1.00, phi = 0.46, significance = 0.001). And 13 religious communes survived for more than a century (gamma = 1.00, phi = 0.32, significance = 0.001).

In the early 1950s, Robert V. Hine ([1953] 1983) found that the same pattern applied to the major utopian movements launched in California from the 1880s through 1950. He wrote, "The average life of religious colonies in California has been over twenty years, while that of the secular colonies has been well under ten." In re-examining Hine's data, we decided to drop one of the 17 communities, a short-lived Mormon colony in San Bernardino, because Hine himself admitted that it was not a utopian venture. Of the other 16, five were religious and eleven were secular.

Ten years after their foundings, four of the religious utopias still functioned, but only one of the secular utopias remained. Because of the small number of cases the results may not be statistically significant, but the association between religion and survival is strong (gamma = 0.95, phi = 0.71). Adding back the Mormon group we excluded from consideration changes results only slightly (gamma = 0.90, phi = 0.60). By the 20-year mark all 11 secular utopias were gone, but three of the 5 (or 6) religious communities continued.

Finally, a study of contemporary "counterculture" communes yields similar findings. Hugh Gardner (1978) visited 12 such groups and then reexamined them three years later. He classified three of these communes as religious, and two of them still functioned after three years. Actually, we consider that the third religious commune continued to exist, because its members had merely moved to a new location, but Gardner counted it extinct. Of the nine secular groups, just three persisted through three years. Moreover, one of the secular groups Gardner considered still living might better be considered dead, because it had shrunk to one couple and their children; a family, yes, but not a commune.

Given that religious communes have much greater life expectancies than secular ones, we should examine more closely the theoretical explanation for this fact. Our approach is sociological but concerns economies—adding intangible rewards to the tangible rewards usually studied by economists.

Economies of Intangibles

Our systematic theory stresses the point that many things people seem to very strongly desire, including victory over death, are not known to be available (Stark and Bainbridge 1985, 1987). If these desires are to be satisfied, the only plausible source of supply lies in the supernatural realm. Promises that one will receive these rewards are not be to fulfilled in the here-and-now, but only later in another world. This is the unique resource of religious institutions: the capacity to issue promises backed by the power of the gods.

Utopian communities are the quintessential human effort to seek rewards not otherwise available. The crucial difference between such efforts based on religion and those based on secular ideologies has to do with when and where the major rewards are to be obtained.

In 1962, Nikita S. Khrushchev, then leader of the Soviet Union, explained to a group of Third World diplomats that communism promises to create "a paradise on this planet, unlike Christianity, which promises paradise after death." Unwittingly, he thus isolated the precise reason that secular efforts at paradise are short-lived. Their hopes are subject to empirical verification. If paradise, or at least an acceptable substitute, fails to arrive, this will be evident to all. As we shall see, secular utopias are forced to pursue goals that cannot be achieved in this world. Ironically, faith in the supernatural frees religious utopians to focus on goals that readily can be achieved, here and now.

Sociologies of the Possible and Impossible

All utopian communities, whether religious or secular, are countercultures in pursuit of a different mode of life. In the case of the religious utopias, however, the new community is not the ultimate aim. Rather, it is simply a preliminary station where members can attempt to live in accord with divine will, while waiting to fulfill their truly utopian life in the world to come. As a result, religious utopias are very likely to limit their social arrangements to those well-known to work, to limit themselves to sociologies of the possible. This is true despite the exotic impression their lifestyle often makes on outsiders.

The Shakers, for example, opted for absolute celibacy, and this might strike many social scientists as trying the "impossible." Difficult, yes, but not impossible. Countless groups through the centuries have successfully fulfilled norms of celibacy. In contrast, many secular utopian ventures have attempted to maintain "free love" or "indiscriminate promiscuity" as Berger (1981) would have it. The results typically have been explosive (Zablocki 1980; Jaffe 1975; Berger 1981).

Taking conventional monasteries and convents as models, we also can see that vows of poverty, norms of frequent prayer, or obedience, and even vows of silence are quite possible social arrangements. Indeed, many of the religious utopian communities that have occurred in America seem mainly to have been outlets for the monastic impulse among Protestants.

On the other hand, few religious utopias have attempted to abandon the family. In most of them the family remained the primary social unit, and families maintained individual households. For example, despite their vows of absolute chastity, the Rappites lived in family units of mixed age and sex. Even among the Shakers, families were not scattered among the various Shaker centers, but overwhelmingly members remained in

the same center, it being the one closest to their place of origin in the outside world (Stein 1992). Secular utopian ventures often have tried to
abandon the family with rather unpleasant results in terms of internal
conflict and neglected children. And Noyes would point out that abandonment of the family means destruction of the most powerful form of
"previous acquaintance of the members," thus violating the chief nonreligious prescription for success of a utopian experiment.

But the central element separating the sociologies attempted by
religious and secular communes involves stratification. Religious
utopias often have aimed to reduce material inequalities, but rarely have
they felt it necessary to attempt to eliminate them entirely. Moreover,
seldom do they seek equality in terms of status and power. Nordhoff
reported that he was surprised to discover, in all but one of the groups
he visited, "the ease and certainty with which brains came to the top."
He found that turnover in leadership was rare and leaders usually had
much authority. Only the Icarians, of those he visited, attempted pure
democracy and had short-term leaders with little authority. Nordhoff
cited these differences as the reason why the Icarians had such miser-
able material conditions and experienced so much disharmony.

Secular utopias are usually animated by the desire to escape stratification. Lacking the resources to postpone achievement of this blessing to
the next life, frequently they attempt to create an unstratified utopia. But,
today not even Marxist sociologists believe it is possible to have organized social life without stratification, at least in terms of power and pres-
tige. If this is so, then all utopias designed to be unstratified are destined
to fail. Thus, if a group attempts unstratified anarchism it will not thereby achieve equality, freedom, and a pleasant life, but rather chaos or the
equality of abject poverty. Members of secular communes will not have
to wait until their next lives to discover this complete disconfirmation of
their utopian theories. In contrast, members of religious communes postpone their most unrealistic hopes until a life after death, which provides
no disproof of faith to those who remain alive. The point is that religious
utopians need not, and often do not, attempt impossible sociologies.
Therefore they have a chance to succeed. Secular utopias, however, are
forced to attempt impossible sociologies, and their failures to achieve
them are evident and distressing to all concerned.

Moreover, because many religious utopias often function very well
on a day-to-day basis, while secular utopias do not, religious utopias

often are able to provide their members with exceptional levels of material and emotional rewards—in many cases a much higher level than members could expect in the outside world. This, of course, greatly reinforces commitment, although in the longer run it may lead the group to abandon its errand into the wilderness.

Economies of Tangibles

Medieval historians are agreed that one of the greatest attractions of monastic life was the relatively high standard of living it provided. Indeed, Johnson (1976: 256) describes the Benedictine abbeys of northern and central Europe in the twelfth century as "a combination of luxury hotel and cultural centre." Monastery fields, vineyards and flocks were vastly more productive than were those of the nobility. The reasons for this include a more dedicated and far better trained labor force and much better educated, able, and more attentive administrators. Management of the great estates of the nobility often suffered when incompetent or indolent heirs took charge, while monasteries could count on a succession of the most able as administrators and upon continuity in long range plans for increasing production. Consequently, the average monk usually ate, drank, and was housed far better than he could have expected in secular life and had real prospects for advancement into administrative positions. Hence, the blessings of faith included a huge portion of tangibles. Moreover, periodic efforts by church authorities to restore asceticism were short-lived, because plenty was too easily at hand.

Like the medieval monasteries, many of the religious utopian communities in America were extremely successful economically and therefore able to provide members with a fine standard of living and, indeed, a life of relative ease. Nordhoff marvelled at the quality of life and the standard of living he found in the religious communes. A very recent and excellent study of the Shakers by Stephen J. Stein (1992) punctures the wholly unreasonable myths spread by a legion of uncritical writers about this group. Despite the occasionally shaky financial situation of certain Shaker communities, the fact remains that Shakers lived better and had far greater security than did the average American citizen. Indeed, Stein's examples of financial difficulties at particular Shaker communes, and even the complete collapse of some of them, demonstrate the tremendously high level of economic security enjoyed by members, because other Shaker communities always came to the rescue.

Aryei Fishman (1982, 1983b, 1983c) has written extensively on the role of religion in creating and sustaining the kibbutz communities of Israel. In one study (1983a) Fishman found 13 religious communal farms to be superior to 83 secular ones in terms of per capita income, savings, and net worth. More recently, many of the nonreligious communities got into serious financial trouble, while the religious ones did not (Fishman and Goldschmidt 1990). There is a sense in which even the "secular" Israeli communes are really religious, because their Zionism is the nearest thing to a supernatural faith. Nordhoff long ago speculated that some creeds that fell just short of being fully religious might give strength to a utopian endeavor (1875: 387). But even in Israel, the nation that seems most hospitable to utopianism, religious communities do better than somewhat more secular ones.

But why were the religious communes so much more potent in the material sphere? Like the medieval monasteries, they enjoyed very high levels of member commitment and morale, bound together by the immense attractiveness of the intangible rewards they offered. Like monks, the religious utopians could more easily sublimate their own narrow interests to the collective good, thus minimizing the "free-rider" problem which haunted the secular communities (Hall 1988; Iannaccone 1992).

We also should note again the immense importance of intense interpersonal attachments. Secular utopias are typically composed of like-minded individuals who collected only at the moment the commune was formed, often as the result of reading an influential book. Religious communes either emerge from pre-existing sects which already constitute cohesive communities, or coalesce gradually over a period of years as individuals develop intense religious fellowship. Strong attachments serve both as tangible rewards for belonging and as a firm basis for collective action. The importance of interpersonal attachments in bringing converts into groups and in maintaining their commitment is well known (Lofland and Stark 1965; Stark and Bainbridge 1980, 1985, 1987). Strong interpersonal bonds make any organization strong. Indeed, such attachments are known to be the primary basis of conformity to norms. If people were more obedient in the religious communities, it was not so much for fear of God as for fear of losing the love and respect of those around them. No such conditions sustain group interests in communities of strangers, and throughout this book we have seen evidence that lack of social cohesion facilitates individual deviance.

Finally, it is because the primary goals of religious utopians are not worldly, that they can be so successful in worldly ways. That is, members of religious utopias are in far less need of immediate material benefits, for they can sustain commitment for a substantial time on the basis of socio-emotional rewards and the immense, if distant, intangible rewards of faith. This makes it possible for the religious utopians to pursue rational, long-range economic strategies. The result is that palpable rewards begin to flow freely within such a community before faith in the supernatural compensators begins to fade. This, ironically, can erode the supernaturalism of a group, transforming the religion in the direction of greater worldliness (Niebuhr 1929) and raising the potential for a reunion with the world and consequent abandonment of utopianism (cf. Barthel 1984).

To this point we have seen both empirical evidence and theoretical analysis demonstrating that religious utopias are far more successful than secular ones. However, we also cast doubt on the proposition that any complete society could really sustain communism for long. One way to clarify the power of religion is to conduct a reconnaissance of one particular movement, seeking more modest effects and keeping aware of the limited nature of data and analytical tools available to us. To that end, we will survey the Shaker movement, including comparison with two other groups, Oneida and Zoar. Together, these three represent one third of Kanter's nine successful cases, and (in all their twenty-five branches) more than a third of the seventy-one religious communes counted by Stephan and Stephan.

The Shaker Experiment

Of all the religious utopian experiments in American history, none is more famous or more deserving of sociological study than that of the Shakers, or United Society of Believers, as they called themselves. When founder Ann Lee brought her tiny band of eight followers to New York in 1774, the sect was in extreme tension with the surrounding sociocultural environment (Green and Wells 1823; Robinson 1893; Andrews 1953). Yet by the middle of the nineteenth century, there were a few thousand members in nearly two dozen colonies, valued and respected by their neighbors. Today, Shaker furniture is regarded with such favor that major museums devote rooms to it, and single pieces sometimes bring prices of several thousand dollars (Pearson and Neal 1974; Shea 1971).

We have personally met a surviving Shaker at the Canterbury, New Hampshire colony, and a group persists at Sabbathday Lake in Maine (Kay 1982; Stein 1992). The wonder is that the Shakers could endure for two centuries, and thrive for half that time, despite a firm rule of celibacy. Every social-scientific study of American utopianism, from Noyes (1870) and Nordhoff (1875) through Kanter (1972), has recognized that the Shakers were the model utopia against which to judge all the others, at the very least because they appeared to have the greatest population. Yet prior to our own research even a wide shelf of scholarly books on the sect had failed to report anything from the single best source of demographic data: the original manuscript enumeration schedules of the United States census.

From 1850 onward, each person in the country is represented by a line of data identified with the person's name, and we had no difficulty finding what we believe to be complete data on all Shaker colonies for 1840, 1850, 1860, 1880, and 1900. The existence of a Massachusetts state census allowed us also to obtain data on the five Massachusetts colonies for 1855 and 1865. Our precise tabulation of names in the 1860 census reveals that there were 3,502 members in that year, not 5,200 or 6,000 as some writers assume (e.g. Desroche 1971: 129; Whitworth 1975). In 1840 there were 3,627 members plus 15 slaves, and in 1850 the total was 3,842. Thus, in the middle of the nineteenth century, the Shaker population fluctuated just below four thousand. After that, the trend was decidedly downward. We counted 1,849 in 1880 and 855 in 1900. The surveys of religious bodies carried out by the Bureau of the Census (1910, 1919, 1930, 1941) show further declines to 516 members in 1906, 367 in 1916, 192 in 1926, and just 92 in 1936.

While we do not have detailed quantitative data for the period of Shakerism's growth, published histories make it very clear that it capitalized on local religious revivals and schisms in established denominations. The early gains came when Shaker leaders were able to exploit the passion and denominational disruptions of two exceptional religious revivals that raged in the surrounding society, in parts of New York and New England around 1779 (Robinson 1893; Blinn 1901: 24–28) and in Kentucky and Ohio around 1801 (MacLean 1975: 19–58;

Neal 1947: 11–19). When the social structure of a community fractured under the pressures of religious enthusiasm, not only would substantial sects break away from the churches, but tiny fragments consisting of a few families and isolated individuals would be catapulted toward the extreme of fanaticism. Some of these could be caught by the Shakers.

The process was not pretty, and many authors of books on the Shakers have so uncritically adored the group that they failed to present accurate pictures of it in its early days. But early nineteenth-century opponents or victims of the Shakers left sufficiently vivid and well-documented accounts that a more balanced view can be achieved (Marshall 1847; Anonymous 1849). From our studies of modern cults, we find nothing implausible in the charge that founder Ann Lee was a drunkard and a petty dictator; perhaps, as her early nineteenth-century detractors said, she was also a whore and a fortune teller. Her successors clearly possessed considerable organizational skills and often had served apprenticeships in other sects. But the movement gained as much from splintered families and community disruption as from the persuasiveness of its leaders and the attractiveness of its lifestyle.

After the 1840s, during which Shakerism attracted some persons inspired by the millenarian hopes of Millerism (White and Taylor 1904: 169), the Shakers were no longer able to maintain their numbers. But, paradoxically, this decline occurred when the group had most perfectly achieved its utopian aims. Life was comfortable, secure, and rendered meaningful by a well-developed ideology communicated through incessant collective rituals. In the religious realm, all the Shakers had lost was the expectation that the end of the world was at hand, a belief hardly compatible with investment in building a terrestrial paradise.

John Whitworth has pointed out that the long-lived utopian sect may typically trade its celestial hopes for earthly comforts, and experience a marked shift in the character of its members, losing dynamic agents of expansion and gaining persons seeking security and peace. He further hypothesized that those who defect or are expelled are likely to be younger adults, who are more enterprising, more talented, and more courageous than those who remain. Those left behind "have little desire to do more than lead comfortably secluded and gratifyingly sanctified lives" (Whitworth 1975: 237). That is, the members most likely to gain rewards by defecting are more likely to do so, while those who maximize their rewards by staying will do that instead. The fact that the

Shakers failed to follow the frontier any farther westward than Ohio and Kentucky, abandoning an outpost in Indiana in 1827, suggests that a shift in the direction predicted by Whitworth had already begun before the period of our census data. But changing age structure after 1840 will chart much of this change.

Table 9.1 shows the age distribution of Shakers at each of four points in time, from 1840 to 1900, compared with distributions in the general White population for the extreme years (Department of State 1841: 100-101; Bureau of the Census 1906: 154). Note first the small proportion who were tiny children among the Shakers, a reflection of the sect's celibacy. The historical records suggest that a Sister who became pregnant would be asked to leave. Many of the sect's children were orphans or foundlings. Others were left by parents in the Shakers' care or came with parents who joined. Thus there was more chance that an older child would find his or her way to the sect, tending to produce a bulge of persons at the threshold of adulthood. In 1840, only 21 percent of the 0–9 age group were under five, while this proportion was just 15 percent in 1900.

Note the precipitous drop among Shakers from the teens to the twenties. Defection was always a serious problem for the sect (Sears 1916: 222), and the Shakers themselves became intensely worried about the loss of members at the end of childhood (Neal 1947: 250). Whitworth's dependency thesis is supported by the fact that the proportion who were young adults dropped significantly over the sixty-year span of the statistics. While 39.1 percent were aged 20–49 in 1840, this fraction declined to 26.5 percent in 1900, and the proportion of the general population in that age group actually increased by over five percentage points. As the years passed, fewer and fewer of the Shakers were in the most vigorous, most economically productive age group. As children accounted for a constant proportion, young adults declined markedly, and older persons increased as a percent of the total.

The increasing sex imbalance among the Shakers is revealed in Table 9.2. Sexual equality was a hallmark of Shaker culture (Green and Wells 1823; Eads 1884), and leadership positions were shared equally between men and women. The very celibacy of the group was part of nineteenth-century women's liberation, because it freed women not only from the pains and dangers of childbirth, but also from sexual domination by men. Having few small children, and raising those communally, the sect also freed most female members from the special

Table 9.1

Shaker Age Distributions, 1840-1900

Age Group	U.S. Whites 1840	Members of Shaker Communities 1840	1860	1880	1900	U.S. Whites 1900
0-9	31.6%	9.1%	7.9%	7.5%	5.4%	23.3%
10-19	23.0%	21.8%	28.4%	21.5%	24.6%	20.3%
20-29	18.1%	13.6%	12.3%	9.7%	11.2%	18.1%
30-39	11.7%	14.4%	9.2%	10.2%	6.9%	14.2%
40-49	7.3%	11.1%	10.3%	10.4%	8.4%	10.4%
50-59	4.4%	10.1%	12.2%	11.6%	11.7%	7.0%
60-69	2.4%	11.4%	10.8%	12.3%	14.6%	4.2%
70-79	1.1%	6.4%	5.3%	12.3%	11.2%	1.9%
80 & over	0.4%	2.2%	3.8%	4.5%	6.0%	0.5%
0-19	54.5%	30.9%	36.2%	29.0%	29.9%	43.6%
20-49	37.2%	39.1%	31.8%	30.3%	26.5%	42.8%
50 & over	8.3%	30.0%	32.0%	40.6%	43.5%	13.6%

Table 9.2

Percent Female by Age Group

Age Group	U.S. Whites 1840	Members of Shaker Communities 1840	1860	1880	1900	U.S. Whites 1900
0-19	49.3%	51.1%	53.4%	68.9%	77.3%	49.6%
20-49	48.0%	62.2%	63.0%	66.0%	73.1%	48.2%
50 & over	49.7%	58.5%	61.7%	60.6%	68.0%	48.5%
All ages	48.8%	57.7%	59.1%	64.5%	72.2%	48.8%

duties of childrearing. Thus, the relative balance of the sexes in Shakerism is of major interest.

Table 9.2 reveals that the proportion female among Shakers was always greater than in the general population, and it increased spectacularly as the years passed. By 1900, the Shakers were 72 percent female. This proportion increased to 79 percent in 1906, 83 percent in 1916, 86 percent in 1926, and 88 percent in 1936 (Bureau of the Census 1910, 1919, 1930, 1941).

Several plausible hypotheses can be suggested for the increasing sex imbalance. First, men may have been more likely to defect, especially upon reaching adulthood. Second, the sect may have been more able to recruit older women seeking a refuge than older men. Third, the women may have lived longer on average than the men. However, the pattern in Table 9.2 is not entirely consistent with these hypotheses. The proportion female is always lower among older members than among those in the 20-49 age group, and the real surprise is that for 1880 and 1900 the proportion female is greatest among the children.

Actually, if quantitatively minded sociologists had paid attention to the data published well over a century ago (Nordhoff 1875: 256), we would have realized that the sex ratio among Shaker children was quite unusual. Nordhoff reports that 695 adult men and 1,189 adult women belonged to the Shakers in 1874, which figures out at 36.9 percent male. He also tabulated 192 boys under age 21, and 339 girls. Among the young, the sex distribution is almost identical to that of adults, 36.2 percent male.

One explanation is that males may have defected heavily prior to age 21, perhaps because males were more able to take advantage of secular sources of rewards in the nineteenth century. Another possibility is that the sex imbalance became a more-or-less conscious choice of the sect. The leaders had great control over which children would be admitted, and often went hunting for children. For example, in January 1843, Urban Jones of the South Union (Kentucky) colony went to New Orleans and brought back eighteen boys given over by the proprietors of an orphanage (Neal 1947: 169). Perhaps the sect came to realize that many boys would defect upon reaching manhood, and anticipated this as the century wore on by accepting progressively fewer boys. The sex imbalance among older Shakers is less extreme because it represents cohorts shaped primarily by conditions that prevailed long before the given census year.

Analysis of Shaker Recruitment and Defection

After 1860, the census records show clear evidence that Shakerism had become a refuge rather than a revolution, even in the outlines of personal stories. For example, the 1880 records show that Sarah Jane Drum had joined the Watervliet (New York) colony—a widow 44 years of age, with her daughters Clara, age 17, Mary, 9, and Cornelia, 5. But by 1900, all four of them had vanished from the colonies. Other fragments of families abound in the records. One commonly sees pairs or groups of siblings without parents. In 1880, the West Family at Union Village (Ohio) contained 28 persons, 15 of whom consisted of 6 widows and their children. This is an extreme example, but mothers who suddenly found themselves without the support of a husband would have been well advised over a century ago to take their children to a Shaker colony, where they would be well fed and educated.

In 1870 a Shaker journal expressed alarm: "Taken away—Mary Ann Austin came & took her 7 girls after our expenses of raising them" (Neal 1947: 250). The sect used the pejorative term "winter Shaker" for anyone who joined in late fall to find refuge with the intention of leaving come spring. Perhaps many Shakers were in truth "winter Shakers" with "winters" several years long. Decades later, the Shakers looked back and tried to find merit in this situation. They authorized the census to report that "in the case of transient members a great but silent work has been accomplished in rescuing, equipping, and inspiring with faith, hope and energy the discouraged and unfortunate, thereby raising numbers of men and women from the ranks of paupers to self-respecting and useful citizens" (Bureau of the Census 1930: II: 445).

Because the manuscript schedules of the censuses from 1850 through 1900 list all the names of the Shakers, along with other identifying information such as age and birthplace, it is possible to analyze recruitment and defection systematically through record linkage and tracking of individuals across the years. Table 9.3 shows the results of tracking all Shakers from 1850 to 1860, with the figures broken down by age and sex.

Altogether, 1,208 females and 658 males who were listed in the 1850 records were found again at Shaker colonies in 1860. These numbers represent retention rates of 54.5 percent for females and 40.5 percent for males, for all age groups combined. Males were more likely to die or defect from every age group, the greatest difference being among those aged ten through nineteen in 1850. For both sexes, the retention rate is lower for this age group than for any other except those eighty or over in 1850 (the youngest of whom would have been ninety if still alive in 1860). While the chief factor responsible for the disappearance of elderly Shakers is mortality, most Shakers who disappeared before their forties undoubtedly defected, and defection seems to have been the rule for younger members.

Three complementary explanations can be offered for the heavy losses of young people. First, the Shakers prohibited sexual relations, a sacrifice that may have been felt most keenly by those whose desires for erotic rewards have just been aroused by the hormonal changes of adolescence. Older members may have joined after bruising experiences which made them happy to abandon sexuality, judging it more costly than rewarding. Others were selected for lower inherent sex drive, and many might experience a diminished drive compared with their younger years.

Much has been made of the idea that the Shakers' ecstatic religious exercises may have satisfied erotic urges, and the historical accounts describe these rituals as emotionally intense and physically exhausting. But the capacity of religion to sublimate sexual urges may be limited, especially for those who feel these urges most strongly. As our theory of

Table 9.3
Shaker Retention Rates by Age and Sex, 1850–1860

Percent of Those Present in the 1850
Census Who Were Present in the 1860 Census

Age in 1850	Males	Females
0-9	36%	45%
10-19	19%	39%
20-29	39%	47%
30-39	51%	64%
40-49	66%	81%
50-59	69%	79%
60-69	52%	56%
70-79	31%	42%
80 & over	7%	16%

religion states, humans prefer rewards to the compensators that merely promise the rewards (Stark and Bainbridge 1987: 37), and religious ecstacies would have to be very powerful to compensate for the loss of sexual rewards. In the 1840s and 1850s, young women were sometimes seized by the "whirling gift," and behavior that would strike many observers as the undirected outpouring of insufficiently sublimated sexual urges was common (Kern 1981).

Second, children typically achieve considerable autonomy and form their adult identities during the years of greatest defection (Erikson 1968). If they stay Shakers through these years of individual decision, they may remain for the rest of their lives. For each separate teenager, this is the time when the greatest proportion of his or her peers defect, and the social maturation of the cohort as well as the psychological maturation of the individual will encourage many to seek wider scope for decision and action outside the community.

The Shakers imposed considerable ideological and social conformity in their schools, incessant religious meetings, heavily supervised residential dormitories, and regulated work activities. The fact that all this concentrated socialization effort availed them nothing with most of the young people should remind us of the strength of individual human needs. It also casts severe doubt on any sociological theories that postulate that religious ritual and formal socialization processes have overwhelming power, in and of themselves.

Third, many young people were taken away by relatives, rather than departing on their own, and relatives might have been more likely to do this when the children were old enough for their labor to be a valuable asset. Roughly 60 percent of members under age five in 1850 vanished by 1860, and surely they did not all walk off on the eves of their fifteenth birthdays. Most, undoubtedly, returned to families who had left them on a trial basis or during a time of difficulty that later passed (cf. Foster 1981: 57).

However, if Shaker religious socialization had been very effective, one would expect the older children to resist removal by family members, especially since, by depositing them with the Shakers in the first place, their families would have partially forfeited their loyalty. Or children taught the Shaker faith should have returned to the colonies when they reached the age of majority. In a theoretical analysis based on behaviorist principles, John Finley Scott (1971) has argued that very few individuals hold to any particular set of norms, unless those norms are continually sustained by their immediate social environment. This is tantamount to saying that intense religious socialization, which the Shakers surely accomplished, is not very robust.

As the years passed, Shakerism drew progressively farther away from its millenarian, schismatic origins. This would mean that the strength of otherworldly compensators must have faded. Thus, one would expect problems of defection to increase as the nineteenth century wore on. The five Massachusetts colonies are ideal for research, because the state conducted censuses in 1855 and 1865 that can be analyzed along with the federal censuses to give five data points from 1850 to 1870.

Table 9.4 reports the rates of retention of Massachusetts Shakers, by age and sex, over the four five-year spans. Retention rates appear higher here than in Table 9.3, but we must remember we are here dealing with five-year periods, rather than ten as before. If a cohort has a retention rate of 70 percent over each of two five-year spans, it will have a retention rate of only 49 percent over the full ten years.

The clearest trend in Table 9.4 is the declining retention rate for males under age twenty. For 1850–1855, this group already has a lower retention rate than any other group for these years, just 32 percent. This drops to 28 percent five years later, then to 18 percent, and finally to 14 percent for 1865–1870. Foster's data on the Second Family at New Lebanon (New York) also indicate that the Shakers' power to hold males declined, although he does not distinguish age groups (1981: 56). Their mean stay was 16.9 years for 1820–1849, 4.9 years for 1850–1859, and 2.1 years for 1860–1869. He notes a parallel shift for females at this New York colony, although the Massachusetts retention rates for girls seem to hold about steady, with only a hint of a decline at the very end.

We performed a third analysis of retention using data from 1880 to 1900. We could not examine 1890 because the original census manuscripts were destroyed in a fire, and poor legibility of some 1880 records forced us to limit our analysis to a subset of colonies containing a majority of members. Of 1,003 Shakers tracked from 1880 to 1900, only 165 could be found again at any of the colonies, for a retention rate of just 16.5 percent. Further, by the end of the nineteenth century, the Shakers had practically lost the capacity to hold children. The twenty-year retention rate for girls was 5.7 percent, and for boys just 1 percent.

Our data can also be used to examine recruitment. A total of 1,636

Table 9.4
Shaker Retention Rates by Age and Sex in Massachusetts Colonies, 1850–1870

| | Percent of Those Present Still Present 5 Years Later | | | |
	1850-55	1855-60	1860-65	1865-70
Males				
0-19	32%	28%	18%	14%
20-29	60%	48%	50%	73%
50 and over	71%	68%	57%	63%
Females				
0-19	47%	50%	48%	40%
20-29	60%	76%	64%	66%
50 and over	65%	75%	74%	69%

Table 9.5
Shaker New Recruits, 1850–1860

| | | | Percent Who Shared Last Name With Other Recruits | |
Age in 1860	Percent	Percent Female	Males	Females
0-19	68.0%	53.1%	63.0%	65.6%
20-49	23.0%	55.4%	35.1%	52.6%
50 and over	9.0%	42.2%	23.5%	24.2%
All ages		52.6%	52.6%	59.5%
n = 1636				

persons who were not residents of Shaker colonies in 1850 appear in the 1860 records, and they are described by Table 9.5. Females outnumbered males among these recruits, 861 to 775, and the imbalance is greatest in the earliest years. However, it would be a misinterpretation of the statistics to conclude that more females than males joined the Shakers during this period. Many people joined after 1850 but defected before 1860. Perhaps equal numbers of males and females joined, but males were more likely to defect, thus producing an excess of females among those who appear for the first time in the 1860 census.

A similar effect cannot be responsible for the excess of children among recruits, however, because Table 9.3 showed rates of loss to be especially high among young people, rather than low. Therefore, the proportion of children among those who joined the Shakers during the decade must have been even higher than indicated by that subset that were still members at the time of the 1860 census. The concluding columns of Table 9.5 sketch the social circumstances under which young people entered.

Foster (1981) examined the names of 284 individuals who entered the Second Family at New Lebanon, and found that 171 (60 percent) shared their surname with at least one other newcomer. This is a good, if imperfect, measure of kinship. Some persons share the same last name by accident, while many close relatives have different last names.

Nearly two-thirds of the 1,112 children who entered in the 1850s came with at least one probable family member. With fair confidence, we can identify parents within family groups as those adult individuals or couples with at least a twelve-year age gap separating them from the next-oldest family members. By this standard, 480 (67 percent) of the 716 children apparently joining with family members entered with siblings only, not accompanied by a parent. Only 39 (5 percent) of the 716 apparently joined with both of their parents. Another 34 (5 percent) came with fathers only, while 163 (23 percent) came with mothers. Indeed, if we remove single parents from consideration, the proportion female aged 20 to 49 among those added since 1850 drops from 55.4 percent to 48.3 percent.

Undoubtedly, a few marriages broke up after one partner joined the Shakers, leaving the other outside, and mothers may have been more likely than fathers to bring children in with them. But reports of marital breakup associated with joining seem limited to the earliest days of the sect, when religious revivals and awakenings disrupted some households (Marshall 1847; Anonymous 1849). Furthermore, much evidence indicates that under normal conditions recruitment to sects spreads through existing social bonds, and thus would have difficulty sundering strong marital relationships.

These statistics make the Shakers appear more like a refuge for broken families than like a utopian community demonstrating a new plan for the ideal society. Even before we take account of the high rates of loss that must reduce the apparent proportion of children among recruits, family problems are implicated in the overwhelming majority of membership gains. If we add the 54 newcomers in their earlier twen-

ties, guessing that they were children at admission, and the 79 probable single parents under age 50, we reach a total of 1,245, or 76.1 percent of the total recruited. While something about Shaker life may have
been attractive to each recruit, and some of these 1,245 may not in fact
have been impelled to join by family dislocation or poverty, some of the
147 older recruits must have been elderly persons choosing the colony
in preference to the poorhouse.

We find a similar picture when we analyze the 537 Massachusetts
recruits who joined between 1850 and 1870 and who show up in at least
one census record. Again, children predominated, constituting 67 percent
of the 260 males and 74 percent of the 277 females. Among those under
age 20 at first appearance in the census records, only 16 percent of males
and 11 percent of females apparently entered in the company of parents.

Shakerism began with millinarian hopes, but it became a monastic
refuge. In the early days, recruits were filled with anticipation that the
world would soon end, and even as they harvested their bountiful crops
they could rely upon intense, otherworldly compensators to make up
for rewards such as individual autonomy and sexuality that they had
forsworn. Most persons who entered the Shakers after 1850 were
apparently driven by family disruption and other social problems of
the surrounding society, rather than being drawn in by a vision of
perfection.

Zoar and Oneida

We promised to compare the Shakers with two other religious communes of nineteenth-century America, Zoar and Oneida. The chief
difference between these two and the Shakers is that Zoar and Oneida
both provided for sexual gratification, although regulating eroticism by
very different means. That is, the three communes handled one of the
important biological drives in very different ways, providing the desired
reward in the cases of Zoar and Oneida and substituting socialization
and compensators in the case of the Shakers. Data on retention rates
for Zoar and Oneida may thus help clarify the capacity of compensators
to substitute for rewards when the reward in question could readily be
obtained by violating the norms of the community. Put another way,
these data can help us discover the limits to the degree of sacrifice a
moral community may demand of its members.

Zoar is representative of stable immigrant communes (Dobbs

1947). While we secured census data for Harmony, Amana, Icaria, and Bishop Hill, the best data for comparison with the Shakers came from Zoar. Icaria and Bishop Hill failed too quickly to provide much scope for tracking of members. We had no trouble locating Harmony records from as early as 1810, but it is not until 1850 that we have data on individual members, and by then the group had ceased vigorous recruitment and was declining rapidly through mortality. To complicate matters further, a schism back in 1832 had carried away en mass a large number of members who were dissatisfied with life at Harmony (Nordhoff 1875: 80).

We were unable to find 1850 records for Amana's original New York colony, perhaps because it was on the Seneca Indian Reservation and was missed by enumerators. Furthermore, it is difficult to track young female members accurately, because many have the same first name, and they acquired new last names at marriage. Scholars who wish to study this important commune in detail can follow the example of Jonathan Andelson (1985) and examine the group's own comprehensive records. We had no difficulty identifying Zoar women after marriage, partly because of their limited numbers and partly because of a custom of new couples living with the bride's family for a few years.

Table 9.6 shows the population of Zoar and rates of retention for 10-year periods. In comparing these data with those from the Massachusetts Shakers, we must be careful to look at patterns rather than particular percentages of retention: the Shaker analysis was for 5-year periods, while the Zoar data are at 10-year intervals.

The Zoar rates for 1850–1860 can be compared directly with Shaker rates for the same decade, in data analyzed for Table 9.3. The retention rates are almost identical for the 20–49 and 50+ age groups, suggesting that the very healthy style of life and consequent longevity for which the Shakers prided themselves was equalled by at least one other commune of the period. But Zoar shows much higher retention rates for persons under age 20. For young females, Zoar has 1.8 times as high a rate as the Shakers, and for young males Zoar's rate is fully 3.3 times as high.

If we look at trends over time in Table 9.6, we see that Zoar maintained its high rates of retention of young people, while the Shakers lost their already faltering grip on the commitment of the young. Furthermore, despite some instability in the figures because of the rel-

Table 9.6

Retention Rates for Zoar by Age
and Sex, 1850–80

| | Percent of Those Present Still Present 10 Years Later | | |
	1850-60	1860-70	1870-80
Males			
0-19	78%	60%	77%
20-49	52%	71%	57%
50 & over	41%	56%	39%
Females			
0-19	73%	71%	75%
20-49	62%	67%	75%
50 & over	56%	60%	27%

atively small numbers of people tabulated, Zoar had no greater trouble holding young men than young women.

If Zoar was a typical German sect, Oneida was without doubt an American-born cult, perhaps the century's preeminent example of a communal cult. Surely its beliefs and practices were substantially novel. In addition to communism, founder John Humphrey Noyes taught that each member should become morally and spiritually perfect. Believing that this perfection would be passed on biologically to subsequent generations, he instituted a system of human breeding, which he called *stirpiculture*. This eugenics experiment demanded special control over sexuality, and he taught men a technique of intercourse that would provide pleasure but prevent pregnancy. Marriages between individuals were forbidden, and any couple that became emotionally "sticky" would be broken up. Adults were encouraged to engage in perpetual courtship, changing partners constantly under the guidance of senior members.

Oneida was the most intellectual of the nineteenth-century religious communes, and in 1870 fully 12 of the 104 men at Oneida and its Wallingford branch worked in publishing, according to the census records. Eighteen of Oneida's 121 women worked in publishing, as well: 15 compositors, a printer, and two women with the job title "editrise." With so many of both sexes involved in printing, the Oneida movement sought to bring its message to the world, and through its publications to lead society into a radically better day. Nordhoff remarked upon the profuse publications of the Oneidans, saying: "I suppose it may be said that they aim to keep themselves and their doctrines before the public. In this respect they differ from all the other Communistic societies now existing in this country (1875: 266)." Table 9.7 shows membership and retention statistics for this radical cult.

Oneida's system of complex marriage, in which all adult members were like spouses to each other, came to an end on August 28, 1879 (Noyes 1937: 164). The census records for the community's headquarters list 89 married persons, 41 (46 percent) of whom had weddings between June 1, 1879 and May 31, 1880. The chaos of the last days of Oneida communism undoubtedly drove a few members out. Carden (1969: 41) counted 288 members for 1875, an increase of about 30 over the previous decade, while we find only 262 for 1880. On June 23, 1879, John Humphrey Noyes himself fled, responding to a threat of criminal prosecution by outsiders who did not appreciate "free love" or communism. Table 9.7 shows that retention rates for Oneida compare favorably with those for Zoar, even for the period 1870–1880, and they are much higher than for the Shakers.

Table 9.7
Retention Rates for Oneida by Age and Sex, 1850–80

	Percent of Those Present Still Present 10 Years Later		
	1850-60	1860-70	1870-80
Males			
0-19	75%	64%	64%
20-49	81%	82%	68%
50 & over	63%	83%	71%
Females			
0-19	87%	85%	56%
20-49	86%	86%	62%
50 & over	73%	67%	66%

Conclusion

A prima facie case exists for the proposition that religion gives strength to communist utopian experiments. Among the famous nineteenth-century American cases, religious communes lasted considerably longer than nonreligious ones. Our theory of religion notes the superior capacity of supernatural movements to provide compensators or intangible rewards. Furthermore, the result of this capacity is often an increased power to provide tangible rewards, as well. However, none of the communes were able to survive indefinitely.

We can also raise the question of whether the successful communes were really complete social systems. There is nothing remarkable about specialized institutions that recruit exceptional individuals from unusual situations and convince them to play extreme roles. Consider how different from the ordinary is life in the army, the merchant marine, or a traveling circus. To the extent that the Shakers were the Protestant equivalent of Catholic monastic orders, they are specialized extensions of a non-communal society, rather than examples of successful communism. Similarly, to the extent that any of the nineteenth-century communes were the temporary results of religious upheavals in the larger society, they do not qualify as societies in their own right. Even the greatest ocean wave is a poor subject for research on the characteristics of islands.

However, these criticisms aside, research on utopian experiments provides at least a rough picture of the boundaries of moral communities. So long as it satisfies basic human biological needs, provides sufficient economic resources, and makes provision for continuation of itself through birth and socialization of children, a moral community can demand much of its members. But when it fails to give people what they need, they will abandon it, either by defecting or by transforming the community.

In the late nineteenth and early twentieth centuries, many members of American communes found it easy to escape to profitable jobs and satisfying family lives in the surrounding cosmopolitan society. Permissive, secular society challenges a moral community to satisfy the basic needs of members while convincing them that forgoing some of their superficial desires will, in the long run, be good for them as individuals and essential for the community as a moral unit. By offering people its valued compensators, religion can accomplish much in this regard; but ultimately even religion cannot do the impossible.

1 0

Brief Reflections on a
Research Agenda

Some years ago, during the first Sunday of duck season, a Lutheran pastor in North Dakota devoted his entire sermon to a blistering attack on all the people who had skipped church that day in order to go hunting. As the congregation filed out afterwards, an elderly women said to the minister "I don't know why *we* had to listen to all that. *We* were here."

Guided by her very sound advice, we will not devote this conclusion to criticizing other social scientists for their overwhelming neglect of the religious factor in both theories and empirical studies of deviance and social control. It is true enough that this book could have been (and should have been) written decades ago. Most of the central ideas were well-known more than a century ago and a lot of the data we have analyzed are nearly as old—and most were available all along in every sizeable university library. However, like those who went to church rather than duck hunting, those of you who have read this book deserve our thanks for doing so. Therefore, to conclude this chapter we would like merely to sketch some lines of future theorizing and research that strike us as promising. In so doing we will stretch the limits of the terms deviance and social control.

Religion and Reform

Perhaps the most neglected of all topics in this general area involves reform—and especially efforts to prevent those in jails and prisons from committing new crimes upon their release. All manor of secular measures have been tried to reduce recidivism. For example, a controlled experiment was conducted to see if payments to help newly released prisoners restart their lives would reduce the likelihood of their arrest for new offenses. After a year, 49 percent of both the experimental and the control groups had been rearrested—payments had no effect whatever (Rossi, Berk, and Lenihan 1980). An incredible number of individual and group therapies have been tried, also without appreciable success—after several generations of effort and billions of dollars, recidivism has not been reduced.

Meanwhile, several religious groups do seem to have had some success with reform. The most obvious example is the Black Muslims, but several evangelical Protestant groups, including the Prison Fellowship founded by Charles Colson, seem to have had some success too. Based on discussions in previous chapters (especially Chapter 5) we can offer a few predictions about how and why these groups might contribute to reform.

It seems likely that prison communities are, like the West Coast, lacking in organized religious participation. That being the case, variations in individual religiousness ought not influence moral behavior of prisoners *unless* they are embedded in a strong prison subculture rooted in common religious commitment. Put another way, it may be of little consequence that a given inmate "finds" religion in prison unless this also involves or is followed by immersion in a like-minded group. Moreover, prison conversions will not have lasting influence unless persons retain or replace religious group support upon their release.

This line of analysis ought to help explain the particular effectiveness of the Nation of Islam—both during and after release. The Muslims have been able to sustain extremely solid subcultures of African-American prisoners, wherein religion is of constant relevance and reference during everyday interactions. Moreover, the Muslims are often successful in relocating prisoners within similarly solid subcultures upon their release. To they extent they have been successful, evangelical Protestant groups also have constructed religious prison subcultures and have passed prisoners into support groups upon their release.

Keep in mind that despite the regional, contextual effects we have identified, it isn't necessary that the whole community be relatively religious for religion to influence moral behavior, but only that people experience an everyday context within which religion is normative. Thus, for example, we would expect that Orthodox Jews in California would be significantly less likely to deviate than most others, despite living in relatively unchurched environments. In similar fashion, a tightly-knit Muslim subculture could achieve low rates of member deviance, regardless of the general religious climate.

As a first step, it ought to be possible to examine some prison populations closely to identify converts to various religions and subsequently to compare their rates of recidivism with other prisoners. If a religious effect on reform can be isolated, then it would seem appropriate to invest in more intensive studies, including field research, to identify the fundamental mechanisms involved.

Family "Deviance"

These days Americans all across the political spectrum are worried about a number of forms of family problems: spousal and child abuse, high divorce rates and the countless fathers who don't pay their child support, and millions of families that never had a father. Once upon a time social scientists studied the causes of "broken homes," of "promiscuity," and of "illegitimacy." Conceivably such topics will once again inspire study. Although we personally have no plans for such research, it may be helpful to others to report that, at the ecological level, we have examined (but not published) data showing that divorce rates are lower in moral communities, as are female-headed families. And at the individual level, the recent General Social Surveys (which have begun to ask many questions about sexual activity) show that there are very marked religious effects both on sexual activity and on approval of such things as extra-marital sex. Studies usefully could pursue these findings and also examine the effects of religion on divorce at the individual level. Moreover, recent overtly religious social movements directed towards increased male responsibility towards wives and children—such as the Promise-Keepers—ought to be studied. To be of any use, however, these can not be "studies" that dismiss these people as merely "fundamentalists."

Indeed, this topic offers fine opportunities for cross-national studies, especially of the impact of the "Protestantization" of many Latin American nations on traditional marital relations. Anecdotal evidence abounds that Latin American men who become Protestants typically become far more reliable and congenial husbands (cf. Martin 1990).

Schools

There is abundant evidence that parochial schools far surpass public schools in terms of student safety, orderly behavior, and academic achievement (Coleman, Hoffer and Kilgore 1982). Moreover, this seems not to simply be a public/private difference or one entirely attributable to selection and retention biases. Although the data mainly pertain to Catholic schools, there is abundant anecdotal evidence to suggest that Protestant "Christian" schools are effective too. How much of this is due to religion? Are there denominational differences? Why and how? Put another way, under what circumstances can schools function as moral communities?

Organizations as Moral Communities

And, if schools can be moral communities, what about other kinds of organizations? What would seem to be required is a relatively high member commitment to a shared moral vision. Typically this would be anchored in religious beliefs, but we leave open the possibility that secular moral visions might suffice (the Marine Corps comes to mind). Moreover, this moral vision must generate or sustain especially strong interpersonal attachments. Both of us have noted extremely strong norms of civility among faculty members at several "religious" universities. Thus, while faculty at Brigham Young University have the same diversity of "interest groups" as do many secular schools, faculty interaction and meetings are conducted with such courtesy and mutual concern that factionalism is minimized and morale remains high. We suspect that similar patterns exist even in commercial organizations if the members have a strong religious bond. That Orthodox Jews enter into complex diamond dealings on the basis of trust alone suggests where this line of study might lead. Indeed, we suspect that there is a very strong, complex, and revealing connection between religious bonds and interpersonal trust.

Religion and Trust

In a recent study, John Orbell and his colleagues (1992) discovered that outcomes in a variant of the famous "prisoner's dilemma" game were very sensitive to religious context. That is, when Mormon subjects in Logan, Utah were used a subjects, the level of cooperation was far higher than normal. Moreover, subjects were more likely to cooperate, the more often they went to church—but this held only in Utah, not when the study was repeated in Oregon. The researchers concluded that because Logan, Utah is overwhelmingly Mormon, the Logan subjects tended to assume they were playing the game with another Mormon and to also assume, therefore, that this person would select the cooperative option, which is not necessarily the one that will yield them the maximum benefit. That is, in this Mormon "moral community" subjects were far more likely to believe their anonymous exchange partner would also do the "right" thing.

In our judgment this study may have uncovered the most basic aspect of moral communities—*trust*. It was trust that sustained the religious communes and a lack of it that condemned the secular communes to rapid failure. It is trust that enables Muslims and evangelical Protestants to build strong bonds within a prison setting. And it is trust that cements strong marital and family bonds.

Trust is, of course, regarded by many as an old-fashioned concept. But then, so are moral community, civility, monogamy, faithfulness, orderly schools, and even religion. Is it possible that these concepts are sufficiently outdated to be useful to a social science suitable for a new century?

Bibliography

Ackerknecht, Erwin H.
1943 "Psychopathology, Primitive Medicine and Primitive Culture," *Bulletin of the History of Medicine* 14:30-67.

Adorno, Theodore W., Else Frankle-Brunswik, Daniel J. Levinson, and R. Nevitt Sanford
1950 *The Authoritarian Personality*. New York: Harper and Sons.

Ahlstrom, Sydney E.
1975 *A Religious History of the American People*. Two volumes. Garden City, New York: Image.

Albrecht, Stan L., Bruce A. Chadwick, and David S. Alcorn
1977 "Religiosity and Deviance: Application of an Attitude-Behavior Contingent Consistency Model,"*Journal for the Scientific Study of Religion* 16:263-274.

Allison, Joes
1968 "Adaptive Regression and Intense Religious Experience," *The Journal of Nervous and Mental Disease* 145:452-463.

Allport, Gordon W.
1950 *The Individual and His Religion*. New York: Macmillan.

Andelson, Jonathan G.
1985 "The Gift to be Single: Celibacy and Religious Enthusiasm In the Community of True Inspiration," *Communal Societies* 5:1-32.

Anderson, Margo J.
1988 *The American Census: A Social History*. New Haven: Yale University Press.

Andrews, Edward Deming
1953 *The People Called Shakers*. New York: Oxford University Press.

189

Angell, Robert C.
  1942 "The Social Integration of Selected American Cities," *American Journal of Sociology*
    47:575-592.
  1947 "The Social Integration of Cities of More than 100,000 Population," *American
    Sociological Review* 12:335-342
  1949 "Moral Integration and Interpersonal Integration in American Cities," *American
    Sociological Review* 14:245-251.
  1974 "The Moral Integration of American Cities-II," *American Journal of Sociology*
    80:607-629.

Anonymous
  1849 *Report of the Examination of the Shakers of Canterbury and Enfield before the
    New-Hampshire Legislature at the November Session, 1846.* Concord, New Hampshire:
    Ervin B. Tripp.

Azzi, Corry and Ronald G. Ehrenberg
  1975 "Household Allocation of Time and Church Attendance, *Journal of Political
    Economy* 83:27-56.

Bachman, Jerome
  1970 *The Impact of Family Background and Intelligence on Tenth-Grade Boys.* Vol. 2. Ann
    Arbor, Michigan: Institute for Social Research.

Bainbridge, William Folwell
  1874 "Discourse Delivered at the Central Baptist Church, Providence." Providence,
    Rhode Island: A. Crawford Greene.
  1875 "The Relation of the Churches to the Temperance Cause." Pp. 11-17 in *The Eighth
    Annual Report of the Rhode Island Temperance Union.* Providence, Rhode Island:
    Providence Press.

Bainbridge, William Sims
  1978 *Satan's Power: A Deviant Psychotherapy Cult.* Berkeley: University of
    California Press.
  1982 "Shaker Demographics 1840-1900: An Example of the Use of Census
    Enumeration Schedules," *Journal for the Scientific Study of Religion* 21:352-365.
  1984 "Religious Insanity in America," *Sociological Analysis* 45:223-239.
  1985a "Cultural Genetics." Pp. 157-198 in *Religious Movements: Genesis, Exodus, and
    Numbers*, edited by Rodney Stark. New York: Rose of Sharon.
  1985b "Utopian Communities: Theoretical Issues." Pp. 21-35 in *The Sacred in a Secular
    Age*, edited by Phillip E. Hammond. Berkeley: University of California Press.
  1987 "Science and Religion: The Case of Scientology." Pp. 59-79 in *The Future of New
    Religious Movements*, edited by David G. Bromley and Phillip E. Hammond. Macon,
    Georgia: Mercer University Press.
  1989 "Religious Ecology of Deviance," *American Sociological Review* 54:288-295.
  1990 "Explaining the Church Membership Rate," *Social Forces* 68: 1287-1296.
  1992a "Crime, Delinquency, and Religion." Pp. 199-210 in *Religion and Mental Health*,
    edited by John F. Schumaker. New York: Oxford University Press.
  1992b *Social Research Methods and Statistics: A Computer-Assisted Introduction.* Belmont,
    California: Wadsworth.
  1992c "The Sociology of Conversion." Pp. 178-191 in *Handbook of Conversion*, edited by
    H. Newton Malony and Samuel Southard. Birmingham, Alabama, Religious
    Education Press.
  1997 *The Sociology of Religious Movements.* New York: Routledge.

Bainbridge, William Sims and Rodney Stark
1979 "Cult Formation: Three Compatible Models," *Sociological Analysis* 40:283-295.
1980 "Sectarian tension," *Review of Religious Research* 22:105-124.
1981 "Suicide, Homicide, and Religion: Durkheim Reassessed," *Annual Review of the Social Sciences of Religion* 5:33-56.
1981 "The Consciousness Reformation Reconsidered," *Journal for the Scientific Study of Religion* 20:1-16.
1981 "Friendship, Religion, and the Occult," *Review of Religious Research* 22:313-327.
1982 "Church and Cult in Canada," *Canadian Journal of Sociology* 7:351-366.

Barron, Milton L.
1954 *The Juvenile in Delinquent Society*. New York: Knopf.

Barthel, Diane
1984 *Amana: From Pietist Sect to American Community*." Lincoln: University of Nebraska Press.

Bastide, Roger
1972 *The Sociology of Mental Disorder*. New York: McKay

Batson, C. Daniel, Patricia Schoenrade and W. Larry Ventis
1993 *Religion and the Individual*. New York: Oxford University Press.

Benedict, Ruth
1934 *Patterns of Culture*. Boston: Houghton Mifflin (1959).

Benson, Peter L.
1992 "Religion and Substance Use." Pp. 211-220 in *Religion and Mental Health*, edited by John F. Schumaker. New York: Oxford University Press.

Berger, Bennett M.
1981 *The Survival of a Counterculture*. Berkeley: University of California Press.

Berger, Peter L.
1963 *An Invitation to Sociology*. Garden City, New York: Doubleday.
1969 *The Sacred Canopy*. Garden City, New York: Doubleday.

Berger, Peter L., and Thomas Luckmann
1966 *The Social Construction of Reality*. Garden City, New York: Doubleday.

Bergin, Allen E.
1983 "Religiosity and Mental Health: A Critical Reevaluation and Meta-Analysis," *Professional Psychology: Research and Practice* 14:170-184.

Bergson, Henri
1932 *The Two Sources of Morality*. New York: Henry Holt (1956).

Blinn, Henry C.
1901 *The Life and Gospel Experience of Mother Ann Lee*. East Canturbury, New Hampshire: Shakers.

Breault, Kevin D.
1986 "Suicide in America," *American Journal of Sociology* 92:628-656.

Breen, Michael
1968 "Culture and Schizophrenia: A Study of Negro and Jewish Schizophrenics," *International Journal of Social Psychiatry* 14:282-289.

Brierley, Peter
   1993 "Europe: Where Christianity Matters and is in Decline," *MARC Newletter* 93(September):2.

Brigham, Amariah
   1835 *Observations on the Influence of Religion upon the Health and Physical Welfare of Mankind*. Boston: Marsh, Capen and Lyon.

Brunner, Edmund deS.
   1927 *Village Communities*, New York: George H. Doran Company.

Bucknill, John Charles and Daniel H. Tuke
   1879 *A Manual of Psychological Medicine*. London: Churchill.

Bureau of the Census
   1906 *Twelfth Census of the United States: 1900 - Supplementary Analysis and Derivative Tables*. Washington: United States

Government Printing Press.
   1910 *Religious Bodies: 1906*. Washington,D.C.: U.S. Government Printing Office.
   1918 *Prisoners and Juvenile Delinquents in the United States -1910*. Washington, D.C.: Government Printing Office.
   1919 *Religious Bodies: 1916*. Washington, D.C.: U.S. Government Printing Office.
   1925 *Prisoners, 1923*. Washington, D.C.: Government Printing Office.
   1927 *Children under Institutional Care - 1923*. Washington, D.C.: Government Printing Office.
   1930 *Religious Bodies: 1926*. Washington,D.C.: U.S. Government Printing Office.
   1941 *Religious Bodies: 1936*. Washington,D.C.: U.S. Government Printing Office.
   1979 *Twenty Censuses: Population and Housing Questions, 1790-1980*. Washington: U.S. Government Printing Office.
   1982 *State and Metropolitan Area Data Book*. Washington, D.C.: U.S. Government Printing Office.
   1983 *County and City Data Book*. Washington, D.C.: U.S. Government Printing Office.

Burkett, Steven R., and Mervin White
   1974 "Hellfire and Delinquency: Another Look," *Journal for the Scientific Study of Religion* 13:455-462.

Calhoun, Charles (ed.)
   1837 *Reports and Other Documents Relating to the State Lunatic Hospital at Worcester, Massachusetts*. Boston: Dutton and Wentworth (also, New York:Arno, 1973).

Carden, Maren Lockwood1969 *Oneida: Utopian Community to Modern Corporation*. Baltimore: Johns Hopkins University Press.

Carroll, Michael P.
   1987 "Praying the Rosary: The Anal-Erotic Origins of a Popular Catholic Devotion," *Journal for the Scientific Study of Religion* 26:486-498.

Cochran, John K., Leonard Beeghley, and E. Wilbur Bock
   1992 "The Influence of Religious Stability and Homogamy on the Relationship between Religiosity and Alcohol Use among Protestants," *Journal for the Scientific Study of Religion* 31:441-456.

Coleman, James S., Thomas Hoffer, and Sally Kilgore
   1982 *High School Achievement: Public, Catholic, and other Private Schools*. New York: Basic Books.

Collins, Randall
1993 "A Theory of Religion," *Journal for the Scientific Study of Religion* 32:402-406.

Comte, Auguste 1896
The Positive Philosophy of Auguste Comte. London: G. Bell.

Cooper, Paulette
1971 *The Scandal of Scientology.* New York: Tower.

Crutchfield, Robert D., Michael R. Geerken, and Walter R. Gove
1982 "Crime Rate and Social Integration: The Impact of Metropolitan Mobility"
Criminology 20:467-478.

Currie, Robert, Alan Gilbert, and Lee Horsley
1977 *Churches and Churchgoers.* Oxford: Oxford University Press.

Dain, Norman
1964 *Concepts of Insanity in the United States, 1789-1865.* New Brunswick, New Jersey:
Rutgers University Press.

Darnton, Robert
1970 *Mesmerism and the End of the Enlightenment in France.* New York: Schocken.

Davis, James A. and Tom W. Smith
1991 *General Social Surveys: 1972-1991: Cumulative Codebook.* Chicago: National
Opinion Research Center.

Department of Health and Human Services
1985 *Vital Statistics of the United States-1980.* Hyattsville, Maryland: National Center for
Health Statistics.

Department of the Interior, Census Office
1860 *Instructions to U.S. Marshals.* Washington: Bowman.

Department of State
1841 *Compendium of the Enumeration of the Inhabitants and Statistics of the United States.*
Washington: Thomas Allen.

Desroche, Henri
1971 *The American Shakers.* Amherst: The University of Massachusetts Press.

Dittes, James E.
1971 "Typing the Typologies: Some Parallels in the Career of Church-Sect and
Extrinsic-Intrinsic," *Journal for the Scientific Study of Religion* 10:375-383.

Dobbelaere, Karel
1987 "Some Trends in European Sociology of Religion: The Secularization Debate,"
Sociological Analysis 48:107-137.

Dobbs, Catherine R.
1947 *Freedom's Will, the Society of Separatists of Zoar.* New York: William Frederick Press.

Douglas, Jack D.
1967 *The Social Meaning of Suicide.* Princeton, N.J.: Princeton University Press.

Douglass, H. Paul and Edmund deS. Brunner
1935 *The Protestant Church as a Social Institution.* New York: Russell and Russell.

Durkheim, Emile
1897 *Suicide: A Study in Sociology,* J. A. Spaulding and G. Simpson, trans. New York: Free
Press (1951).

1915 *The Elementary Forms of the Religious Life*. London: Allen and Unwin.
1961 *Moral Education*. New York: Free Press.

Eads, H. L.
1884 *Shaker Sermons*. South Union, Kentucky: United Society of Believers.

Earle, Pliny
1841 *A Visit to Thirteen Asylums for the Insane in Europe*. Philadelphia: Dobson.
1848 *History, Description and Statistics of the Bloomingdale Asylum for the Insane*. New York: Egbert, Hovey and King.
1863 "Insanity, and Hospitals for the Insane," pp. 54-60 in *The National Almanac and Annual Record for the Year 1863*. Philadelphia: George W. Childs.
1867 *An Address Delivered before the Berkshire Medical Institute*. Utica, New York: Roberts.
1886 *The Curability of Insanity*. Philadelphia: Lippincott.

Edgerton, Robert B.
1966 "Conceptions of Psychosis in Four East African Societies," *American Anthropologist* 68:408-424.

Elifson, Kirk W., David M. Petersen, and C. Kirk Hadaway
1983 "Religiosity and Delinquency," *Criminology* 21:505-527.

Ellis, A.
1980 "Psychotherapy and Atheistic Values," *Journal of Consulting and Clinical Psychology* 48:635-639.

Ellison, Christopher G.
1993 "Religion, the Life Stress Paradigm, and the Study of Depression." Pp. 78-121 in *Religion in Aging and Mental Health*, edited by Jeffrey S. Levin. Thousand Oaks, California: Sage.

Empey, LeMar T. and M. L. Erickson
1972 *The Provo Experiment*. Lexington, Massachusetts: Lexington.

Erikson, Erik H.
1968 *Identity, Youth and Crisis*. New York: Norton.

Evans-Pritchard, Edward E.
1965 *Theories of Primitive Religion*. Oxford: Clarendon Press. 1981 *A History of Anthropological Thought*. New York: Basic Books.

Federal Bureau of Investigation
1980 *Uniform Crime Reports*. Washington,D.C.: U.S. Government Printing Office.

Feuerbach, Ludwig
1841 *Das Wesen des Christentums*. Stuttgart, Germany: Reclam (1974).

Finke, Roger, and Rodney Stark
1992 *The Churching of America 1776-1990*. New Brunswick, New Jersey: Rutgers University Press.

Finkel, Norman J.
1976 *Mental Illness and Health*. New York: Macmillan.

Fischer, Claude S.
1975 "Toward a Subcultural Theory of Urbanism," *American Journal of Sociology* 80:1319-1341.

Fishman, Aryei
  1982 "'Torah and Labor': The Radicalization of Religion within a National Framework,"
      Studies in Zionism 6:255-271.
  1983a "Judaism and Modernization: The Case of the Religious Kibbutzim," *Social Forces*
      62:9-31.
  1983b "Moses Hess on Judaism and Its Aptness for a Socialist Civilization," *Journal of
      Religion* 63:143-158.
  1983c "The Religious Kibbutz: Religion, Nationalism and Socialism in a Communal
      Framework." Pp. 115-123 in *The Sociology of the Kibbutz*, edited by Ernest Krausz and
      David Glanz. New Brunswick, New Jersey: Transaction.

Fishman, Aryei, and Yaaqov Goldschmidt
  1990 "The Orthodox Kibbutzim and Economic Success," *Journal for the Scientific Study of
      Religion* 29:505-511.

Fitzpatrick, Joseph P.
  1967 "The Role of Religion in Programs for the Prevention and Correction of Crime
      and Delinquency." Pp. 317-330 in *Juvenile Delinquency and Youth Crime*, Task force on
      Juvenile Delinquency, The President's Commission on Law Enforcement and
      Administration of Justice. Washington, D.C.: U.S. Government Printing Office.

Fodor, Nandor
  1971 *Freud, Jung and Occultism*. New Hyde Park, New York: University Books.

Foster, Lawrence
  1981 *Religion and Sexuality*. New York: Oxford University Press.

Frank, Jerome
  1961 *Persuasion and Healing: A Comparative Study of Psychotherapy*. Baltimore: Johns
      Hopkins Press.

Freud, Sigmund
  1927 *The Future of an Illusion*. Garden City, New York: Doubleday (1961).
  1930 *Civilization and its Discontents*. New York: Norton (1961).

Gallup Organization
  1978 *The Unchurched American*. Princeton: The Princeton Religious Research Center.

Gardner, Hugh
  1978 *The Children of Prosperity*. New York: St. Martin's Press.

Gardner, Martin
  1957 *Fads and Fallacies in the Name of Science*. New York: Dover.

Gay, John D.
  1971 *The Geography of Religion in England*. London: Duckworth.

Gillispie, Charles Coulston
  1959 *Genesis and Geology*. New York: Harper and Row.

Girard, Chris
  1988 "Church Membership and Suicide Reconsidered: Comment on Breault," *American
      Sociological Review* 93:1471-1479.

Glock, Charles Y., and Rodney Stark
  1965 *Religion and Society in Tension*. Chicago: Rand McNally.

Glueck, Sheldon, and Eleanor Glueck
  1952 *Delinquents in the Making: Paths to Prevention*. New York: Harper.

Goffman, Erving
1961 *Asylums*. Garden City, New York: Anchor.

Goldenweiser, Alexander A.
1915 "Review of Le Forms," *American Anthropologist* 17:719-735.

Goode, Erich
1969 "Marijuana and the Politics of Reality," *The Journal of Health and Social Behavior* 10:83-94.

Gordon, Ernest
1943 *The Wrecking of the Eighteenth Amendment*. Francestown, New Hampshire: Alcohol Information Press.

Greeley, Andrew
1974 *Ethnicity in the United States*. New York: John Wiley.
1989 "Protestant and Catholic," *American Sociological Review* 54: 485-502.

Green, Calvin and Seth Y. Wells
1823 *A Summary View of the Millennial Church, or United Society of Believers*. Albany, New York: Packard and Van Benthuysen.

Guerry, André Michel
1833 *Essai sur la Statistique Morale de la France*. Paris: French Royal Academy of Science.

Gurrslin, Orville R., Raymond G. Hunt and Jack L. Roach
1959 "Social Class and the Mental Health Movement," *Social Problems* 7:210-218.

Gusfield, Joseph R.
1963 *Symbolic Crusade: Status Politics and the American Temperance Movement*. Urbana: University of Illinois Press.

Hadaway, C. Kirk, Kirk W. Elifson, and David M. Petersen
1984 "Religious Involvement and Drug Use among Urban Adolescents," *Journal for the Scientific Study of Religion* 23:109-128.

Halbwachs, Maurice
1930 *Le Causes du Suicide*. Paris: Felix Alcan.

Haley, Jay
1963. *Strategies of Psychotherapy*. New York: Grune and Stratton.

Hall, John R.
1988 "Social Organization and Pathways of Commitment: Types of Communal Groups, Rational Choice Theory, and the Kanter Thesis," *American Sociological Review* 53:679-692.

Harris, Anthony
1977 "Sex and Theories of Deviance: Toward a Functional Theory of Deviant Script Types," *American Sociological Review* 42:3-16.

Hartshorne, Hugh, and Mark A. May
1928 *Studies in Deceit*. New York: Macmillan.

Healy, William, and Augusta F. Bronner
1936 *New Light on Delinquency and Its Treatment*. New Haven, Connecticut: Yale University Press.

Henry, Andrew F. and James F. Short
1954 *Suicide and Homicide*. Glencoe, Illinois: Free Press.

Hexham, Irving, Raymond F. Currie and Joan B. Townsend
  1985 "New Religious Movements." In *The Canadian Encyclopedia*. Edmonton: Hurtig.

Higgins, P. C. and G. L. Albrecht.
  1977 "Hellfire and Delinquency Revisited," *Social Forces* 952-58.

Himmelfarb, Milton, and David Singer (eds.)
  1980 *American Jewish Year Book - 1981*. Philadelphia: Jewish Publication Society of America.

Hindelang, Michael J.
  1978 "Race and Involvement in Common Law Personal Crimes." *American Sociological Review* 43 (1):93-109.

Hindelang, Michael J., Travis Hirschi, and Joseph Weiss
  1979 "Correlates of Delinquency: The Illusion of Discrepancy between Self-Report and Official Measures," *American Sociological Review* 44 (6) 995 1014.
  1981 *Measuring Delinquency*. Beverly Hills: Sage.

Hine, Robert V.
  1953 *California's Utopian Colonies*. Berkeley: University of California Press (1983).

Hirata, Lucie Cheng
  1979 "Free, Indentured, Enslaved: Chinese Prostitutes in Nineteenth-Century America," *Signs: Journal of Women in Culture and Society* 5:3-29.

Hirschi, Travis
  1969 *Causes of Delinquency*. Berkeley: University of California Press.

Hirschi, Travis and Michael J. Hindelang
  1977 "Intelligence and Delinquency: A Revisionist Review," *American Sociological Review* 42 (3) 571-587.

Hirschi, Travis, and H. Selvin
  1967 *Delinquency Research*. New york: Free Press.

Hirschi, Travis, and Rodney Stark
  1969 "Hellfire and Delinquency," *Social Problems* 17:202-213.

Hobbes, Thomas
  1996 *Leviathan*. New York: Cambridge University Press.

Hoge, Dean R., and Ernesto De Zulueta
  1985 "Salience as a Condition for Various Social Consequences of Religious Commitment," *Journal for the Scientific Study of Religion* 24:21-37.

Hollingshead, August B. and Frederick C. Redlich
  1958 *Social Class and Mental Illness*. New York: Wiley.

Homans, George C.
  1967 *The Nature of Social Science*. New York: Harcourt, Brace and World.

Howard, George Elliott
  1918 "Alcohol and Crime: A Study in Social Causation," *American Journal of Sociology* 24:61-80.

Hubbard, L. Ron
  1950a "Dianetics: The Evolution of a Science," *Astounding Science Fiction* 45 (May):43-8⁻
  1950b *Dianetics, the Modern Science of Mental Health*. New York: Paperback Library.

Hurd, Henry M. ed.
   1917 *The Institutional Care of the Insane in the United States and Canada*, Volume IV. Baltimore: Johns Hopkins Press.

Iannaccone, Lawrence R.
   1991 "The Consequences of Religious Market Structure," *Rationality and Society* 3:156 177.
   1992 "Sacrifice and Stigma: Reducing Free-Riding in Cults, Communes, and Other Collectives," *Journal of Political Economy* 100:271-291.

Jaffe, Dennis
   1975 *Couples in Communes*. New Haven: Yale University, Ph.D. dissertation.

Jarvis, Edward
   1850 "On the Comparative Liability of Males and Females to Insanity," *American Journal of Insanity* 7:142-171.
   1852 "On the supposed Increase of Insanity," *American Journal of Insanity* 8:333-364.
   1855 *Report on Insanity and Idiocy in Massachusetts by the Commission on Lunacy under Resolve of the Legislature of 1854*. Boston: William White (also, Cambridge: Harvard University Press, 1971).

Jensen, Gary F. and Maynard L. Erickson.
   1979. "The Religious Factor and Delinquency: Another Look at the Hellfire Hypothesis." Pp. 157-77 in *The Religious Dimension*, edited by Robert Wuthnow. New York: Academic Press.

Johnson, Barclay D.
   1965 "Durkheim's One Cause of Suicide," *American Sociological Review* 30:875-886.

Johnson, Douglas W., Paul R. Picard, and Bernard Quinn
   1974 *Churches and Church Membership in the United States - 1971*. Washington, D.C.: Glenmary Research Center.

Johnson, Paul
   1979 *A History of Christianity*. New York: Atheneum.

Johnson, R. Christian
   1978 A procedure for sampling the manuscript census schedules." *Journal of Interdisciplinary History* 8:515-530.

Johnson, Stephen D. and Joseph B. Tamney
   1988 "Factors Related to Inconsistent Life-Views," *Review of Religious Research* 30:40-46.

Kanter, Rosabeth Moss
   1972 *Commitment and Community*. Cambridge: Harvard University Press.

Kay, Jane Holtz
   1982 "Last of the Shakers," *Historic Preservation* 34 (March/April): 14-21

Kennedy, Joseph C. G. ed.
   1864 *Population of the United States in 1860*. Washington: Government Printing Office.

Kern, Louis J.
   1981 *An Ordered Love*. Chapel Hill, North Carolina: University of North Carolina Press.

Kett, Joseph F.
   1968 *The Formation of the American Medical Profession*. New Haven: Yale University Press.

.ev, Ari
   .972 *Transcultural Psychiatry*. New York: Free Press.

Kirkpatrick, Lee A., and Ralph W. Hood, Jr.
    1990 "Intrinsic-Extrinsic Religious Orientation: The Boon or Bane of Contemporary Psychology of Religion?" *Journal for the Scientific Study of Religion* 29:442-462.

Kosmin, Barry A.
    1991 *Research Report: The National Survey of Religious Identification.* New York: CUNY Graduate Center.

Kox, Willem, Wim Meeus, and Harm t'Hart
    1991 "Religious Conversion of Adolescents: Testing the Lofland and Stark Model of Religious Conversion," *Sociological Analysis* 52:227-240.

Kvaraceus, William C.
    1954 *The Community and the Delinquent.* Yonkers-on-Hudson, New York: World Book Company.

La Barre, Weston
    1969 *They Shall Take Up Serpents.* New York: Schocken.

Laing, R. D.
    1967 *The Politics of Experience.* New York: Balantine.

LaMore, George, E.
    1975 "The Secular Selling of a Religion," *Christian Century* 10:1133-1137.

Langfeldt, Gabriel
    1939 *The Schizophreniform States.* Copenhagen: Munksgaard.

Laslett, Barbara
    1977 "Social Change and the Family: Los Angeles, California, 1850-1870," *American Sociological Review* 42:268-291.

Le Bon, Gustave
    1895 *The Crowd.* New York: Viking (1960).

Legoyt, A.
    1881 *Le Suicide, Ancien et Moderne.* Paris: A. Drouin.

Lenski, G.
    1961 *The Religious Factor.* Garden City, New York: Doubleday.

Lewis, Ioan M.
    1971. *Ecstatic Religion.* Baltimore: Penguin.

Lipset, Seymour Martin and Earl Raab
    1970 *The Politics of Unreason: Right-Wing Extremism in America, 1790-1970.* New York: Harper.

Loether, Herman J. and Donald G. McTavish
    1974 *Descriptive and Inferrential Statistics.* Boston: Allyn and Bacon.

Lofland, John, and Rodney Stark
    1965 "Becoming a World-Saver: A Theory of Conversion to a Deviant Perspective," *American Sociological Review* 30:862-875.

Mackay, Charles
    1852 *Memoirs of Extraordinary Popular Delusions and the Madness of Crowds.* London: National Illustrated Library.

MacLean, John Patterson
    1975 *Shakers of Ohio.* Philadelphia: Porcupine (1907).

Malko, George
1970 *Scientology: The Now Religion*. New York: Delacorte.

Maris, Ronald W.
1969 *Social Forces in Urban Suicide*. Homewood Illinois: Dorsey.

Marshall, Mary (Mary M. Dyer)
1847 *The Rise and Progress of the Serpent from the Garden of Eden*. Concord, New Hampshire, Mary Marshall.

Masaryk, Thomas G.
1881 *Suicide and the Meaning of Civilization*. Chicago: University of Chicago Press (1970).

Medvedev, Zhores A. and Roy Medvedev
1971 *A Question of Madness*. New York: Vintage.

Melcher, Marguerite Fellows
1941 *The Shaker Adventure*. Princeton: Princeton University Press.

Melton, J. Gordon
1978 *Encyclopedia of American Religions*. Two volumes. Wilmington, North Carolina: McGrath (A Consortium Book).
1989 *The Encyclopedia of American Religions*. Third edition. Detroit, Michigan: Gale Research.

Merton, Robert K.
1968 *Social Theory and Social Structure*. New York: Free Press.
1970 *Science, Technology and Society in Seventeenth-Century England*. New York: Harper and Row.

Merz, Charles
1932 *The Dry Decade*. Garden City, New York: Doubleday, Doran.

Meyer, John W., David Tyack, Joane Nagel, and Audri Gordon
1979 "Public Education as Nation-Building in America: Enrollments and Bureaucratization in the American States, 1870-1930," *American Journal of Sociology* 85:591-613.

Miller, Russell
1987 *Bare-Faced Messiah: The True Story of L. Ron Hubbard*. New York: New York: Holt.

Morselli, Henry
1879 *Suicide: An Essay on Comparative Moral Statistics*. New York: Appleton (1882).

Muncy, Raymond Lee
1973 *Sex and Marriage in Utopian Communities*. Bloomington: Indiana University Press.

National Commission on Law Observance and Enforcement
1931 *Commission Reports*. Washington, D.C.: U.S. Government Printing Office.

Neal, Julia
1947 *By Their Fruits - The Story of Shakerism in South Union, Kentucky*. Chapel Hill: University of North Carolina Press.

Neumeyer, Martin H.
1955 *Juvenile Delinquency in Modern Society*. Princeton, New Jersey: D. van Nostrand.

Newman, William M., and Peter L. Halvorson
1984 "Religion and Regional Culture," *Journal for the Scientific Study of Religion* 23:304-315.

Niebuhr, H. Richard
1929 *The Social Sources of Denominationalism*. New York: Henry Holt.

Nock, David A.
1987 "Cult, Sect, and Church in Canada: A Reexamination of Stark and Bainbridge," *Review of Sociology and Anthropology* 24:514-525.

Nordhoff, Charles
1875 *The Communistic Societies of the United States*. London: John Murray.

Noyes, John Humphrey
1870 *History of American Socialisms*. Philadelphia: Lippincott.

Noyes, Pierrepont
1937 *My Father's House: An Oneida Boyhood*. New York: Farrar and Reinhart.

Noyes, Russell
1968 "The Taboo of Suicide," *Psychiatry* 31:173-183.

Opler, Marvin K. (ed.)
1959. *Culture and Mental Health*. New York: Macmillan.

Opler, Marvin K. and Jerome L. Singer
1956 "Ethnic Differences in Behavior and Psychopathology: Italian and Irish," *International Journal of Social Psychiatry* 2:11-22.

Orbell, John, Marion Goldman, Matthew Mulford, and Robyn Dawes
1992 "Religion, Context, and Constraint Toward Strangers," *Rationality and Society* 4:291-307.

Ostow, Mortimer
1990 "The Fundamentalist Phenomenon: A Psychological Perspective." Pp. 99-125 in *The Fundamentalist Phenomenon*, edited by Norman J. Cohen. Grand Rapids, Michigan: Eerdmans.

Pagano, Robert R., Richard M. Rose, Robert M. Stivers, and Stephen Warrenburg
1976 "Sleep During Transcendental Meditation," *Science* 191:308 310.

Parsons, Talcott
1964a "Evolutionary Universals in Society," *American Sociological Review* 29:339-357.
1964b "Definitions of Health and Illness in the Light of American Values and Social Structure." Pp. 257-291 in *Social Structure and Personality*. New York: Free Press.

Pearson, Elmer R. and Julia Neal
1974 *The Shaker Image*. Boston: New York Graphic Society.

Peek, Charles W., Evans W. Curry, and H. Paul Chalfant
1985 "Religiosity and Delinquency Over Time," *Social Science Quarterly* 66:120-131.

Perlmann, Joel
1979 "Using Census Districts in Analysis, Record Linkage, and Sampling." *Journal of Interdisciplinary History* 10: 279-289.

Peterson, William
1962 "Religious Statistics in the United States," *Journal for the Scientific Study of Religion* 1:165-178.

Pickering, W. S. F.
1984 *Durkheim's Sociology of Religion*. London: Routledge and Kegan Paul.

Pope, Whitney
1976 *Durkheim's Suicide: A Classic Analyzed*. Chicago: University of Chicago Press.

Pope, Whitney, and Nick Danigelis
1981 "Sociology's 'One Law,'" *Social Forces* 60:495-516.

Porterfield, Austin L.
1952 "Suicide and Crime in Folk and in Secular Society," *American Journal of Sociology* 57:331-338.

Prinzing, Friedrich
1906 *Handbuch der Medizinischen Statistik*. Jena, Germany: Gustav Fischer.

Quinn, Bernard, Herman Anderson, Martin Bradley, Paul Goetting, and Peggy Schriver
1982 *Churches and Church Membership in the United States, 1980*. Atlanta, Georgia: Glenmary Research Center.

Ray, Isaac
1863 *Mental Hygiene*. Boston: Ticknor and Fields.
1871 *Treatise on the Medical Jurisprudence of Insanity*. Boston: Little, Brown and Company.

Rhodes, Albert Lewis, and Albert J. Reiss
1970 "The 'Religious Factor' and Delinquent Behavior," *Journal of Research in Crime and Delinquency* 7:83-98.

Rieff, Philip
1966 *The Triumph of the Therapeutic*. New York: Harper and Row.

Robbins, Thomas and James Beckford
1988 "Introduction." Pp. 1-23 in *Cults, Converts and Charisma*, edited by Thomas Robbins. Beverley Hills: Sage.

Roberts, James S.
1984 *Drink, Temperance and the Working Class in Nineteenth Century Germany*. Boston: Allen and Unwin.

Robinson, Charles Edison
1893 *A Concise History of the United Society of Believers*. East Canterbury, New Hampshire: United Society of Believers.

Robison, Sophia M.
1960 *Juvenile Delinquency: Its Nature and Control*. New York: Holt, Rinehart and Winston.

Rossi, Peter H., R. A. Berk, and K. J. Lenihan
1980 *Money, Work, and Crime*. New York: Academic Press.

Rothman, David J.
1971 *The Discovery of the Asylum*. Boston: Little, Brown and Company.

Schafer, Stephen and Richard D. Knudten
1970 *Juvenile Delinquency: An Introduction*. New York: Random House.

Schauffler, A. F.
1891 Untitled. *New York City Mission Society Monthly* November.

Scheff, Thomas J.
1966 *Being Mentally Ill*. Chicago: Aldine.

Scott, Ann Herbert
1968 *Census, U.S.A.: Fact Finding for the American People, 1790–1970*. New York: Seabury Press.

Scott, John Finley
1971 *Internalization of Norms*. Englewood Cliffs, New York: Prentice-Hall.

Sears, Clara Endicott
1916 *Gleanings from Old Shaker Journals*. Boston: Houghton Mifflin.

Secretary of the Interior
1866 *Statistics of the United States in 1860*. Washington, D.C.: Government Printing Office.

Selvin, Hanan C.
1958 "Durkheim's *Suicide* and Problems of Empirical Research," *American Journal of Sociology* 63: 607-619.

Shaw, Clifford R. and Henry D. McKay
1929 *Delinquency Areas*. Chicago: University of Chicago Press.
1931 *Report on the Causes of Crime*. Washington, D.C.: National Commission on Law Observance and Enforcement 12:13.
1942 *Juvenile Delinquency in Urban Areas*. Chicago: University of Chicago Press.

Shea, John Gerald
1971 *The American Shakers and their Furniture*. New York: Van Nostrand.

Singh, Parmatma (Howard Weiss)
1974 *Spiritual Community Guide, 1975–76*. San Rafael, California: Spiritual Community Publications.

Stack, Steven
1983 "The Effect of the Decline in institutionalized Religion on Suicide, 1954-1978," *Journal for the Scientific Study of Religion* 22:239-252.
1992 "Religiosity, Depression, and Suicide." Pp. 87-97 in *Religion and Mental Health*, edited by John F. Schumaker. New York: Oxford University Press.

Stack, Steven and Ira Wasserman
1992 "The Effect of Religion on Suicide Ideology: An Analysis of the Networks Perspective," *Journal for the Scientific Study of Religion* 31:457-466.

Stack, Steven and Mary Jeanne Kanavy.
1983 "The Effect of Religion on Forcible Rape," *Journal for the Scientific Study of Religion* 22:67-74.

Stark, Rodney
1968 "Age and Faith: A Changing Outlook or an Old Process," *Sociological Analysis* 29:1-10.
1971 "Psychopathology and Religious Commitment," *Review of Religious Research* 12:165-176.
1980 "Estimating Church-Membership Rates for Ecological Areas," National Institute of Juvenile Justice and Delinquency Prevention., LEAA, U.S. Department of Justice. Washington, D.C.: U.S. Government Printing Office.
1981 "Must all Religions be Supernatural?" Pp. 159-177 in *The Social Impact of New Religious Movements*, edited by Bryan Wilson. New York: Rose of Sharon.
1984 "Religion and Conformity: Reaffirming a *Sociology* of Religion," *Sociological Analysis* 45:273-282.

1985a "From Church-Sect to Religious Economies." Pp. 139-149 in *The Sacred in a Post-Secular Age*, edited by Phillip E. Hammond. Berkeley: University of California Press.

1985b "Europe's Receptivity to Religious Movements." Pp. 301-343 in *New Religious Movements: Genesis, Exodus, and Numbers*, edited by Rodney Stark. New York: Paragon.

1986 "Correcting Church Membership Rates: 1971 and 1980," *Review of Religious Research* 29:69-77.

1991 "Normal Revelations: A Rational Model of 'Mystical' Experiences," *Religion and Social Order* 1:239-251.

1992 "A Note on the Reliability of Historical U.S. Census Data on Religion," *Sociological Analysis* 52:91-95.

1996 *The Rise of Christianity: A Sociologist Reconsiders History*. Princeton: Princeton University Press.

Stark, Rodney, and William Sims Bainbridge
1979 "Of Churches, Sects, and Cults," *Journal for the Scientific Study of Religion* 18: 117-131.

1980a "Networks of faith," *American Journal of Sociology* 85: 1376-1395.

1980b "Towards a Theory of Religion: Religious Commitment," *Journal for the Scientific Study of Religion* 19:114-128.

1980c "Secularization, Revival, and Cult Formation," *Annual Review of the Social Sciences of Religion* 4:85-119.

1981 "Cult Membership in the Roaring Twenties," *Sociological Analysis* 42: 137-162

1981 "Secularization and Cult Formation in the Jazz Age," *Journal for the Scientific Study of Religion* 20:360-373.

1985 *The Future of Religion*. Berkeley: University of California Press.

1987 *A Theory of Religion*. New York: Peter Lang (Reprinted by Rutgers University Press, 1996).

Stark, Rodney, William Sims Bainbridge, and Daniel P. Doyle
1979 "Cults of America: a Reconnaissance in Space and Time," *Sociological Analysis* 40:347-359.

Stark, Rodney, William Sims Bainbridge, Robert Crutchfield, Daniel P. Doyle, and Roger Finke
1983 "Crime and Delinquency in the Roaring Twenties," *Journal of Research and Crime and Delinquency* 20:4-21.

Stark, Rodney, Daniel P. Doyle, and Lori Kent
1980 "Rediscovering Moral Communities: Church Membership and Crime." Pp. 43-52 in *Understanding Crime: Current Theory and Research*, edited by Travis Hirschi and Michael Gottfredson. Beverly Hills, California: Sage.

Stark, Rodney, Daniel P. Doyle, and Jesse Lynn Rushing
1983 "Beyond Durkheim: Religion and Suicide," *Journal for the Scientific Study of Religion* 22:120-131.

Stark, Rodney and Laurence R. Iannaccone
1993 "Rational Choice Propositions About Religious Movements," Pp. 241-261 in *Religion and the Social Order* (Vol. 3-A): *Handbook on Cults and Sects in America*, edited by David G. Bromley and Jeffrey K. Hadden. Greenwhich, Connecticut: JAI Press.

1994 "A Supply-Side Reinterpretation of the `Secularization' of Europe," *Journal for the Scientific Study of Religion* 33:230-252.

Stark, Rodney, Laurence R. Iannaccone, and Roger Finke
1996 "Religion, Science and Rationality," *American Economic Review* (papers and proceedings):433-437.

Stark, Rodney, Lori Kent, and Daniel P. Doyle
1982 "Religion and Delinquency: The Ecology of a 'Lost' Relationship," *Journal of Research in Crime and Delinquency* 18:4-24.

Stark, Rodney and Charles Y. Glock
1968 *American Piety*. Berkeley: University of California Press.

Stein, Stephen J.
1992 *The Shaker Experience in America*. New Haven, Connecticut: Yale University Press.

Stephan, Karen H. and G. Edward Stephan
1973 "Religion and the Survival of Utopian Communities," *Journal for the Scientific Study of Religion* 12:89-100.

Stier, Hans-Erich, Ernst Kirsten, Heinz Quirin, Werner Trillmich, and Gerhard Czybulka
1956 *Westermanns Grosser Atlas zur Weltgeschichte*. Braunschweig, Germany: Georg Westermann.

Strauss, Anselm, Leonard Schatzman, Rue Bucher, Danuta Ehrlich, and Melvin Sabshin
1964 *Psychiatric Ideologies and Institutions*. New York: Free Press.

Stump, Roger W.
1984 "Regional Migration and Religious Commitment in the United States," *Journal for the Scientific Study of Religion* 23:292 303.

Szasz, Thomas
1961 *The Myth of Mental Illness*. New York: Delta.
1970 *The Manufacture of Madness*. New York: Harper and Row.

Tappan, Paul W.
1949 *Juvenile Delinquency*. New York: McGraw-Hill.

Tennov, Dorothy
1975 *Psychotherapy: The Hazardous Cure*. New York: Abelard Schuman.

Timberlake, James H.
1963 *Prohibition and the Progressive Movement, 1900-1920*. Cambridge: Harvard University Press.

Tittle, Charles R., and Michael R. Welch
1983 "Religiosity and Deviance: Toward a Contingency Theory of Constraining Effects," *Social Forces* 61:653-682.

Toulmin, Stephen
1982 *The Return to Cosmology*. Berkeley: University of California Press.

Turk, Austin T.
1969 *Criminality and the Legal Order*. Chicago: Rand-McNally.

Wagner, Adolf Heinrich Gotthilf
1864 *Die Gesetzmässigkeit in den Scheinbar Willkürlichen Menschlichen Handlungen vom Standpunkte der Statistik*. Hamburg: Boyes und Geisler.

Wallace, Robert Keith
1970 "Physiological Effects of Transcendental Meditation," *Science* 167:1251-1754.

Wallis, Roy
1976 *The Road to Total Freedom*. New York: Columbia University Press.
1986a "Figuring Out Cult Receptivity," *Journal for the Scientific Study of Religion* 25:494-503.
1986b "The Caplow-DeTocqueville Account of Contrasts in European and American Religion: Confounding Considerations," *Sociological Analysis* 47:50-52.

Wallis, Roy and Steve Bruce
1984 "The Stark-Bainbridge Theory of Religion: A Critical Analysis and Counter Proposals," *Sociological Analysis* 45:11-27.

Warner, R. Stephen
1993 "Work in Progress toward a New Paradigm for the Sociological Study of Religion in the United States," *American Journal of Sociology* 98:1044-1093.

Watters, Wendell W.
1993 *Deadly Doctrine: Health, Illness, and Christian God-Talk*. Buffalo, New York: Prometheus.

Welch, Kevin W.
1981 "An Interpersonal Influence Model of Traditional Religious Commitment," *Sociological Quarterly* 22:81-92.
1983 "Community Development and Metropolitan Religious Commitment: A Test of Two Competing Models," *Journal for the Scientific Study of Religion* 22:167-181.

Welch, Michael R., and John Baltzell
1984 "Geographic Mobility, Social Integration, and Church Attendance," *Journal for the Scientific Study of Religion* 23:75-91.

Welch, Michael R., Charles R. Tittle, and Thomas Petee
1991 "Religion and Deviance among Adult Catholics: A Test of the 'Moral Communities' Hypothesis," *Journal for the Scientific Study of Religion* 30:159-172.

Westfall, Richard S.
1958 *Science and Religion in Seventeenth-Century England*. New York: Columbia University Press.

White, Anna and Leila S. Taylor
1904 *Shakerism, Its Meaning and Message*. Columbus, Ohio: Heer.

White, John
1976a "A Critical Look at TM," *New Age Journal* (January):68-73.
1976b "Second Thoughts: What's Behind TM?" *Human Behavior* (October):70-71.

Whitworth, John McKelvie
1975 *God's Blueprints*. London: Routledge and Kegan Paul.

Woodward, Samuel B.
1840 *Hints for the Young in Relation to the Health of Body and Mind*. Boston: George W. Light (also, New York: Arno: 1973).

Wuthnow, Robert
1978 *Experimentation in American Religion*. Berkeley: University of California Press.

Wuthnow, Robert, and Kevin Christiano
1979 "The Effects of Residential Migration on Church Attendance in the United States." Pp. 257-276 in *The Religious Dimension*, edited by Robert Wuthnow. New York: Academic Press.

Zablocki, Benjamin
1980 *Alienation and Charisma*. New York: The Free Press.

Index

Ackerknecht, Erwin H.,132
Adorno, Theodore W., 152
affect, 22
affiliation, 25, 55, 117
African Americans, 56, 60-61, 184
agnostics and atheists, 151
Ahlstrom, Sydney, 137
Albrecht, G. L., 70-71, 76
Albrecht, Stan L., 70, 73
alcohol, 70, 81-99
alienists, 130, 132, 145-146
Allport, Gordon W., 152-153
altruism, 158
Amana, 179
Andelson, Jonathan G., 179
Anderson, Margo J., 28
Andrews, Edward Deming, 166
Angell, Robert C., 18, 54-55
Anglican Church, 38, 40
animal magnetism, 106
Annuaire Statistique de la France, 35-36, 38
anomie, 6, 18-19, 50, 158; defined, 19
arrest, 66
asceticism, 164
astrology, 120, 127
attachments, 4-6, 24-25, 165, 186

Austria, 33, 47-50
authoritarianism, 152-153
autocorrelation, 107, 117
Azzi, Corry, 28

Baha'i, 109-111
Bainbridge, William Folwell, 86
baptism, 145
Baptists, 39, 145
Barker, Eileen, 122
Barron, F., 154
Barthel, Diane, 166
Bastide, Roger, 132
Beckford, James, 120, 125
belief in God, 78
Benedict, Ruth, 132
Benedictines, 164
Benson, Peter L., 81
Berger, Bennett M., 162
Berger, Peter L., 19
Bergin, Allen E., 153
Bergson, Henri, 149
Besant, Annie, 109
Bible, 55, 85
Black Muslims, 184, 187
Blavatsky, Helena Petrovna, 109

Blinn, , Henry C., 167
bootleggers, 87, 89
brainwashing, 152
Breault, Kevin D.,19, 31
Breen, Michael, 147
Brierley, Peter, 127
Brigham, Amariah, 143-145
Bronner, Augusta F., 68
Bruce, Steve, 120
Brunner, Edmund deS., 153
Bucknill, John Charles, 138, 148
Buddhism, 123
Bureau of the Census, 28, 131
burial, 16
Burkett, Steven R., 2, 70, 73, 80, 96

Calhoun, Charles, 134
camp meetings, 143-145
Canada, 90, 93-94, 105, 112, 117-119, 127
Capone, Al, 87
Carden, Maren Lockwood, 181
Carroll, Michael P., 150
Catholic schools, 36, 186
Catholic Yearbook, 34
Catholicism and alcohol, 82-83, 90-95, 99;
    and suicide, 23-24, 27, 30, 35, 46-51;
    condemns suicide, 12, 16; relative, 41
celibacy, 162, 167, 169
census manuscript schedules, 63, 167
child abuse, 185
Christian Science, 106-117, 122
church attendance, 44, 66, 69-70, 75, 77-
    78, 91-95, 97, 119
church membership rates, 20, 25-26, 51, 55,
    66, 78; and alcoholism, 82-83; and crime,
    56-65; and cults, 105, 197-108, 115-116;
    and suicide, 22-23, 27-29, 42-43
cirrhosis of the liver, 82-83, 88-89, 91-92
city size, 60, 108
Cochran, John K. 96
Coleman, James S., 186
Colson, Charles, 184
commitment mechanisms, 159
communism, 158-159, 161-162, 166,
    181-182
compensators, 22, 174-175, 182
complex marriage, 181
Comte, Auguste, 1, 13, 129
conservative Protestants, 44, 70, 93-95
control theories of deviance, 25

convents, 162
Cooper, Paulette, 114
coping strategies, 147
County and City Data Book, 62
crime, 56-66; and attachments, 5;
    organized, 87; statistics, 21, 56
criminology, 2
Crutchfield, Robert D., 27, 53, 57-58
cults, 103-128, 150; defined, 104
Currie, Raymond F., 126
Currie, Robert, 38

Dain, Norman, 138
Danigelis, Nick, 31
Darnton, Robert, 141
Davis, James A., 64
death, 161-163
defection, 169, 171, 174-175
delinquency, 2, 67-80; and attachments, 5
delirium tremens, 82-83, 142
denaturing, 87
Denmark, 35
denomination effect, 95
depression, 25
desires, 22
despair, 18, 25, 30
Desroche, Henri, 167
Dianetics, 114
disappointment, 22
dissent, 24
Dittes, James E., 153
Divine Science, 109-111
divorce, 59-61, 185
Dobbelaere, Karel, 120
Dobbs, Catherine R., 178
dogmatism, 155
Douglas, Jack D., 20
Douglass, H. Paul, 153
Doyle, Daniel, 11, 53, 67
drugs, 70, 81-99
Durkheim, Emile, 4, 26, 30, 158; attitude
    toward religion, 14; reconsidered, 14-19;
    suicide research evaluated 31-51

Eads, H. L., 169
Earle, Pliny, 131, 134-138, 141-142, 145, 147
ecological effect, 74, 78
ecological fallacy, 43, 64, 93
ecological units, 3
economic conflict, 84

economic development, 35
economic success, 164
Eddy, Mary Baker G., 106
Edgerton, Robert B., 132
education, 17, 38, 50
egoism, 158; defined, 18-19
Ehrenberg, Ronald G., 28
Ellis, A., 150
Ellison, Christopher G., 154
Empey, L. T., 74
Encyclopedia Britannica, 54
England, 31, 37-41
enthusiasm, 168
equality, 163
Erickson, M. L., 74
Erikson, Erik H., 174
ethnicity, 70, 84
eugenics, 180
Europe, 138; alcoholism in, 91; cults in, 105, 119-127; Eastern, 3; suicide in, 31-41
Evangelical Protestants, 184, 187
Evans-Pritchard, Edward, 54, 151
evolutionary universals, 159
exciting causes, 141

false consciousness, 1, 6, 15
family, 60, 162-163, 177, 185
fanaticism, 143, 158, 168
fatalism, 18
Fate magazine, 112-114, 116
Feuerbach, Ludwig, 53-54
Finke, Roger, 53, 68
Finkel, Norman J., 132
Finland, 33
Fischer, Claude S., 108
Fishman, Aryei, 165
Fitzpatrick, Joseph P., 68, 157
Fodor, Nandor, 155
Foster, Lawrence, 174-175, 177
France, 12, 31, 35-37, 50
Frank, Jerome, 155
Franklin, Benjamin, 137
free enquiry/inquiry, 13, 17, 32
free love, 162, 181
free rider problem, 165
Freud, Sigmund, 129, 151, 155
fundamentalism, 150, 152
funeral services, 16
Furfey, Paul Hanly, 120

Gallup Poll, 55
Gardner, Hugh, 161
Gardner, Martin, 114
Gay, John D., 40
gender differences, in delinquency, 68; in religiousness, 79
General Social Survey, 44, 64, 93, 185
Germany, 13, 33, 47-50
Gillispie, Charles Coulston, 132
Girard, Chris, 31
Glock, Charles Y., 56, 71
Glueck, Eleanor, 68
Glueck, Sheldon, 68
Goffman, Erving, 146
Goldenweiser, Alexander, 54
Goldschmidt, Yaaqov, 165
Goode, Erich, 132
Gordon, Audri, 28
Gordon, Ernest, 88
Green, Calvin, 158, 166, 169
Guerry, André Michel, 12, 16, 32
Gurrslin, Orville R., 132
Gusfield, Joseph R., 84, 90

Halbwachs, Maurice, 45
Haley, Jay, 132
Hall, John R., 165
hallucinations, 129
Hare Krishna, 126
Harmony, 179
Harris, Anthony, 75
Hartshorne, Hugh, 67
Healy, William, 68
Heaven, 157
Hellfire effect, 2, 69-72
Henry, Andrew F., 18
heredity, 141, 148-149
Herfindahl index, 41
Hexham, Irving, 126
hierarchy, 38
Higgins, P. C., 70-71, 76
Hindelang, Michael J., 21, 75-76, 78
Hinduism, 104, 109
Hine, Robert V., 160
Hirata, Lucie Cheng, 131
Hirschi, Travis, 2, 69-71, 75-76, 78, 80
Hobbes, Thomas, 4
Hoffer, Thomas, 186
Hollingshead, August B., 132
Homans, George C., 51

Hood, Ralph W., 153
Howard, George Elliott, 85
Hubbard, L. Ron, 114
human ecology, 54
Hurd, Henry M., 144
hysteria, 146-147

Iannaccone, Lawrence R., 24, 41, 68, 103, 165
Icaria, 163, 179
illiteracy, 38, 41
imitation, 143
immigration, 179
immortality, 17, 22
importation of religion, 104
impulse crimes, 58
incarceration rates, 63-64
individualism, 18, 38
innovation of religion, 104
insane asylums, 130, 133-135, 145, 149;
    English and French, 138
intemperance, 82-83
intentional communities, 157
interaction, 51
irrationality, 149
ISKCON (International Society for
    Krishna Consciousness), 121, 125
Israel, 165

Jackson, Daniel H., 114
Jaffe, Dennis, 162
Jarvis, Edward, 13, 141-142, 146
Jehovah's Witnesses, 121
Jesus, 22, 55
Jewish communities, 17
Johnson, Barclay D., 19
Johnson, Douglas W., 20
Johnson, Paul, 164
Johnson, R. Christian, 131
Johnson, Stephen D., 152

Kanavy, Mary Jeanne, 2
Kant, Immanuel, 11
Kanter, Rosabeth Moss, 159, 167
Kay, Jane Holtz, 167
Kennedy, Joseph C. G., 131, 134,
    137-138, 148
Kent, Lori, 67
Kern, Louis J., 174
Kett, Joseph F., 145-146
Khrushchev, Nikita S., 161

kibbutz communities, 165
Kiev, Ari, 132
Kilgore, Sally, 186
kinship, 177
Kirkpatrick, Lee. A., 153
Klass, Philip, 113
Knudten, Richard D., 68
Kosmin, Barry A., 126
Kox, Willem, 105
Kurtz, Paul, 113
Kvaraceus, William C., 68-69

La Barre, Weston, 151
labeling theory, 63, 146
Laing, R. D., 146
LaMore, George, E., 114
Langfeldt, Gabriel, 147
Laslett, Barbara, 131
Latin America, 185
Le Bon, Gustave, 143
Lee, Ann, 166, 168
Legoyt, A., 48-49
Lenski, G., 70
Lewis, Ioan M., 147
Liberal Catholic Church, 109-111
liberal Protestants, 44, 70, 93-95
Library of Congress, 45
Lipset, Seymour Martin, 84
Loether, Herman J., 50
Lofland, John, 105, 165
London, 12
Luckmann, Thomas, 19

Mackay, Charles, 143
MacLean, John Patterson, 167
Malko, George, 114
Mann, Horace, 39-40
marijuana, 95-99
Marine Corps, 186
Maris, Ronald W., 19
Marshall, Mary (Mary M. Dyer),
    169, 177
Marx, Karl, 6, 15, 17
Marxist sociologists, 163
Masaryk, Thomas G., 12, 14, 18
mass hysteria, 143
masturbation, 139-142
maturation, 174
May, Mark A., 67
McKay, Henry D., 54

McTavish, Donald G., 50
medicine, 145-146
Medvedev, Roy, 132
Medvedev, Zhores A., 132
Meeus, Wim, 105
Melton, J. Gordon, 121-123
mental competency, 145
mental illness, 129-155
mental retardation, 23
Merton, Robert K., 1, 31, 132
Merz, Charles, 87
Mesmerism, 106, 141
Methodists, 39, 145
Meyer, John W., 28
migration, 59, 109; see also population
    turnover
Miller, Russell, 114
Millerism, 136, 145, 168
minority religions, 13
miracles, 143
mobility, 73
modernization, 14, 18, 35, 49
monasteries, 162, 164-166, 178
moral causes of insanity, 139, 141
moral climate, 76-77
moral community, 15, 54-56, 73, 80, 119,
    157, 178, 182, 187
moral integration 5-7; and anomie, 18; and
    crime, 60-61, 65; and cults, 103, 107-
    108, 111, 115-116, 118-119
moral statistics, 32, 45
Mormons, 39, 70, 73, 75, 106, 121-123,
    127, 145, 160-161, 187
Morselli, Henry, 12-14, 16, 18, 32-35, 39,
    47-49
Mountain Region, 79

Nagel, Joane, 28
Nation of Islam, 184
Neal, Julia, 167-169, 171-172
Neo-Pagans, 104
nervous breakdown, 147
nervous exhaustion, 141
Neumeyer, Martin H., 68
neurosis, 129
New Age Movement, 112-113, 115
New England, 56, 59, 62, 112
New Thought, 106
Niebuhr, H. Richard, 166
Nock, David, 117

non-conforming Protestant churches, 38, 40
Nordhoff, Charles, 158, 163, 165, 167,
    171, 179
norms, 72
Noyes, John Humphrey, 158, 163, 167,
    180-181
Noyes, Pierrepont, 181

Oberg, James E., 113
occult, 112-113
offense rates, 63
Oneida, 166, 178, 180-181
Opler, Marvin K., 132, 147
orphans, 169, 171
Orthodox Jews, 185-186
Ostow, Mortimer, 150

Pacific region, 66, 78-79
Pagano, Robert R., 114
paradise, 162, 168
Paris, 12
Parsons, Talcott, 1, 132, 159
Pearson, Elmer R., 167
Perlmann, Joel, 131
Picard, Paul R., 20
Pickering, W. S. F., 37, 53
Poggi, Isotta, 122
Poland, 3
poorhouses, 133, 178
Pope, Whitney, 19, 31, 33-34, 49-50
population growth, 26, 90-92
population turnover, 25-27, 30 55
Porterfield, Austin L., 19-20, 28
poverty, 60-61, 178
prayer, 56, 150, 162
predisposing causes, 141
Presbyterians, 39
previous acquaintance, 158, 163
Prinzing, Friedrich, 49
prisoner's dilemma, 186-187
prisons, 63
Prohibition, 84-92
Promise Keepers, 185
property crimes, 57, 62
prosperity, 18
Protestant-Catholic comparison, 31, 36-37,
    46, 51, 70
Protestantism and high suicide rates, 13,
    14, 31, 37, 46-51
Provo, Utah, 74-75

psychiatric ideologies, 132, 134, 146-147, 154-155
Psychoanalysis, 154-155
psychological model of religious effects, 71
publishing, 180
puritanism, 88, 139

Quakers, 39
Quetelet, Adolphe, 45
Quimby, Phineas Parkhurst, 106
Quinn, Bernard, 20

Raab, Earl, 84
Randi, James, 112
Rappites, 162
Ray, Isaac, 141, 144, 146
recidivism, 184-185
recruitment, 175-177, 179
Redlich, Frederick C., 132
reform, 184
refuge, 171-172, 177-178
Reiss, Albert J., 70-71
religion, as cultural epiphenomenon, 6, 30; comforts, 22, 30; defined, 54; sustains moral order, 1-2, 182; symbolizes society, 15, 53
religious climate, 71-74, 80, 82, 96
religious ecology, 73-74
religious excitement, 131, 134-136, 138
religious pluralism, 15, 37, 39, 41
retention rates, 172-176, 178-181
revivals, 137, 141, 143, 147, 149, 153, 167, 177
rewards, intangible, 160-161, 182
Rhodes, Albert Lewis, 70-71
Richmond, California, 73, 77
Rieff, Philip, 155
rituals, 143
Robbins, Thomas, 120, 125
Roberts, James S., 85
Robinson, Charles Edison, 166-167
Robison, Sophia M., 67
Rothman, David J., 147
Rushing, Jesse Lynn, 11
Russia, 3

Satanism, 117
Scandinavia, 38
Schafer, Stephen, 68
Schauffler, A. F., 6

Scheff, Thomas J., 146
schism, 155, 167, 179
schizophrenics, 142
schools, 36, 186
science and religion, 132
science fiction, 114
Scientology, 112-116, 123, 125-127
Scott, Ann Herbert, 20
Scott, John Finley, 174
scripture reading, 56
Sears, Clara Endicott, 169
Seattle, Washington, 76-77
sects, 103-104, 143, 149, 165
secular society, 182
self-esteem, 22, 151, 154
self-sacrifice, 158
Seventh Day Adventists, 121
sex ratio 171
sexual equality, 169
sexual urges, 173, 178
Shakers, 158, 162, 164, 166-179, 182
Shaw, Clifford R., 54
Shea, John Gerald, 167
Short, James F., 18
sin, 16, 23, 69, 73, 107
Singer, Jerome L., 147
Singh, Parmatma (Howard Weiss), 113
Smith, Tom W., 64
social facts, 51
social integration, 3-5, 15, 17, 24-30, 35, 59; and alcohol, 90-91; and crime, 60-61, 65; and cults, 108, 111, 115-116, 118-119; and egoism, 18; defined, 4; supports church membership, 26
social networks, 24, 51
social reinforcement, 55
social science bias against religion, 14, 22, 30, 51, 68, 149-155, 183
social status, 84
socialization, 174, 182
societal reaction, 130
sociology replacing religion, 1
solidarity, 15, 35
soul, 144
Soviet Union, 161
Spencer, Herbert, 37
spirit possession, 147
Spiritual Community Guide, 113, 115-116
spiritual rappings, 135
Spiritualism, 131, 136, 138-139, 145

spuriousness, 47, 59, 79, 124
Stack, Steven, 2
Standard Metropolitan Statistical Areas
    (SMSAs), 20, 27, 55, 62
statistics biased, 20
status politics, 88
Stein, Stephen J., 163-164, 167
Stephan, G. Edward, 160
Stephan, Karen H., 160
Stier, Hans-Erich, 33
Stiles, Ezra, 137
stratification, 22, 163
Strauss, Anselm, 132
stress, 147
Study of High School and Beyond, 78, 95-96
suffering, 22
Sufis, 109-110
suicide, 11-51; attitudes, 44; covered up, 21;
    notes, 12, 16; rates 11-12
Sunday School, 67-69, 72
supernatural, 22, 153, 155, 161-162, 166
Sweden, 96
synagogue membership, 20, 28
Szasz, Thomas, 132, 146

Tamney, Joseph B., 152
Tappan, Paul W., 68
Taylor, Leila S., 168
Temperance Movement, 82, 84-86
Ten Commandments, 5
Tennov, Dorothy, 155
tension with the sociocultural environment,
    146, 166
t'Hart, Harm, 105
theology, 15-16, 23, 71, 144
theoretical propositions, 5, 7, 105
Theosophy, 109-111
Thomas, W. I., 22
threshold effect, 76
Timberlake, James H., 85
Toulmin, Stephen, 132
Townsend, Joan B., 126
Transcendental Meditation, 105, 112-116
trust, 187
Tuke, Daniel H., 138, 148

Turk, Austin, 86
Tyack, David, 28

Unchurched Belt, 73, 76-77
Unification Church, 104
Uniform Crime Report, 56
urbanization, 6, 73
utopian communities, 157-182

victimization surveys, 21
violent crimes, 57, 60, 62
vital statistics, 20
vows of silence, 162

Wagner, Adolf, Heinrich Gotthilf, 32, 36,
    45-51
Wales, 37
Wallace, Robert Keith, 114
Wallis, Roy, 114, 120, 125-126, 155
Ward, Gary L., 122
Watters, Wendell W., 150-151
Weber, Max, 49
Wedgwood, James, 110
Weiss, Joseph, 76, 78
Welch, Kevin W., 6
Wells, Seth Y., 158, 166, 169
West Coast, 2, 73-74, 77-78, 80, 96, 106, 184
Westfall, Richard S., 132
White, Anna, 168
White, John, 114
White, Mervin, 2, 70, 73, 80, 96
Whitefield, George, 137
Whitworth, John McKelvie, 167-169
Wilson, Warren H., 153
winter Shaker, 172
Woodward, Samuel B., 139, 141
World Values Surveys, 96
worldliness, 166
Wuthnow, Robert, 114

Yogi, Maharishi Mahesh, 114

Zablocki, Benjamin, 162
Zen Buddhism, 123
Zoar, 166, 178-181